UNION INTERNATIONALE DES SCIENCES PRÉHISTORIQUES ET PROTOHISTORIQUES
INTERNATIONAL UNION OF PREHISTORIC AND PROTOHISTORIC SCIENCES

PROCEEDINGS OF THE XVI WORLD CONGRESS (FLORIANÓPOLIS, 4-10 SEPTEMBER 2011)
ACTES DU XVI CONGRÈS MONDIAL (FLORIANÓPOLIS, 4-10 SEPTEMBRE 2011)

VOL. 10
Actes des session 27 et 42
Proceedings of sessions 27 and 42

uispp

I0086040

Technology and Experimentation in Archaeology

Edited by

Sara Cura

Jedson Cerezer

Maria Gurova

Boris Santander

Luiz Oosterbeek

Jorge Cristóvão

BAR International Series 2657
2014

Published in 2016 by
BAR Publishing, Oxford

BAR International Series 2657

Proceedings of the XVI World Congress of the International Union of Prehistoric and Protohistoric Sciences
Actes du XVI Congrès mondial de l'Union Internationale des Sciences Préhistoriques et Protohistoriques

Secretary of the Congress: Rossano Lopes Bastos; President of the Congress National Commission:
Erika Robrhan-Gonzalez; Elected President: Jean Bourgeois; Elected Secretary General: Luiz
Oosterbeek; Elected Treasurer: François Djindjian; Series Editors: Luiz Oosterbeek, Erika Robrhan-
Gonzalez; Volume title: Technology and Experimentation in Archaeology; Volume editors: Sara
Cura, Jedson Cerezer, Maria Gurova, Boris Santander, Luiz Oosterbeek, Jorge Cristóvão

Technology and Experimentation in Archaeology

ISBN 978 1 4073 1299 6

Contacts: General Secretariat of the U.I.S.P.P. – International Union of Prehistoric and Protohistoric
Sciences; Instituto Politécnico de Tomar, Av. Dr. Cândido Madureira 13, 2300 TOMAR; Email:
uispp@ipt.pt

BAR Publishing is the trading name of British Archaeological Reports (Oxford) Ltd.
British Archaeological Reports was first incorporated in 1974 to publish the BAR
Series, International and British. In 1992 Hadrian Books Ltd became part of the BAR
group. This volume was originally published by Archaeopress in conjunction with
British Archaeological Reports (Oxford) Ltd / Hadrian Books Ltd, the Series principal
publisher, in 2014. This present volume is published by BAR Publishing, 2016.

Printed in England

BAR
PUBLISHING

BAR titles are available from:

BAR Publishing
122 Banbury Rd, Oxford, OX2 7BP, UK
EMAIL   info@barpublishing.com
PHONE   +44 (0)1865 310431
FAX   +44 (0)1865 316916
www.barpublishing.com

Table of Contents

i

List of Figures and Tables

B. DE S. BARRETO; M.P. CABRAL: The Lithic Technology of Laranjal do Jari I: a Koriabo Site at South Amapá

M.J. RODET et al.: Les industries des sites du haut rio São Francisco: outilllage "simple", ou "complexe"? Le cimetière de Buritizeiroetl'abriBibocas de Jequitai

G.N. POPLEVKO: Methodology for integrated research flint products of the Neolithic site Old Voitkovichi 1 in Belarus

Introduction

This volume includes papers presented during the XVI world congress of UISPP (Florianópolis 2011) in session 27 (Opportunistic flaking and complex procedures) and in session 42 (Technology and experimentation).

Experimental Archaeology as an hypothesis contrast method, focusing on technological studies, is not new in archaeological research procedures. Since the early 1970s, as a consequence of the application of *châine-operatoire*/reduction sequence concepts within the framework of Palaeoethnological investigation, or within the actualistics studies highly developed in the framework of Processual Archaeology, the experimentation and utilization of artefact replicas have been used in the search for answers regarding technological procedures and their functional aspects.

However, since the 1990s the research interface between technology and experimentation, worldwide, has increased, resulting in a renewal of procedures and interest in the incorporation of such studies particularly in the field of techno-functional analysis of prehistoric artefacts.

Nevertheless the criticisms on experimental procedures are abundant, questioning its theoretical fundamentals and explanation validity. These remarks result both from the morphotypological approaches to artefact assemblages, but also from a lack of understanding on the range and goals of such studies.

The session Technology and Experimentation promoted the discussion on the present applicability and future perspectives of experimental procedures applied to the study of prehistoric technology studies, through the presentation of reflections and/or study cases regarding the modification, utilization and discard of varied raw materials employed in the fabrication of prehistoric artefacts (clay, stone, bone, vegetal material).

Throughout prehistory we verify that in different moments and regions there are lithic assemblages with technically simple processes of production. In many cases we face opportunistic flaking schemes having their origins in the beginning of lithic tool production. Nevertheless, depending on multiple variables (such as raw material economy, nature of the occupations, tools functionality, cultural choices, etc) these simple technical choices are part of rather complex adaptive and cultural behaviors that go beyond their technical expression. This is an apparent opposition that must be discussed, aiming to bring together technical options and behavioral issues.

Stefano Grimaldi discusses the epistemological implications of experimental approaches. Experimentation on lithics are discussed in the papers of S. Cura, P. Cura, S. Grimaldi and E. Cristiani; G.N. de Souza and Â.P. Lima; B. de S. Barreto and M. P. Cabral; M.J. Rodet, A. Prous, J. Machado and L.F. Bass; G.N. Poplevko). Other papers discuss experimentation in the production of beads (M. Gurova, C. Bonsall, B. Bradley, E. Anastassova and P. Cura), new protocols on ceramics experimentation (J.F. Cerezer), ethnographic ceramic technology (R.T. Bortolin and V. Fróis), bone industry (B. Santander; C. Costa, N.

Almeida, H. Gomes, S. Cura and P. Cura) and rock art engravings (N.S. da Rosa, S. Cura, S. Garcês and P. Cura).

HOW MUCH SKILLED SHOULD BE AN EXPERIMENTAL ARCHAEOLOGIST AND WHO IS THE REFEREE? EPISTEMOLOGICAL REFLECTIONS OF A FLINTKNAPPER

Stefano GRIMALDI

Universitá degli Studi di Trento, Quaternary and Prehistory group of GeoSciences Center Unit (uID73 – FCT), Italy
stefano.grimaldi@unitn.it

Abstract: *Archaeology is a professional activity which is deeply characterized by subjective thought and conventions. This subjectivity, particularly evident in prehistoric archaeology where the researcher aims to understand human societies without evidences unless those coming from excavation, should be positively considered. Here we can identify a "tacit knowledge" acquired through personal practice and experience which can't be explicitly articulated. The "tacit knowledge" is one of the most significant and interesting components of prehistoric research in association, not in contraposition, with the formative homogeneity that distinguishes and simultaneously ties one or more generations of researchers.*

Key-words: *"Tacit knowledge", subjectivity, experimental archaeology*

Résumé: *L'Archéologie est une activité professionnelle profondément caractérisée par la pensée subjective et par des conventions. Cette subjectivité, bien évidente en archéologie préhistorique dans laquelle le chercheur essaye de comprendre les sociétés humaines en absence de toute évidence sauf celles résultant des fouilles, devrait être considérée positivement. Ici on peut identifier une "connaissance tacite" acquise a travers la pratique personnelle et l'expérience, qui ne peut pas être articulée de façon explicite. Cette "connaissance tacite" est une des composantes les plus signifiantes et intéressantes de la recherche préhistorique en association, pas en contradiction, avec l'homogénéité formative laquelle, en même temps, distingue et uni une ou plusieurs générations de chercheurs.*

Mots-clés: *"Connaissance tacite", subjectivité, archéologie experimental*

Some years ago I received as a gift my own caricature (Fig. 1). We can see that I produce a small but valuable lithic artifact – a Christmas tree – after an enormous waste of raw material.

Figure 1. Caricature of Stefano Grimaldi as a flintknapper

This image triggered long personal reflections, still ongoing, with the purpose of answering to questions that are rarely found in the literature: how proficient should be an experimental activity to allow the use of the data in the interpretation of archaeological artifacts? How can we evaluate such proficiency? And who can be the evaluator?

In this paper I intent to present my current reflections and results hoping that they can be of wide interest.

FIRST REFLECTION: THE "SUBJECTIVE" OBJECTIVITY OF ARCHAEOLOGICAL RESEARCH

The success of a theory (model, hypothesis… in any field of scientific research, for example prehistoric archaeology, should be found in the joint presence of an objective and subjective component. On one side, a research methodology must be shared by all or great part of the scientific community, according to the concept of paradigm and its methodological consequences in the field of science evolution, as stated in Khun 1995. On the other side, the subjective component refers to the sensibility and analytical capacity that each researcher "tacitly" develops along his/her life, as described by Polanyi 1958.

The need of these two components in a research activity only apparently looks like a contradiction. An example can be given by the studies on species evolution.

If we theoretically imagine an objective approach-based research approach, we will face a situation where the scientific community mechanically applies a common methodology to interpret a variety of case-studies that must be compared (probably obtaining homogenous results) or a restricted variety of case-studies that can be compared (probably obtaining identical results). The creationist paradigm, by offering a single methodology based on the enunciation of the principle that "all life forms are created by God", determines a research only characterized by the objective component. In this situation, the results obtained through the "research activity" are necessarily similar, frequently identical, regardless the researchers and the different analyzed contexts.

On the contrary, if we imagine a research approach only based on a subjective component we are forced to delineate a very confusing scenario where the scientific community is represented by multiple schools of thought – some of them eventually assigned to individual researchers – in competition with each other. Each researcher will be suggesting one or more theories that found their validity only in the personal (subjective) vision of the phenomena, not allowing the confrontation between methods and results. A good example of the incommensurability of the different subjective theories produced under this "confusing" scenario and based on personal research experience is given by the scientists-philosophers of ancient classical civilizations – see for instance the references of Xenophanes of Colophon and Herodotus to explain the existence of fossilized bones.

The theory proposed by Charles Darwin on the species evolution is a very good example of a research where the objective components (among others, the phenotypic variability) is associated to the subjective experience of each researcher involved in studies on Evolutionism. In this case, we observe the outcome of this field of research through the proliferation of models and observations useful to interpret, adapt or even modify the original Darwinian model.

First conclusion

The contemporary presence of objective and subjective components in a scientific research should be seen as the "perfect cocktail" as far as the validity and the success of the research is concerned.

In Prehistory studies, beyond the formal personal training – which is more or less standardized within the same or several generations of researchers, in other words: "we all studied by reading the same books" – the development of a individual "tacit knowledge" must be improved. This one is acquired trough practice and personal experience and cannot be explicitly articulated. It helps the prehistory archaeologist to elaborate and develop ideas, theories and hypothesis that can be compared, discussed, improved. Any attempts to produce an objective archaeology, deprived of any reference to the individual "tacit knowledge", should determine the failure of the research, since the possibility of discussion between different researchers' tacit knowledge is eliminated. Finally, we may also conclude that it also prevents the improvement of theories and methods.

SECOND REFLECTION: THE "OBJECTIVE" SUBJECTIVITY OF THE ARCHAEOLOGICAL RESEARCH

How is it possible to evaluate the validity of a theory (model, hypothesis…) in a subjective-based discipline as

Prehistoric archaeology and, particularly, in the study of prehistoric artifacts?

An example may help us to reach the answer:

I am glad to state that I "fortunately" belong to a generation of researchers who – at the end of the '80s – directly lived the great emotion and the methodological impact in the scientific community provoked by the original technological approach of E. Böeda (Böeda, 1994). I say "fortunately", because I recall a period characterized by an extreme intellectual vivacity among us, young students, who saw on those new ideas the perfect tool to tear apart from the «old» typological approach that held – and still do in some research centers – the monopoly of the academic training. In this period, there was the diffusion and exchange of numerous original publications, significant in the results and innovative in the methodology (among others, Meignen, 1988; Delagnes, 1990; Pelegrin, 1991; Van Peer, 1992; Mourre, 1994).

In my personal opinion, the main shared feature of these papers was that each one of them gave an original contribution by adapting a common research methodology to the particularities of the studied lithic assemblage. At the same time, the interpretative and methodological potentialities of Böeda method seemed to be infinite when we were trying to apply them to the studied archeological contexts (in my case, the lower and middle Paleolithic lithic assemblages of central Italy).

I can point the end of this semi anarchical, turbulent and proliferous period in the meeting "The definition and interpretation of Levallois technology" that had place in Philadelphia in 1993 (Dibble & Bar Yosef, 1995). In this meeting, different generations of researchers needed to share the understanding of the methodological principles of the Böeda method, those principles previously acquired and assimilated by a restricted number of persons who had enough time to share also their own personal knowledge. Consequently, it was necessary to adapt the principles of Boeda method in order to put them in a understandable and recognizable form. The result is the very well known, schematic, easy-to-read, aseptic – in one word, "objective" – drawing where the Levallois technical characteristics are reproduced. Regardless the critics, I remember very well the growing enthusiasm of many participants when they could understand how simple and fructiferous was the application of the few schematic technological laws of the Böeda method in the study of lithic assemblages. Obviously, the Böeda method consolidated its initial success and was quickly accepted by researchers of different nationalities and schools of thought.

This example can be interpreted through a very well know phenomenon in the history of scientific discoveries. The fast diffusion of a theory among the scientific community allows it, regardless its degree of scientific validation, to acquire a major role in the literature over other theories. The reasons of the success can be found mainly in the methodological (but not necessarily theoretical) simplicity which allows an easy application (but not necessarily comprehension). In this way, the theoretical principles of the dominant theory will be accepted, the methodology will be mechanically applied, and the results will be aseptically published by an ever-increasing number of researchers.

In other words, the phenomenon determines its own success: the largest is the number of researchers promoting a theory, the bigger will be the number of researchers of the scientific community that want accept it. In archaeology the examples of such phenomenon are numerous: the "site catchment" analysis, the Thiessen polygons technique, the logic of Laplace or Bordes typology, the diffusion hypothesis of agriculture and megalithic societies, the Böeda method.

THIRD AND LAST REFLECTION: THE "OBJECTIVE TRUTH" AND THE EXPERIMENTAL RESEARCH

We can briefly approach some questions related with the experimental activities in prehistoric archaeology.

Since the 80's, the Böeda method achieves an organic methodology in the study of lithic industries, structured with a rational theoretical model, which can be applied in almost all contexts. At the ground of such methodology there is an unquestionable and significant experimental activity, developed along many years by E. Böeda.

The relevance of the experimentation and, mainly, its meaning is underlined by anyone who, in this field of research, have the reputation of being carriers of the "objective truth". According to these researchers the experimentation should be a subjective experience, carried out in order to improve and develop their own personal knowledge.

"(…) ce n'est pas la méthode (…) du tailleur X qui peut servir de référence pour le classement ou l'étude d'une collection donnée. Ce serait confondre l'object de la recherche." (p. 59). "L'expérimentation (…) ne mesure jamais directement un phénomène archéologique. (p. 61)

(Jacques Pelegrin, 1991)

"Expérimenter, c'est mettre à la disposition de la recherche préhistorique une méthode heuristique supplémentaire. Ces rapports sont dus à deux modes de raisonnement, inductif et deductif, entre lesquels existe une évidente interaction. (…). Il s'en suit un retour au matériel archéologique qui suscite de nouveaux tests expérimentaux. Ces différents modes de raisonnement nous permettent, entre autres, (…) de dégager de la tradition technique la part des contraintes techniques." (p. 16)

(Eric Böeda, 1994)

Nevertheless, in all the bibliography that I know and which refers to the Böeda method I never found references/quotations/descriptions to a long and exhaustive experimental activity like the one that originated the Böeda method. Actually, in the bibliography were the technological study of lithic artifacts is complemented by experimental activities, the results of the experimentation are hardly described exhaustively or in detail. In my opinion, the examples that I know, by several reasons, lead to the belief that a major part of the scientific community conceives the experimental activity as an imitation activity. This one has nothing to do with scientific research or with the resolution of scientific requirements; contrary of what is suggested by the carriers of the "objective truth", experimental activity is conceived as an objective tool that confirms or even demonstrate a given archaeological evidence.

My opinion is that there is a real misunderstanding about the meaning of archaeological artifacts and of experimental activities.

The study of archaeological artifacts is interpreted has a field of research in which the presumed objectivity of the researcher should be assured independently of the technological and morphological variability of the studied lithic assemblage. That's why researchers take refuge in old habits such as the typological approach or in an innovative and widely accepted theory such as the "Böeda method". Accordingly, the experimental activity is generally interpreted as a rational, aseptic tool which clearly aims to prove the interpretations suggested after having analyzed the archaeological evidence.

I am convinced that the – typological and/or technological – analysis of lithic artefacts should be done by giving much more importance to the peculiarities of the analysed lithic industry, usually discarded as "*Divers*" in the Bordes's typological list or in the "waste debitage", following the technological terminology.

The experimental activity is a highly subjective process of research and useful for the researcher to develop its personal skills in order to better understand and objectively recognize the technical characteristics in the lithic assemblages.

References

BÖEDA, Eric (1994) – *Le concept Levallois: variabilité des methods*, CNRS.

DELAGNES, A. (1990) – Analyse technologique de la méthode de débitage de l'Abri Suard, *Paléo*, 2, p. 81-88.

DIBBLE, H.L. and BAR-YOSEF, O. (eds) (1995) – *The Definition and Interpretation of Levallois Technology*, Monographs in World Archaeology 23.

KUHN, T.S. (1962) – The *structure of scientific revolution*, Chicago.

MEIGNEN, L. (1988) – Un exemple de comportement technologique différentiel selon les matières premières: Marillac, couches 9 et 10. In: Otte, M. (Ed) *"L'homme de Neandertal: la technique"*, Liege, ERAUL, p. 71-79.

MOURRE, V. (1994) – *Les industries en quartz au Paléolithique moyen. Approche technologique de séries du Sud-Ouest de la France*, Mém. de Maitrise, Université de Paris X.

PELEGRIN, J. (1991) – Aspects de démarche expérimentale en technologie lithique. In *25 ans d'études technologiques en Préhistoire: bilan et perspectives. XIème rencontres internationales d'Archéologie et d'Histoire d'Antibes*. Juan-les-Pins, APDCA, 1991, p. 57-63

POLANYI, M. (1958) – *Personal knowledge*, Chicago.

VAN PEER, P. (1992) – *The Levallois reduction strategy*, Monographs in World Archeology, 13, Prehistory Press, Madison.

EXPERIMENTATION AND MORPHOTECHNOLOGICAL ANALYSES OF THE MIDDLE PLEISTOCENE LITHIC ASSEMBLAGE OF RIBEIRA DA PONTE DA PEDRA SITE (CENTRAL PORTUGAL)

Sara CURA, Pedro CURA

Museu de Arte Pré-Histórica de Mação, Quaternary and Prehistory group of GeoSciences Center Unit (uID73 – FCT)

0saracura0@gmail.com   0pedrocura@gmail.com

Stefano GRIMALDI

Universitá degli Studi di Trento, Quaternary and Prehistory group of GeoSciences Center Unit (uID73 – FCT)

stefano.grimaldi@unitn.it

Emanuela CRISTIANI

Marie Curie Fellow, McDonald Institute for Archaeological Research, University of Cambridge

ec484@cam.ac.uk

Abstract: *The results obtained from a experimental program carried out in order to investigate morphotechnical features (repeated "informal" retouches – marginal, coarse and irregular) of a Middle Pleistocene lithic industry are presented. The assemblage, made from local quartzite pebbles, comes from the Ribeira Ponte da Pedra site (Central Portugal); it is characterized by abundant worked peblles, cortical and non cortical flakes, few cores and rare bifacial implements. The first results indicate that most of the edges described as "informal" retouched can be the result of functional activities linked to different subsistence tasks.*

Keywords: *Experimentation, Quartzite tools, Middle Pleistocene*

Résumé: *Les résultats obtenus d'après un programme d'expérimentation misé sur l'investigation d'évidences morphotechniques (retouches « informelles » répétées – marginales, grossières et irrégulières) d'une industrie du Paléolithique Moyen, sont présentés. L'ensemble, produit sur des galets locaux en quartzite, provient du site de Ribeira da Ponte da Pedra (Portugal central); il est caractérisé par l'abondance de galet aménagés, des éclats corticaux et non-corticaux, des rares nucleus et des outils bifaciaux rares. Les premiers résultats indiquent que la majorité des tranchants décrits comme retouche « informelle »peuvent être le résultat d'activités fonctionnelles associées a de différentes tâches de subsistance.*

Mots-clés: *Experimentation, outils en quartzite, Pleistocène Moyen*

INTRODUCTION

The Ribeira Ponte da Pedra (also known as Ribeira da Atalaia) archaeological site is located in the valley of Ribeira (=stream) da Ponte da Pedra, a right tributary of the Tagus River in Central Portugal. It is in a region extending along the middle/lower Tagus River valley, thus known as Alto Ribatejo (Fig. 1).

This region comprises three principal geological units: 1) The Pre-Cambrian and Palaeozoic schist-metamorphic complex (Ancient Massif) 2) The "Estremenho" Limestone massif, which is essentially Mesozoic with some Cenozoic deposits 3) The Cenozoic Tagus sedimentary basin.

The regional quaternary deposits are composed of recent alluvial sediments, Pleistocene fluvial terraces, karstic cave fillings (in the limestone massif), and detritic covers.

This hydrological network is shaped by regional tectonics and accordingly, the larger Tagus tributaries come from

the North. The small Ponte da Pedra stream also flows from North to South and its valley has been totally excavated within the Tagus sedimentary basin and hence is constituted by detritic fluvial-lacustrine sediments from the Cenozoic (Miocene).

Until the Middle Pleistocene, the valley was longer than at present and held continuity with the Nabão Valley (Mozzi 1998). Presently, the stream valley is only a few kilometres (8-9 km) shorter.

The landscape around Ribeira Ponte da Pedra site is characterized by fluvial terraces covering the slopes of the nearby low hills that are less than 140 m in height.

The archaeological site has been excavated since 1999. A trench of (27) meters length was excavated from the top to the bottom of a hill formed by lower and middle terrace levels of the Tagus superimposed to Miocene deposit. The main goal of the excavation is to define the stratigraphic correlation between: a) lower and middle terraces, b) between terraces and substratum, and finally

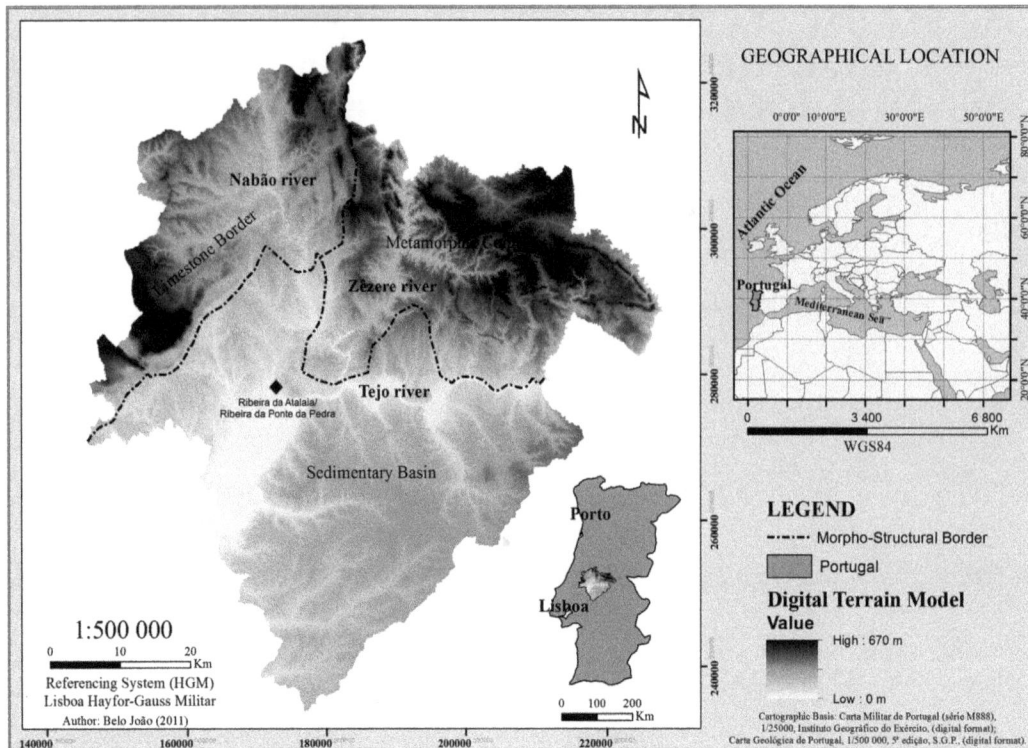

Figure 1. Geographic localization of the archaeological site of Ribeira da Atalaia/Ribeira da Ponte da Pedra

c) between these deposits and the colluviums (Grimaldi and Rosina 2001). Archaeological remains found in both terraces (only lithic industries, mainly in local quartzite and quartz pebbles) have been attributed to Lower-Middle Palaeolithic; however an Upper Palaeolithic hearth was discovered in the colluvium's sediments.

Until now, the excavation activities identified four geological units (from the oldest to the youngest): Miocene substrate, bottom of T4 fluvial terrace, top of Q4a fluvial terrace and colluvium's covering.

The Q3 bottom (from where the artifacts approached here are provinient) is formed by, at least, four different depositional morphologies: a bar (formed by reddish coarse sand and pebbles); a channel (filled with big pebbles and cobbles, until 35 cm, and reddish coarse sand) that cuts the bar; flood plain fine grains deposits (grey to yellow); and transverse channels (filled with reddish sand and pebbles, until 10 cm) that have a very erosive contact with the floodplain deposits.

According to previous attribution (Rosina 2002, 2004), partially confirmed by TL and OSL datings (Dias *et al.*, 2010, Martins *et al.*, 2010), the T4 bottom formation could be associated with i.s. 9 and 7, T5 top match up with i.s. 5, and the oldest colluviums could be related with i.s. 2.

THE REFERENTIAL LITHIC ASSEMBLAGE

The lithic industry found at the bottom of the T4 terrace (1252 artefacts), is essentially characterized by three major groups: worked pebbles; non retouched blanks; "retouched like" blanks (flakes and pebbles).

These groups should be considered together as the technological result of a main reduction sequence: pebbles have been knapped in order to produce flakes (mainly cortical or half-cortical ones), eventually these pebbles are also knapped to produce heavy duty tools. The main debitage method is usually the unidirectional with hard hammer direct percussion.

This assemblage is also characterized by the absence of the "expected" Acheulean artefacts – handaxes and cleavers – and the rarity of picks. Nevertheless, we highlighted the presence of some bifacial tools and a unifacial artefact which presents a more refined and equilibrated morphology.

The scars on the worked pebbles and cores rarely outnumber 4 removals. This probably means a quick production of large/massive blanks and may also indicate a functional need based over quantity rather than quality of the blanks. When the percentage frequencies of blank categories are compared, we observe a lower percentage incidence of non cortical blanks (Cura and Grimaldi, 2009).

"Retouched-like" blanks are mainly cortical or half cortical flakes and some worked pebbles (Fig. 2 and Tab. 1). Their percentage decreases along with the reduction of cortex presence, being less among non cortical flakes. This seems to suggest that blanks showing modified edges were mainly needed in the cortical blanks category. However, the implements analyzed so far present a

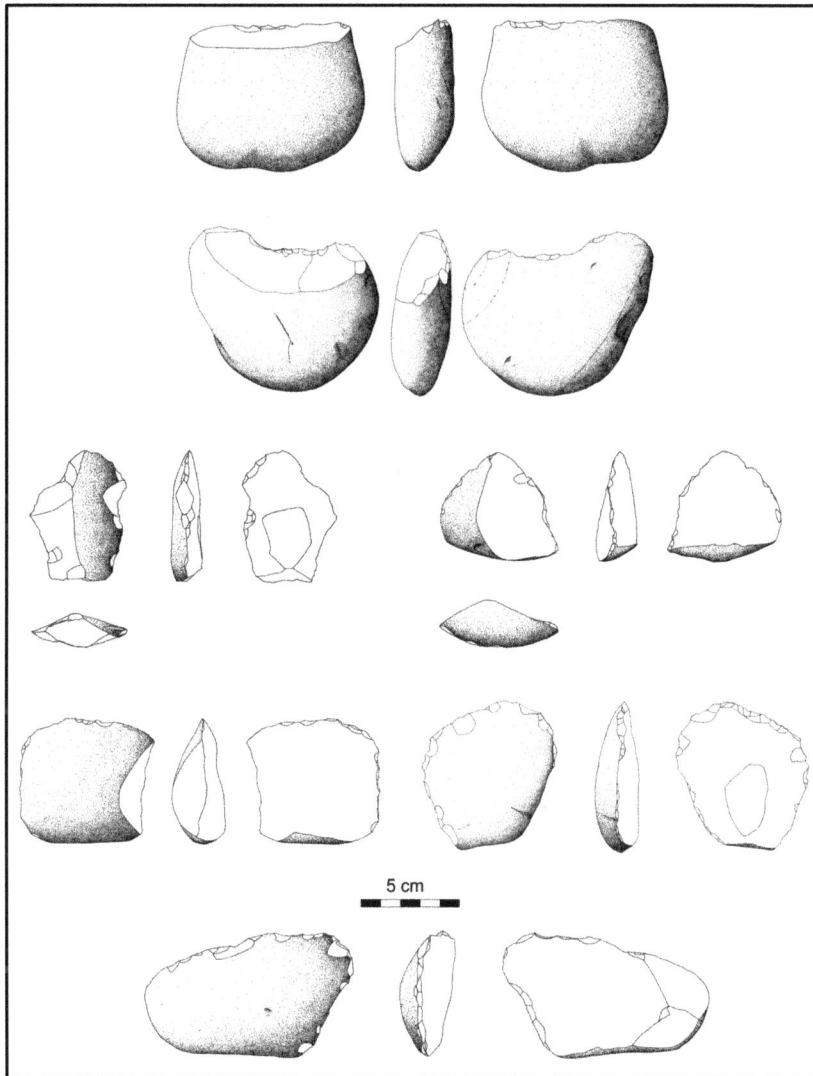

Figure 2. "Informal" Edges modification – Unifacial Worked pebbles and cortical flakes (Quartzite)

Table 1. Distribution of edge modification among the main blanks of the lithic industry

Blank	Non retouched		Retouched		"Informal" retouch		Total	
	N°	%	N°	%	N°	%	N°	%
Worked pebble	96	12%	9	4%	12	5%	117	9%
Retouched pebble			67	29%	26	11%	93	7%
Flake	459	58%	131	57%	177	76%	769	61%
Core	37	5%			2	3%	39	3%
Bifacial tools	2	0,30%			2	1%	4	0%
Others	203	25%	21	9%	13	6%	237	19%
Total	797	63%	228	18%	232	18%	1259	100%

marginal, coarse and "informal" retouch, quite variable in its position and localisation and not resulting on "classic types" of formal tools. A possible explanation for this behaviour could be due to blanks produced mostly to obtain functional edges to cut or scrape, but without the need of being retouched (Meireles and Cunha-Ribeiro, 1991-92).

Considering the fluvial context of the lithic assemblages we can't exclude eventual edge modifications resulting from post-depositional proccess (Chambers, 2003; Hosfield and Chambers, 2002), however, even if informal, these modifications don't occur in all blanks and observing its technical and functional features they don't ressamble the consequence of this type of phenomena. It is not like the isolated abrupt removals in the more fragile margins as the fluvial transport and chock provokes. Besides the exclusion of this hypotheses seems to be confirmed by the experimental studies we present here and previous functional studies (Cristiani *et al.*, 2010) done in a sample of 53 flakes.

It is in this context that we bring up the question of whether these features are an intentional edge modification by retouch or, on the other hand, are mechanical alterations as a consequence of its utilization. To clear out such issue, our goal is to find parameters which allow a clear attribution of the mentioned edge features.

We divided the "retouched-like" implements into five groups (Fig. 2)

a) Notches

b) Denticulates (edge modification on the upper surface)

c) Denticulates (edge modification on the lower surface)

d) A more regular modification (looking like a "true" retouch).

e) "Informal", varied on it's position and irregular retouch

THE EXPERIMENTAL ACTIVITY

To verify and describe the nature of the edge modifications observed in Ribeira da Ponte da Pedra/Atalaia quartzite implements, we set up an experimental procedure characterised by different activities over different materials. The goal was to produce a varied series of experimental edge modifications to be compared with the archaeological ones. To enlarge as much as possible the variety of resulting modifications, as well as to point out precisely their origin, the experiments were carried out using hard and soft materials with different gestures and time spans (Cura *et al.*, 2008).

Although corresponding to the specific scope of this paper, these experiments are part of a larger research framework, involving several research projects (Oosterbeek 2008a and b), aiming the study of quartzite lithic assemblages in the Portuguese Tagus Valley. Within these projects all experiments are preceded by a macroscopic characterization of the lithic raw material. Such description is done over large samples of quartzite clasts collected in different fluvial deposits in the Tagus Valley, from the actual alluvial plain to the most ancient terraces. Features like texture (granulometry, inclusions…), morpho-volumetry (size, shape, angles…) are registered in order to sort out the inner variability of this rock, as well as to set up its influence in technology, function and use of tools.

All implements used in the experiments were made out of 8 quartzite pebbles of medium-fine texture. The pebbles

where knapped with direct percussion using a hard hammer (also quartzite). In total 68 flakes and 7 worked pebbles ("choppers" like morphology) were selected and used. The experiments were systematically photographed and partially video logged and every tool was individually registered following specific parameters according to the nature of the activity (Cura *et al.*, 2008).

Experimentation with worked pebbles

To perform the wood and bone work experiments – cutting *Quercus ilex* and *Salix alba* branches and fracture *of Bos taurus* long bones -we used 7 fine to medium quartzite texture pebbles reproducing identical morphotechnical features of the archaeological ones.

5 branches of oak (*quercus ilex*) and willow (*Salix alba*) were chopped down using 5 of the worked pebbles resulting from the experimental production of blanks (Tab. 2). These worked pebbles have a chopper like morphology and though having several sizes and morphologies all proved to be functional for the purpose (Fig. 3). We believe that the first utilization was longer as the experimenter was getting at ease with the manipulation of such tool, sorting out the best way to handle it (which was much easier after using a leather protection to absorb the strike vibration and shock) and the best angle to chop down the wood branch. According to his report, the Worked Pebbles 2 and 3 (Fig. 3) were the most efficient in combining edge morphology and weight; however the manipulation was more difficult given the dimensions of these pebbles. For these purposes it's interesting to mention that the irregularity caused by the removals limits in upper surface of this kind of tool is of great utility while handling it, since it allows a firm grip. Although these "tools" weren't microscopically observed it is important to refer that the pebble cores, especially those that aren't extensively knapped result in morphologies suitable to these kinds of tasks. Moreover, we remark that the intensive edge modification after the use of the Worked Pebble 3 (Fig. 3) results on features easily deluded for edge regularization or maintenance.

21 *Bos Taurus* bones were fractured (Fig. 3 and Tab. 2), the observations are similar to those of wood work, adding the difficulties of handling the tools as they became covered with bone grease. We registered extensive edge modifications and loss of the active margin, but it's necessary to mention that all fractures were done over a anvil of stone. Nevertheless the edges modifications are similar to the archaeological tools, namely the removals on the inverse surface of the tool (Fig. 3).

Experimentation with flakes

The resulting branches were sectioned in smaller parts, some were left on open air to dry and others were worked 2 hours after being collected. The fresh and dry wood branches were scraped and cut with different movements and angles

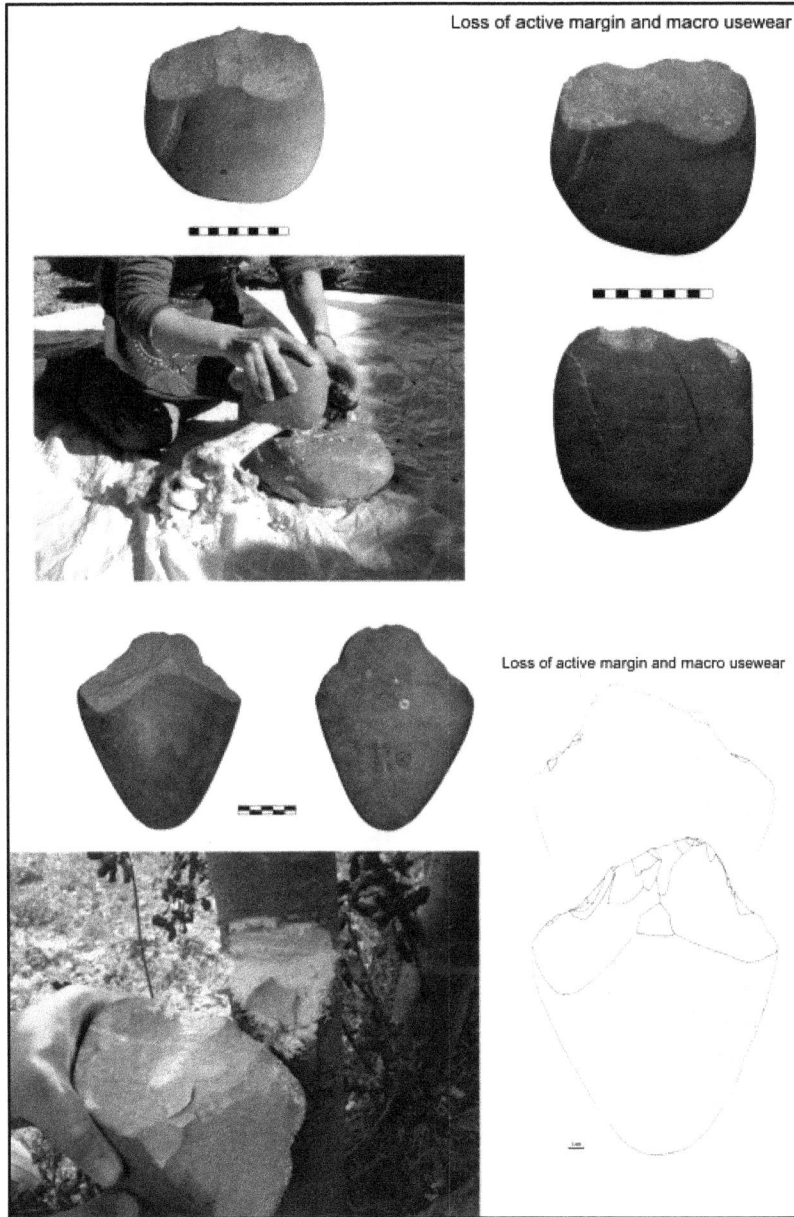

Figure 3. Use of experimental worked pebbles and resulting edge modification

Table 2. Wood cut and bone fracture with experimental worked pebbles

Technology	Worked Material	Action	Use	Nº of strokes	Time	Macro use wear
Unifacial worked pebble 1	Fresh *Quercus ilex*	Cutt	Hand axe like	469 (13 cm diameter)	11 min 04 sec	yes
Unifacial worked pebble 2				208 (9 cm diameter)	4 min 55 sec	yes
Unifacial worked pebble 3				583 (20 cm diameter)	6 min 15 sec + 6 min 38 sec	yes (very visible)
Unifacial worked pebble 4	Fresh *Salix alba*			1416 (29 cm diameter)	48 min 17 sec	yes (very visible)
Unifacial worked pebble 5	2 femur,2 tibia, 2 humerus, 2 radius ulna of fresh *Bos taurus*	Fracture		204	20 min	yes
Unifacial worked pebble 6	1 femur, 2 tibia, 2 radius-ulna of fresh *Bos taurus*			136	36 min	yes
Unifacial worked pebble 7	1 femur, 2 tibia, 3 humerus, 3 radius-ulna (after cooking)			247	42 min	yes (very visible)

Table 3. Experimental wood work with flakes

Implement Technology	Worked Material	Action	Use	Outer bark contact	Time	Macro use wear (naked eye observation)
Cortical Flake G1L1	Fresh *quercus ilex* with outer bark	Scrap with unidirectional movement (from distal to proximal extremities towards the experimenter)	Ventral surface towards the experimenter with 45° angle in the same direction	yes	10 min	yes (very visible)
Cortical Flake G1L2				yes	20 min	yes
Cortical Flake G1L3				no	40 min	yes (not much visible)
Cortical Flake G2L1			Ventral surface towards the experimenter with 90° angle in the same direction	yes	10 min	yes (very visible)
Cortical Flake G2L2				yes	20 min	no
Cortical Flake G2L3				yes	40 min	yes (not much visible)
Cortical Flake G3L1		Scrap with bi-directional movement	Ventral surface towards the experimenter	yes	10 min	yes
Cortical Flake G3L2				yes	20 min	yes (not much visible)
Cortical Flake G3L3				no	40min	yes (very visible)
Half cortical G4L1		Cutting with bi-directional movement	Left upper surface in the right hand of the experimenter (or vice versa in left handed experimenters)	yes	10min	yes (very visible)
Half cortical G4L2				yes	20 min	no
Half cortical G4L3				no	40 min	yes (not much visible)
Half cortical G4aL1				ind.	10 min	yes (very visible)
Half cortical G4aL2				ind.	20 min	no
Half cortical G4aL3				yes	40 min	yes (not much visible)
Cortical Flake G6L1	Dry *quercus ilex* with outer bark	Scrap with unidirectional movement (from distal to proximal extremities towards the experimenter)	Ventral surface towards the experimenter with 45° angle in the same direction	yes	10 min	yes (very visible)
Cortical Flake G6L2				yes	20 min	Não
Cortical Flake G6L3				ind.	40 min	yes (not much visible)
Cortical Flake G7L1			Ventral surface towards the experimenter with 90° angle in the same direction	yes	10 min	yes (not much visible)
Cortical Flake G7L2				yes	20 min	Sim
Cortical Flake G7L3				yes	40 min	yes (not much visible)
Cortical Flake G8L1		Scrap with bi-directional movement	Ventral surface towards the experimenter	yes	10 min	yes (very visible)
Cortical Flake G8L2				yes	20 min	yes (very visible)
Cortical Flake G8L3				no	40 min	yes (not much visible)
Half cortical G9L1		Sawing with bi-directional movement	Left upper surface in the right hand of the experimenter (or vice versa in left handed experimenters)	yes	10 min	yes (very visible)
Half cortical G9L2				yes	20 min	Sim
Half cortical G9L3				no	40 min	yes (not much visible)

(Tab. 2). While using the experimental implements, the several experimenters remarked the importance of the dimensions and suitability to one's hand, since in the best conditions the movements are more regular and thus more efficient.

Concerning the angles of use, a 45° angle seems to be more efficient on irregular surfaces (removing outer bark, for example), while angles of 90° are better on regular surfaces.

The dry wood requires more effort in all activities, resulting in most of the cases on visible edge modifications. These, however, according to the experimenters' observations improve the efficiency of the tool, since more irregular edges with more open angles (similar to notches and denticulates) are better to work over dry wood, particularly to remove the outer bark.

The experimental bone work with flakes was performed using fresh and cooked cow bones. In total 18 implements were employed: 1 flake to fracture, 9 flakes were used to scrap, 3 to cut and 3 to engrave. The activities and use modes were similar to those applied on wood work, plus engraving. In general, according to the experimenters, all blanks were efficient.

The experimental flakes were also used in butchering activities. A skilled butcher performed the activities using quartzite flakes of fine texture and he accomplished the entire slaughtering of *Capra Hircus 1* in 47 min 30sec (Tab. 5). The other slaughterings took more time due to the bigger size of the animals (*Capra hircus 2* – 58 min, 38 sec; *Capra hircus 3* – 126 min, 38 sec; *Ovies aires* – 77 min; *Sus scrofa* – 177 min).

Even though the quartzite used for these tasks was of fine texture, almost no visible edge modifications resulted

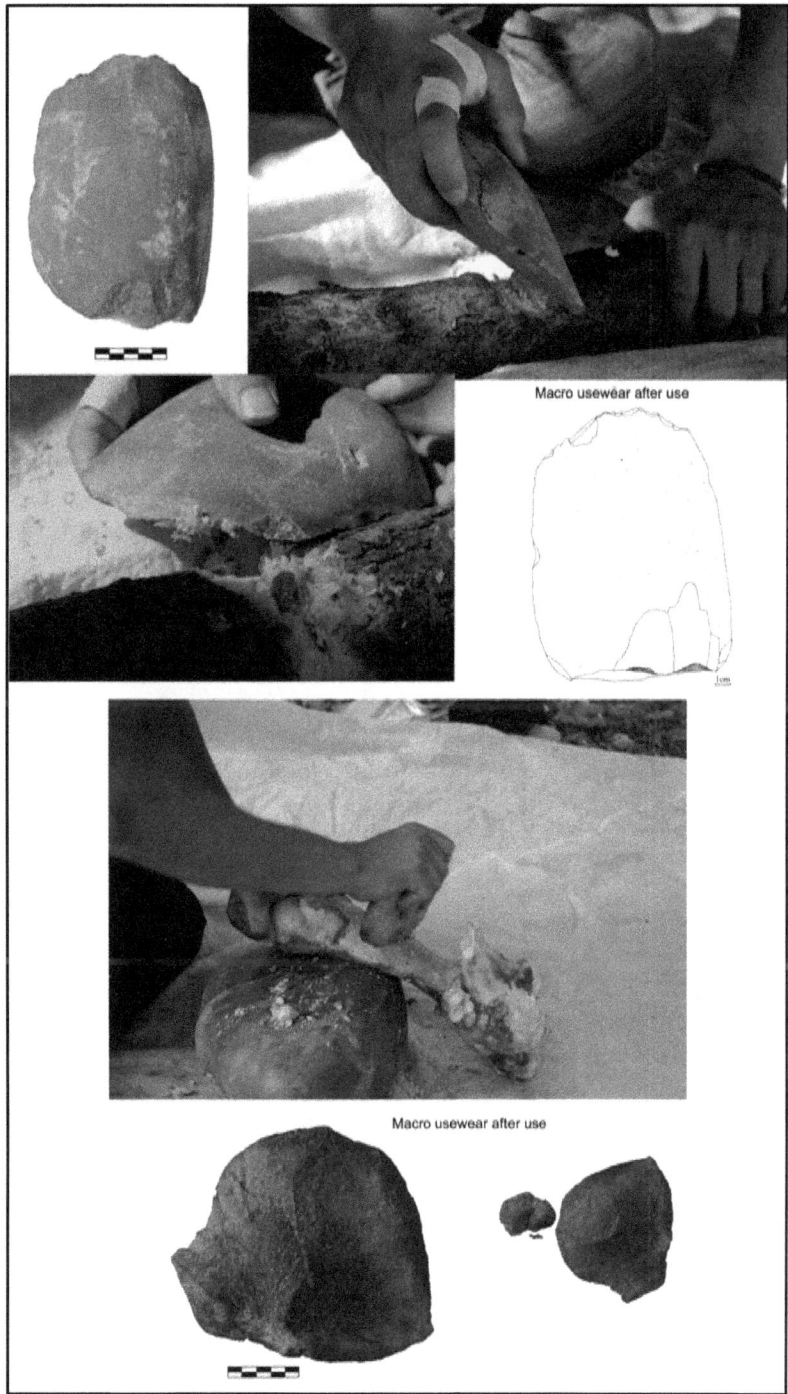

Figure 4. Wood cutting and bone fracture with experimental cortical quartzite flakes

from the experiments, excepting the reduction of cutting edges. Actually, according to the butcher, all the flakes were still quite sharp in the end of the utilization, being replaced only by reasons of equilibrium between size, action and manipulation. These observations are valid for all the other butchering activities.

The skin removed after butchering *Capra hircus 1* was fixed to a wood structure and proccessed fresh and after drying. The major fat removals where done immediately after butchering, but the main scraping was done one day after (Tab. 6). All the work was carried out with the hide on a vertical position (Fig. 6).

FUNCTIONAL ANALYSIS

The analysis of the 39 experimental tools (selected from the mentioned 68) has shown that processing medium and hard materials (like wood and bone) by means of direct resting percussion (scraping/sawing) produces an intense loss of material along the functional edges and the formation of a "denticulated" profile of the edges characterised by invasive hinge and stepped use-retouches. These latter detachments are mainly produced at the beginning of the functional activity and their morphology can be compared to the technological retouch type "b" and "c" (denticulated type)., If these

Table 4. Experimental work with cow bones

Implement Technology	Worked Material	Action	Use	Time	Macro use wear (naked eye observation)
Cortical flake 1	1 femur, 1 tibia, 1 humerus, 1 radius ulna	Fracture	Upper surface in the right hand of the experimenter with na angle of 90º to 70º	10 min	Yes (very visible)
Cortical Flake G10L1	Fresh cow bone (femur)	Scrap with unidirectional movement (from distal to proximal extremities towards the experimenter)	Ventral surface towards the experimenter with 45º angle in the same direction	10 min	Yes (not much visible)
Cortical Flake G10L2				20 min	Yes
Cortical Flake G10L3				40 min	Yes (very visible)
Cortical Flake G11L1			Ventral surface towards the experimenter with 90º angle in the same direction	10 min	No
Cortical Flake G11L2				20 min	Yes
Cortical Flake G11L3				40 min	Yes
Cortical Flake G12L1		Scrap with bi-directional movement	Ventral surface towards the experimenter	10 min	Yes
Cortical Flake G12L2				20 min	Yes (very visible)
Cortical Flake G12L3				40 min	Yes (very visible)
Half cortical G13L1		Sawing with bi-directional movement	Left upper surface in the right hand of the experimenter (or vice versa in left handed experimenters)	10 min	Yes (not much visible)
Half cortical G13L2				20 min	Yes (very visible)
Half cortical G13L3				40 min	Yes (very visible)
Half cortical G13a L1				10 min	Yes (not much visible)
Half cortical G13a L2				20 min	Sim
Half cortical G13a L3				40 min	Yes (not much visible)
Flake with a pointed edge G14L1		Engraving	Burin like	10 min	No
Flake with a pointed edge G14L2				20 min	Yes (point fracture)
Flake with a pointed edge G14L3				40 min	Yes (point fracture)

Table 5. Experimental butchering process with quartzite flakes

Implement Technology	Animal	Butchering stage	Action	Time	Macro use wear (naked eye observation)
Half cortical flake G15L15	*Capra hircus 1*	Cut skin from flesh	Cutting with the lateral cortical edge	19 min	No
Residual cortical flake G15L5		Sever head from body ,viscera removal (contact with the sternum bone), dismember	Cutting with convergent non cortical edges	9 min 30 sec	No
Residual cortical flake G15L16		Cut flesh and tendons, dismember	Cutting with cortical/ non cortical edge	12 min	No
		Cut skin from flesh	Cutting with the lateral cortical edge	19 min	No
Non cortical flake 1	*Capra hircus 2*	Cut skin from flesh	Cutting with the lateral edges	31 min 38 seg	Reduction of 2 mm in both edges
Non cortical flake 2		Sever head from body, viscera removal (contact with the sternum bone), dismember	Cutting with the lateral edges	25 min	Reduction of 2 mm in right edge and 1mm in left edge
Non cortical flake 3		Cut flesh and tendons, dismember	Cutting with left edge	32 min	Reduction of 3 mm in left edge
Hal cortical flake 1	*Capra hircus 3*	Cut skin from flesh	Cutting with left edge	29 min	No
Hal cortical flake 2		Sever head from body , viscera removal (contact with the sternum bone), cut flesh and tendons, dismember	Cutting with the lateral edges	49 min 38 seg	Reduction of 3 mm in left edge
Hal cortical flake 3		Cut flesh and tendons, dismember	Cutting with the left edge	48 min	No

Implement Technology	Animal	Butchering stage	Action	Time	Macro use wear (naked eye observation)
Non cortical flake 1	*Ovis aries* 1	Cut skin from flesh, cut flesh and tendons	Cutting with the left edge	35 min	No
Hal cortical flake 2		Dismember	Cutting with the distal edge	10 min	Reduction of 3 mm
Hal cortical flake 3		Sever head from body, dismember, viscera removal	Cutting with the distal edge	12 min	No
Non cortical flake 1	*Sus scrofa* 1	Dismember, cut flesh and tendons	Cutting with the right edge	20 min	No
Non cortical flake 3		Cut skin from flesh	Cutting with the distal edge	57 min 35 seg	No
Cortical flake 2		Dismember, cut flesh and tendons	Cutting with the distal edge	68 min 19 seg	No
Cortical flake 3		Sever head from body, dismember, viscera removal, cut flesh and tendons	Cutting with the right edge	52 min 33 seg	No

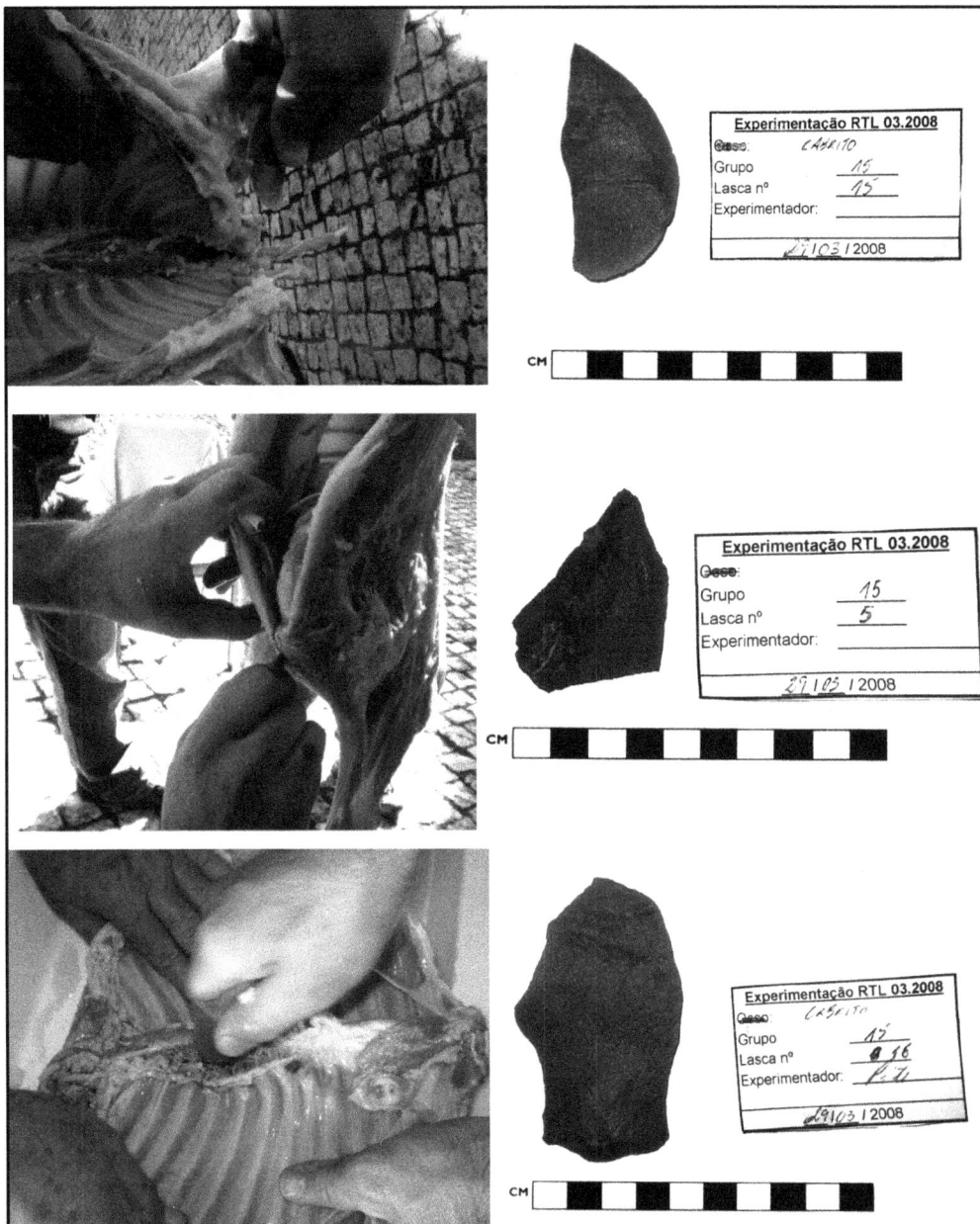

Figure 5. Flakes used in the slaughtering of Capra hircus 1

Table 6. Experimental hide processing with quartzite flakes

Implement Technology	Hide process	Action	Time
Half cortical flake G15L17	Wood structure preparation	Cut vegetal fibers/ perfurate skin	–
Distal cortical edge G15L3	Cut fleshy tissue and fat remains	Cutting with cortical edge in bidirectional movments	7 min 50
Distal cortical edge G15L9	Fat scraping	Scraping with distal cortical	11 min
Distal cortical edge G15L18	Thining scraping (Dry)	Scrap with dorsal surface towards the experimenter	65 min

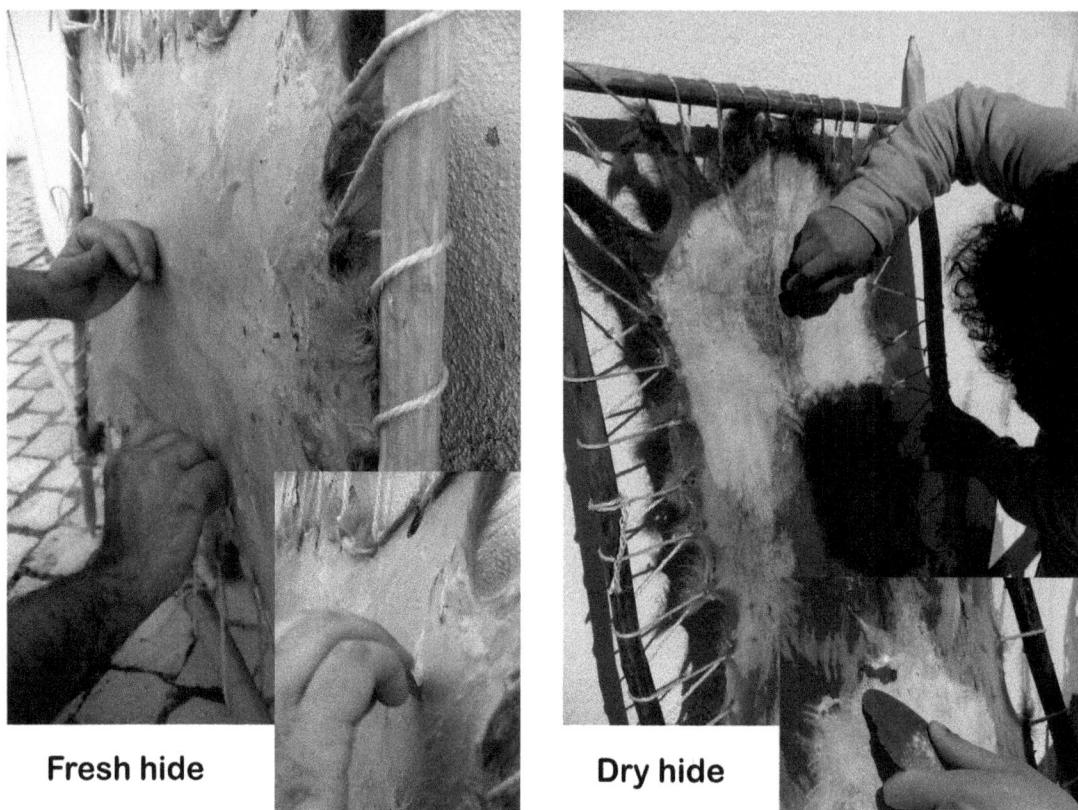

Fresh hide   **Dry hide**

Figure 6. Details of the experimental hide processing

Table 7. Macro and micro usewear traces of experimental tools

		WOOD	BONE	HIDE	BUTCHERING
CUTTING/ SCRAPING		**Macro** – Substantial loss of material on the edge – Denticulate profile of the edge due to invasive mechanical features – Large and deep use-retouches on the lateral part of the used edges, often characterised by hinge termination	**Macro** – Invasive hinge and stepped use-retouches – Microscopic linear features	**Macro** – Mechanical rounding – Circular and half-moon oriented macro use-retouches	**Macro** – Low rate of mechanical features and use-wear characteristics
		Micro – *Furrow* type mechanical linear features – Linear arrays of impact pits (500x≥1000x) – Gentle ondulation of the surface topography	**Micro** – Developed rounding – Furrow striations characterised by irregular edges and comet shaped impact pits (400x) – "Fluid" aspect of the bone polish (400x)	**Micro** – Badly defined irregular striations with a ground plane characterised by irregular lenticular pits (400x magnification). – Smoothing of the edge (200x)	**Micro** – Broad shallow striations clustered in groups on the lateral edge of the tools (400x) – Irregular furrow striations (confirmed by SEM analysis) due to the contact with hard material (bone)

Table 8. Use wear results

Worked Material	Cutting		Scraping		Cutting+Scraping	
	macro	macro+micro	macro	macro+micro	macro	macro+micro
Hard/medium hard material	1	2	2	7	1	2
Soft material	–	1	–	–	–	–
Multifunction	–	–	–	–	–	1

detachments are located on the very lateral end of the used edges they can be similar to the technological atypical retouches described as "notches" (type "a").

Tanning and butchering activities haven't produced a loss of material along the edges, but mainly a mechanical rounding of them. More, the formation of circular and half-moon oriented macro use-retouches have been identified especially in association to hide cutting.

Butchering is the experimental activity which creates the less developed mechanical traces and use-wear characteristics. Micro-traces from this activity have been identified only at 400x magnification using both metalographich and ESEM microscopy. They appear as broad shallow striations clustered in groups on the lateral edge of the tools.

Archaeological use-wear

As stated above, the functional analysis of archaeological tools, still in course, has been carried out with the aim of verifying the "nature" of the atypical retouches/edges modifications characterizing some of the Ribeira da Ponte da Pedra / Atalaia tools. So far, among the 47 selected archaeological tools, 17 flakes characterised by less developed post-depositional alteration were analysed and are presented in this paper.

Up to now, 4 archaeological tools show macroscopic mechanical features and 13 show macro and micro traces. It must be stated that the observed micro-traces never show a well developed characteristics but their aspect and orientation seem to confirm what was observed at low magnification.

On the base of our experimental results, evidences for hard material cutting have been identified on 3 artefacts. The mechanical features on one of them can be connected to bone contact.

Furrow striations, conchoidal step detachments and roundings characterise 9 of the analysed artefacts. At least 1 of them shows abrasion areas and linear arrays of impact pits with more regular edges, which could be typical of wood scraping tools.

On one tool, characterised by continuous series of choncoidal retouches, we observed the presence of a well developed abrasive wear, extensive smoothing patches with defined circumference and straight sided striations

with a ground plane consisting of lenticular pits. For this tool we suggest an interpretation as hide scraper. Only one tool presents both scraping and cutting wear traces.

FINAL REMARKS

The results of the experimental activity and use-wear analysis (both in terms of macro and micro traces) allow us to conclude that most of the edges described as "informal" retouched – and therefore attributed to the four types of edge-modifications – can be the result of functional activities linked to different subsistence tasks, namely those involving hard materials like wood and bone.

Authors agree that the assumptions reported here require further confirmation. A wider experimental reference collection of macro and micro traces resulting from more extensive activities in all kind of materials is required. This is particularly needed in the case of butchering activities where the mechanical processes linked to the edges modifications are less invasive.

This will be one of the objectives of the experimental research we aim to develop in the near future.

References

CHAMBERS, J.C. (2003) – Like a rolling stone? The identification of fluvial transportation damage signatures on secondary context bifaces. *Lithics* 24, p. 66-77.

CRISTIANI, E.; CURA, S.; GRIMALDI, S.; GOMES, J.; OOSTERBEEK, L.; ROSINA, P. (2010) – Functional analysis and experimental archaeology: the Middle Pleistocene site of Ribeira da Atalaia, (Central Portugal). In: Araujo Igreja M., Clemente Conte I. (Eds.). Proceedings of the workshop on "Recent Functional Studies on Non-Flint Stone Tools, Methodological Improvements and Archaeological Inferences". (Lisbon 2008), [CD-ROM] http://www.workshop-traceologia-lisboa2008.com

CURA, S.; OOSTERBEEK, L.; GRIMALDI, S.; CRISITANI, E.; CURA, P.; CUNHA, A.; CEREZER, J. (2008) – Indústrias líticas e comportamento humano pré-histórico no Alto Ribatejo – Uma abordagem Experimental, in Zahara, nº12, p. 71-80.

CURA, S.; GRIMALDI, S. (2009) – The intensive quartzite exploitation in Midlle Tagus Valley

Pleistocene open air sites – the example of Ribeira da Ponte da Pedra. In: Grimaldi, S.; Cura, S. (Eds.), Technological Analysis on Quartzite Exploitation, Proceedings of the XV World Congress UISPP (Lisbon, 4-9 September 2006). BAR Int.Series. 1998, 49-56.

DIAS, M.I; PRUDÊNCIO, M.I.; FRANCO, D.; CURA, S.; GRIMALDI, S.; OOSTERBEEK, L.; ROSINA, P. (2010) – Luminescence dating of a fluvial deposit sequence: Ribeira da Ponte da Pedra – Middle Tagus Valley, Portugal. In: M.I. Prudêncio; M.I. Dias (Eds.), Archaeometry, Proceedings of the XV World Congress UISPP (Lisbon, 4-9 September 2006) Oxford, BAR Publishing, BAR International Series 2045, pp. 103-113.

GRIMALDI, S.; ROSINA, P. (2001) – O Pleistoceno Médio Final no Alto Ribatejo (Portugal, centro): o sítio da Ribeira da Ponte da Pedra. In: Territórios, mobilidade e povoamento no Alto-Ribatejo. II: Santa Cita e o quaternário da região / coord. Ana Rosa Cruz, Luiz Oosterbeek. – Tomar: CEIPHAR – Centro Europeu de Investigação da Pré-História do Alto Ribatejo, p. 89-116.

HOSFIELD, R.T.; CHAMBERS, J.C. (2002) – Processes and Experiences – Experimental Archaeology on a River Floodplain. In Macklin, M.G.; Brewer, P.A.; Coulthard, T.J. eds. River Systems and Environmental Change in Wales: Field Guide. Aberystwyth: British Geomorphological Research Group, p. 32-39.

MARTINS, A.A.; CUNHA, P.P.; ROSINA, P.; OOSTERBEEK, L.; CURA, S.; GRIMALDI, S.; GOMES, J.; BUYLAERT, J.-P.; MURRAY, A.S.; MATOS, J. (2010) – Geoarcheology of Pleistocene open-air sites in the Vila Nova da Barquinha – Santa Cita area (lower Tejo river basin, central Portugal).

Proceedings of the Geologists Association, Elsevier Science Publishers. 121, p. 128-140.

MEIRELES, J., CUNHA-RIBEIRO, J.P. (1991-92) – Matérias-primas e indústrias líticas do Paleolítico Inferior português: representatividade e significado, In Cadernos de Arqueologia, Série II, p. 31-41.

MOZZI, P. (1998) – Evoluzione Geomorfologica della bassa valle del fiume Nabão, Arkeos. vol. 4, p. 37-58.

OOSTERBEEK, L. (2008a) – Territórios, Mobilidade e Povoamento no Alto Ribatejo II – relatório final In: L. Oosterbeek – coord. (2008), In Territórios, Mobilidade e Povoamento no Alto Ribatejo V – Balanço e perspectivas no ano do centenário do Museu de Francisco Tavares Proença Júnior, Tomar, CEIPHAR, p. 9-37.

OOSTERBEEK, L. (2008b) – Paisagens de transição: povoamento, tecnologia e crono-estratigrafia da transição para o agro pastoralismo no Centro de Portugal In: L. Oosterbeek – coord. (2008), In Territórios, Mobilidade e Povoamento no Alto Ribatejo V – Balanço e perspectivas no ano do centenário do Museu de Francisco Tavares Proença Júnior, Tomar, CEIPHAR, p. 173-180.

ROSINA, P. (2002) – Stratigraphie et géomorphologie des terrasses fluviatiles de la moyenne Vallée du Tage (Haut Ribatejo, Portugal). In Territórios, mobilidade e povoamento no Alto-Ribatejo. IV: Contextos macrolíticos / coord. Ana Rosa Cruz, Luiz Oosterbeek. – Tomar: CEIPHAR – Centro Europeu de Investigação da Pré-História do Alto Ribatejo, p. 11-52.

ROSINA, P. (2004) – I depositi quaternari nella Media Valle del Tago (Alto Ribatejo, Portogallo centrale) e le industrie litiche associate. Thèse de Doctorat soutenue auprès de l'Université de Ferrara. 204 p.

EXPERIMENTAL ARCHAEOLOGY ON BRAZILIAN POLISHED ARTIFACTS: MAKING ADORNMENTS, HAFTING BLADES AND CUTTING TREES

Gustavo Neves de SOUZA

Doctoral scholarship CAPES at Universidade de São Paulo, Brazil
gustavo_ns@yahoo.com.br

Ângelo Pessoa LIMA

Master scholarship CAPES at Universidade Federal do Pará, Brazil
lima.angelo@gmail.com

Abstract: *In this work we are going to present some of the results we achieved through the experimental archaeology on three different tasks. First, the making of adornments, that were commonly used on lips (called tembetás), using different rocks as raw materials for the adornments and for the polishing basin. Second, the hafting of one blade in a peculiar way (known trough secondary sources) called "organic hafting". Third, our job of cutting wood with a second polished stone blade, cutting that living branch where the first one was hafted helping us to understand the efficiency on its use.*

Keywords: *Polished artifacts, experimental archaeology*

Résumé: *Dans ce travail nous allons présenter certains des résultats nous avons atteint la cuvette archéologie expérimentale sur les trois tâches différentes. Tout d'abord, la fabrication d'ornements, qui étaient couramment utilisés sur les lèvres (appelées tembetás), en utilisant différentes roches comme matières premières pour la parure et pour le bassin de polissage. Deuxièmement, l'emmanchement d'une lame d'une manière particulière (sources connus sous secondaire) a appelé «l'emmanchement organique». Troisièmement, notre travail de coupe de bois avec une seconde lame de pierre polie, couper cette branche vivante où la première a été emmanchées, nous aidant à comprendre l'efficacité de son utilisation.*

Mots-clés: *Piéces Polie, archéologie expérimentale*

INTRODUCTION

The main focus of this work was to produce data that could help in a broader understanding on the ways of life of the South American societies before the arrival of Europeans. For this purpose we chose as starting point two categories of archaeological artifacts on which very little attention has been given; the adornments and the polished stone blades. Through a work of experimental archeology, which involves the reproduction (in the case of adornments) and use (in the case of blades), we intend to produce data that may allow us to better assess the role that these artifacts played in the daily life, and eventually, in the minds of people.

The chronological depth to which this study intends to refer reaches the last 4000 years, with the expansion of horticultural groups, bearers of these polished blades, and possibly the ornaments in question. However, we will focus our attention in the more direct relationship we can establish between these artifacts and some specific horticulturalist groups that were spread throughout Brazil in the sixteenth century. Our guidelines are essentially the relationships that we can trace, through ethnohistorical and ethnographic data, between these artifacts, and those groups that would have belonged to the Tupi-Guarani linguistic family.

We are aware of the fact that often there is a large temporal gap between the people we see today (or that were seen in recent decades and even centuries) making use of artifacts like these, that are the subject of this work, and the people from more than five centuries ago, whose sites and artifacts we analyze. Even when the region is the same, that the supposed cultural relationship with the contemporary group is well established and ways of life may have been similar, we should be aware of limitations in our capability of making references, inferences and analogies.[1] Cultural groups change throughout space and time.

We will start our approach with the artefactual category of adornments, making reproductions of them, using different raw materials, both in the manufacture of the artifacts as in the support used for polishing. These supports are polishing basins and the so called calibrators. The general goal would be to understand the efforts involved in the manufacturing process, searching for clues that may help understand the prestige that those artifacts were imbued with. The more specific goal is to evaluate the performance of different techniques in the manufacture of the artifacts.

---

[1] David & Kramer, 2001.

The second task will be experimentation of hafting a polished stone blade, commonly called stone axe. We will carry out a part of the "organic hafting", which consists on inserting a blade into the branch of a still living tree, waiting for the growth of the branch itself to make the blade firmly attached to it. This experimentation will not follow the same systematization of the first one, since it consists of a single experiment; however it brings us the first experimental data on this kind of hafting. The aim is to evaluate the time involved in such activity. It will provide us with data on the possible value that could be associated with a tool hafted in this way. Perhaps, it may help on our evaluation on the possible relationship those groups would have established between the time involved in the process and the prestige associated with the artifact.

Finally, we will describe the process of removing the organic haft, which at a first look consists in little more than a branch tied to a tree. For this purpose we used a polished stone blade, hafted in the way called "embedded", about which we have good references. The objective is to evaluate the efficiency of the use of the blade, according to the time spent in the activity.

THE EXPERIMENTATIONS WITH THE ADORNMENTS

Some caution must be taken when using of the sixteenth century sources in our studies (as we said), but lots of information collated from those writings are really precious, allowing us to understand the association between the adornments in question and the Tupi groups. These adornments are called *tembetás* (also labrets), a Tupi language word, formed by the junction of *tembé*, which means *lower lip*, plus *itá*, which means *stone*. Within this category two morphologies are clearly distinguishable (Figs. 1 and 2), whose productions are associated with specific raw materials. In both cases that we see in the drawings (and in many written sources) the items are indicatives of high status. Both of the persons represented are amongst the most prestigious of their villages. Different sources agree that their prestige, among other things, is associated with the ownership and use of these adornments.

One simple description of the morphologies is enough to make clear the distinction between the two kinds of *tembetás*. First we have the long type, "T" shaped, usually made of quartz (Fig. 1b), which would look hung in the lip, somewhat like a finger from the outside of the mouth (Fig. 1a). The second type is characterized by flatter and wider adornments (Fig. 2b), which would look like a button when viewed from the outside of the mouth (Fig. 2a). They are frequently made of amazonite or similar green stones.

The manufacture of these adornments has been frequently associated with some artifacts known as calibrators. These consist of supports that can be made of rock or ceramics (in this case, reutilized pot sherds) with

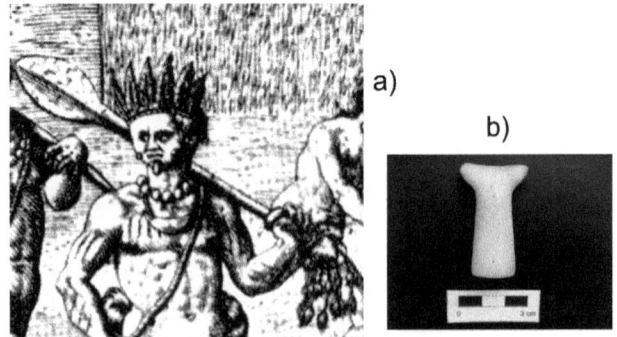

Figure 1. a) Adapted from Staden, H. (1968);
b) Gustavo Neves de Souza

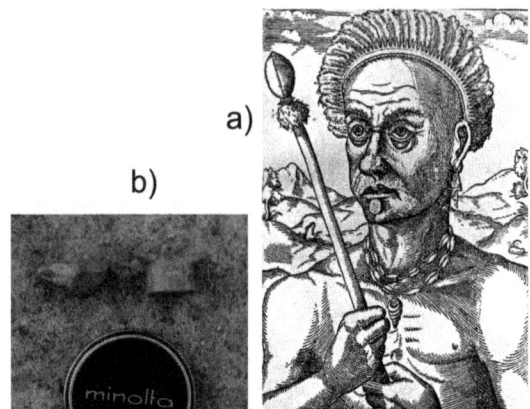

Figure 2. a) Adapted from Thévet, A. (1944)

Figure 3. a) Adapted from Mazière, G. & Maziére, M.
(1997); b) Adapted from Vilhena-Vialou, A. (1980)

channels. There is a quite large variety of them, both in size and number of channels as much as position of then and even in the size of the supports (Fig. 3). The production of adornments on these supports, which is suggested as being part of their manufacturing process, will also be useful to compare the traces observed in the archaeological record with those produced trough experimental work.

To a better understanding of the traces left by the manufacturing of an elongated *tembetá* (as the flat and wider type in no way could have left such channels), we used different supports, both fixed and mobile (which imply in different gestures, as they allow or not the use of the arms along with body weight), made of ceramics and rock of different granulometries. The raw material chosen to produce the adornment was a quartz crystal, often

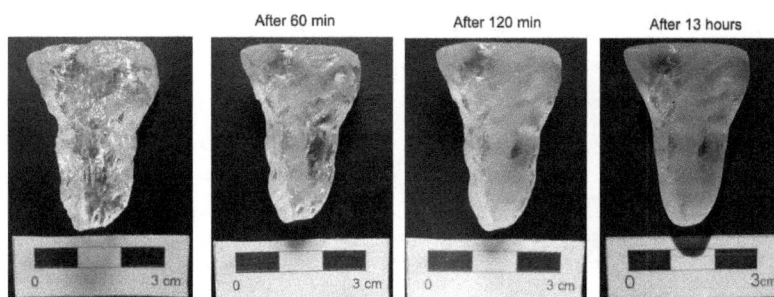

Figure 4. Gustavo Neves de Souza

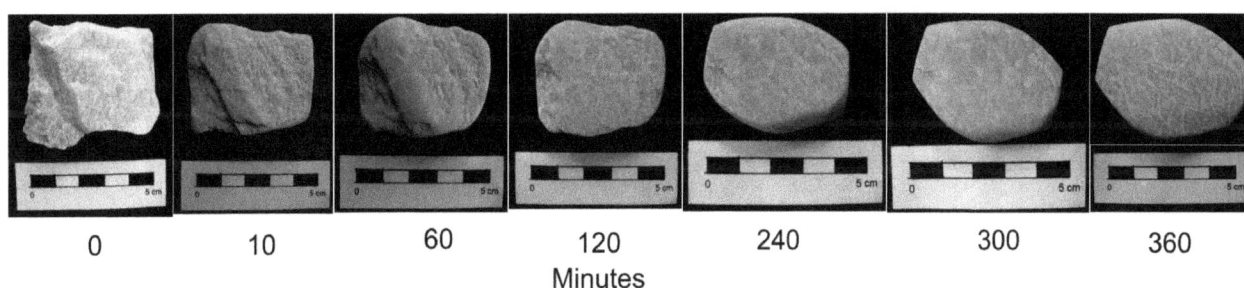

0   10   60   120   240   300   360

Minutes

Figure 5. Gustavo Neves de Souza

chosen by Tupi people when related to the production of those artifacts.

THE MANUFACTURE OF A QUARTZ CRYSTAL TEMBETÁ

During the experiment we used a pre-form of quartz crystal, taken from a crystal by percussion with a hammer stone over an anvil and subtly retouched by direct percussion (Fig. 4). The raw materials that were used as supports, to polish the *tembetá*, were the gneiss (used as fixed polishing basin), a granitous gneiss (as mobile support), that is more friable than the other, and sandstone. The ceramic fragments used were different in terms of antiplastic (or temper) particle size, divided between those of coarse grain (clearly visible in the paste), and those fine-grained (antiplastic discrete in the paste). The addition of water is frequently referred in ethnohistorical and ethnographic data. All were used without addition of water and with the addition of water. The more structured gneiss (less friable) was tested with the addition of sand and water.

Experiments consisted in different working activities, with 60 minutes spent on each one. The sequence was; gneiss as fixed support, with the addition of sand and water, followed by granitous gneiss as mobile support, dry and with the addition of water; gneiss, dry and with the addition of water, ceramics with coarse-grained antiplastic, dry and with the addition of water; ceramics with fine-grained antiplastic, dry and with the addition of water; sandstone, dry and with the addition of water, and finally, again with the dry granitous gneiss. The productivity in each of the raw materials can be seen in Tab. 1 (last page). The result seen in the artifact is

relatively discreet, taking into account the time spent at work (Fig. 4).

THE MANUFACTURE OF THE AMAZONITE TEMBETÁ

In this experiment we used a "flake" taken from a block of amazonite over the anvil. Each activity, again, was to evaluate the work of 60 minutes (however, the measures were carried out every 10 minutes). The piece was used initially on a fixed gneiss polishing basin and then on a fixed sandstone polishing basin, which already had a mild depression before its use in this experiment. This is a kind of artifact or *site furniture*[2] commonly found on the banks of water courses. In both cases the supports were tested dry and with the addition of water, but also with the addition of sand and water. The results are shown in Tab. 2 (last page) and the surface treatment, resulting from the work of the artifact is notorious (Fig. 5).

THE ORGANIC HAFTING

Various forms of hafting are known, both ethno-historically and ethnographically. A few of them are also present in the archaeological record, such as a haft found at the archaeological site Lapa do Boquete, in the Cavernas do Peruaçu National Park, Minas Gerais state, Brazil (Fig. 6). Based on this type of hafting we started our experiment of hafting a polished stone blade. The type of hafting in question, called embedded, consists of a deep depression carved into the wood, where the blade

_____

[2] Schiffer, 1999.

Figure 6. Gustavo Neves de Souza

will be introduced, usually with the addition of some kind of resin, twine (bast) and/or beeswax.

Though, the type of hafting we are trying to get a better knowledge is not as well described in the sources as the common embedded one we explained above. This situation led us to make the attempt to reproduce it, the way it was probably made, allowing us to estimate the time involved in the process. It consists on excavating a cavity[3] in a living branch (Fig. 7), inserting the blade, tying it, in order to keep it pressed against the bottom of the cavity (with the biding wrapping the edge of the blade and the opposite side of the trunk), and wait until it gets firmly attached, due to the growth of the tree.

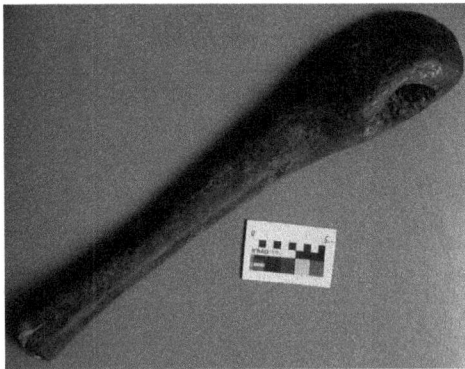

Figure 7. Gustavo Neves de Souza

The blade chosen to be hafted at the living branch is archaeological, with only very scarce information about it. No site or exact place of origin was present. The only information in fact is that it came from Minas Gerais state. It reduces drastically the approaches that can be directed to it. The triangular morphology it presents is also very common in the central region of the state and is easily adaptable to the proposed hafting model. That was a good chance to make and it shed some light at archaeological knowledge of the organic hafting.

For more information on excavating with traditional techniques see Souza & Figueiredo, 2003.

The blade was embedded in a branch of a native tree, the guava (*Psidium guajava*), before the raining season, hoping that during that season, when it is expected to have more log growth, it would be easier to get it firmly held. The blade was introduced in the branch at the end of August. Until the month of April, in the following year, it was not completely attached yet. We decided to monitor the situation for some more time. In fact, it was early June when it became well attached to the b ranch (Fig. 8).

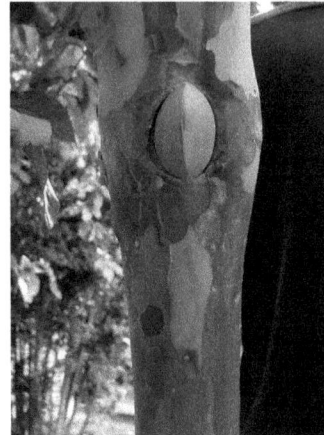

Figure 8. Gustavo Neves de Souza

Finally, with the blade firmly attached to the branch, it was ready to be removed from the tree. For this job we used a second polished stone blade, hafted as embedded. That blade, which was also an archaeological one, had the same problems of information the first one had.

Three non expert woodcutters took turns in the process of taking down the branch the blade was hafted in. The tree is considered to be of small size (about 3 m high) which posed no special difficulties. Then, the smaller branches that were higher and grew from the main branch (where the blade was hafted), were separated from it.

Within about eight minutes the branch the blade was hafted in was separated from the rest of the tree. It was cut at its base (near the log) which consisted in a cylindrical piece of wood of about 15 cm diameter. Certainly the weight of the tree's crown (which had two very large branches growing from it), assisted in the felling. Furthermore, another interesting thing was noticed; a bit of sap flowed through the hole where the blade was hafted during the blows with the axe.

In addition, another 3 minutes were spent on the removal of one of the branches from the upper part (the thickest one), and 2 minutes to remove the smaller one. Another 2 minutes were spent twisting the fibers to separate them from the branch. Meanwhile, about 5 minutes were distributed in short pauses for rest.

The distribution of time spent per woodcutter occurred as follows: 4 minutes with the first woodcutter, 3 minutes with the woodcutter 2, and 1 more minute with the same, spent on the removal of the tree branch. After that 3 more minutes were spent by the third woodcutter on the removal of thicker branches from the tree's crown. This activity was carried out after the removal of the branch from the tree. Finally another 2 minutes were spent removing the second branch, with the first woodcutter in action. In the whole procedure less than 15 minutes were spent, leaving the haft removed from the tree and ready for final preparation.

We started the final preparation of the haft with a concave scraper, aiming to remove the outermost part of the wood. With about 5 minutes of work we realized that a good amount of material had been removed (Fig. 9). We decided to reserve the cable, so we could resume the experiment later with the wood already dried, allowing to evaluate the difference in efficiency.

Figure 9. Gustavo Neves de Souza

Some months later, when we went back to work, we realized that the wood had become so hardened that it would not be possible to proceed with the work using fragile instruments, like the scraper that we had prepared. The work now would require some kind of robust instrument, perhaps like a polished stone chisel, a tool that was not available. We then ended the experiment, which could not be completed, as originally intended. But the information it brought is important, indicating that the final preparation of the haft was probably made with the wood still "green", soon after taking it from the tree, or other polished instruments would have been necessary to finish that task (and they are rare in the archaeological record).

DISCUSSION

After analyzing the data, some points can be highlighted regarding the use of calibrators to make a quartz *tembetá*. First, it has shown clearly the difference between rocky and ceramic supports in terms of efficiency. The ceramic supports did not provide any reduction in weight at the artifact worked on them (which would reflect the amount of material removed during work). In addition, the possible better surface treatment in the piece was only barely observable, with a polishing slightly finer.

A second important point concerns the difference in efficiency observed between the fixed supports and the mobile ones. The fixed supports are much more efficient, up to six times, compared to the mobile ones. Certainly it is due to the comfort in the gesture applicable at the fixed supports, in which we can use the weight of the body and arms with greater dexterity. Mobile supports, as its name indicates, are not stable, often having to be handled with one hand (or feet) to remain in place. This difference in the gesture decreases the amount of force that can be applied to work.

A third important point is related to use of water. The simple addition of water does not seem to have a decisive effect on the efficiency. However, when adding the sand, which makes the efficiency grows, the water becomes crucial, for it is what keeps the sand cohesive, preventing it from spreading and being lost, also allowing the piece to slip on the mass formed by the wet sand.

About the work with amazonite other points can be posed. In matter of efficiency we observed that the use of gneiss as fixed polishing basin, with the addition of water, stands out in the table (Tab. 1). However, we must keep in mind that this is the initial phase of work, when the artifact in production has more edges and hence is expected to miss much more matter, resulting in a higher apparent efficiency of the technique. When compared with the following technique, using a polishing basin of sandstone, with addition of water, the efficiency is now about 20% lower. Nevertheless, water occupies a more important role here, keeping the grains of sand that are detached from the support also usable in the process, providing a surface treatment slightly finer. This is certainly due to the fact that the grains were already slightly rolled during the polishing at the basin.

A curious observation, that presented no easy explanation, was the considerable loss of efficiency of the gneiss with the addition of water and sand over the sandstone with the addition of water. It was expected that the performance would be higher and, although the surface treatment had suggested that, with deep grooves and appearance of coarse polishing only, the observed in the balance told us otherwise. We are not able to explain the reason for this performance, although it is clear that this is the expected performance in the later stages of work, as can be seen in relation to the use of water in the sandstone at the following steps.

The "exceptional" efficiency presented by sandstone with the addition of sand and water can be explained by the strong action of the sand, along with the grains that detached from the sandstone basin, now in greater quantity. This allowed achieving efficiency similar to that observed in the early stages of work, like the first use of sandstone with addition of water. However, as the surface treatment was very coarse, similar to that observed in the use of gneiss with sand and water, we decided to spend the time using the sandstone, only with the addition of water.

The good performance combined with good surface treatment showed that the sandstone, along with water, and the support already with the shape of a polishing basin, has shown up as important elements for the efficient production of these polished artifacts.

As regards the compared efficiency between quartz and amazonite, worked on all the different supports, a clear difference appears. After 13 hours of work (780 minutes) on quartz, only 0.9 grams were removed, with a relatively fine surface treatment, but with the artifact very much incomplete yet. In the case of the amazonite, after 6 hours of work (360 minutes), and 20.2 grams lost, the surface treatment was fine enough and the process was much closer to completion (Figs 4 and 5).

Finally we get back to the question of organic hafting and the use of a polished stone blade. The first noticeable observation is that the growth of the branch around the place the blade was introduced is quite large, making that part much heavier and robust (Figs 7 and 8). This feature, in turn, makes it expendable the robustness of the blade itself, since the weight of this part provides sufficient mass for the proper use of the tool. Probably the blade would also be much better attached than in any other form of conventional hafting, with the addition of wax, resin or twine.

Another important point about this hafting is the time involved in the process. The removal of the branch from the tree, for the final preparation was relatively fast (less than 15 minutes), which shows also a good efficiency of the polished stone blade. The hafted blade used to cut the tree worked fine; neither broke up nor lost the edge (which actually was not very sharp, around 90°). Moreover, it became clear that the final preparation of the organic haft should be made as soon as possible, before the wood becomes too dry and therefore too hard to a less extenuating work. However, the period of ten months for a tool to be ready for use is a time span that we are not used to wait. This point leads us to think about the relationship the indigenous people would have established with time and the prestige that could be associated with a tool hafted this way.

With these experimentations we can understand a little better the processes involved in the production of *tembetás* and the organic hafting, allowing, for example, a finer evaluation of the time that the production of a small adornment (or a specific haft) would have occupied in the lives of its pre-colonial producers. About 8 hours to produce a *tembetá* of amazonite, or about 20 hours for a quartz *tembetá* are reasonable estimatives. If we take into account that those hours would have been distributed over many days we can create a more reliable image of how these artifacts were occupying the minds of people who lived among them. These informations furnish us a better understanding on the appreciation that the natives had for those pieces, something that the chroniclers clearly testified. These data also help us to understand the

prestige associated with these items. In the first case (made of quartz), the prestige of the *tembetá* is probably more related to their "cost" of production and, sometimes, also to the aesthetic appeal (case of rock crystal). In the second case (made of amazonite), it is probably more related to a shortage of raw material combined to the aesthetic appeal provided by its green color.

Finally, but not less important, the experiments brought information about another kind of artifacts. The experiments with the quartz *tembetá* helped understanding the calibrators, artifacts commonly thought to be associated with their production. We observed a very low efficiency in its use, no matter the support chosen. Moreover, the channels produced are completely different from the archeological ones. While the archaeological calibrators have regular and straight edges, besides regular bottom in all length, the experimental ones were irregular in all cases, no matter the support, in cases used with or without the addition of water (Fig. 10 Archaeological and Fig. 11 Experimental). Together, these observations lead us to the conclusion that the calibrators should not be used for this purpose (manufacturing or finishing of the *tembetá*), but for the calibration of stems (most likely) or objects others than the *tembetás*.

Figure 10. Henrique Piló

Figure 11. Ângelo Pessoa Lima

Table 1.

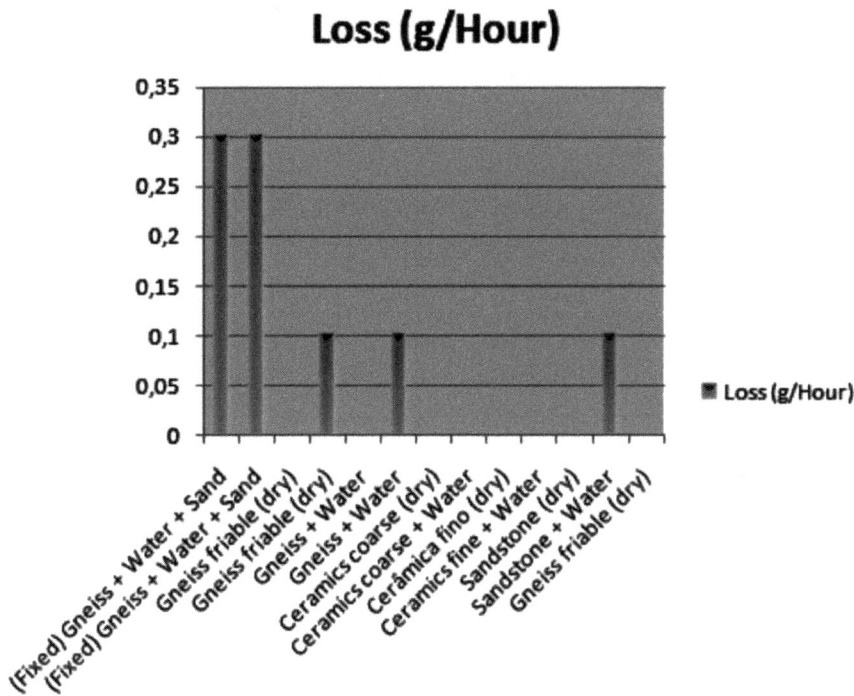

Loss (g/Hour)

Table 2.

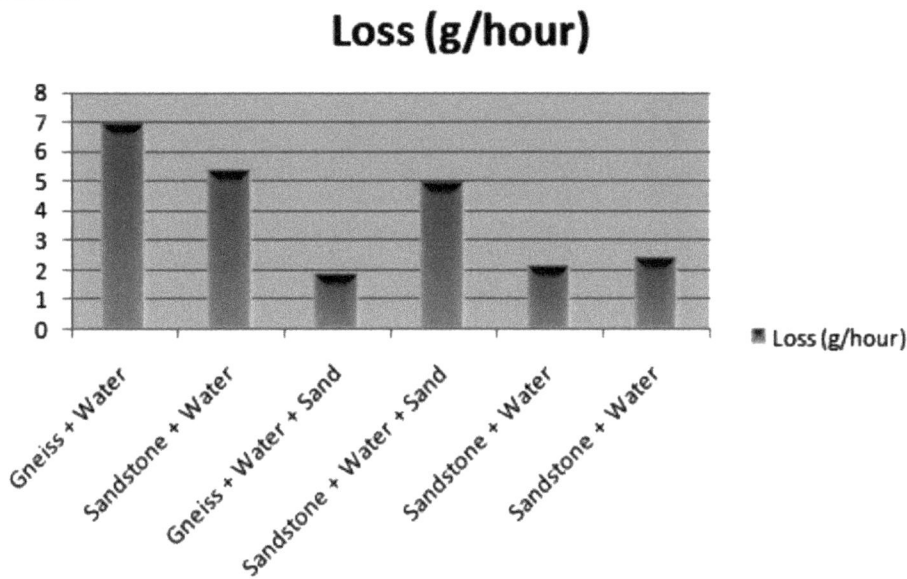

Loss (g/hour)

Acknowledgements

We would like to thank Prof. Dr. André Prous for the discussions and for orientation about the experimental process, always incentivizing us to keep going with the job.

We also want to thank Márcio Alonso and Filipe Figueiredo for the help with experiments of hafting the blade, borrowing their arms and hands.Finally, we would like to thank Prof. Dr. Joel Queménéur for the identification of the raw materials utilized in the experimentations.

References

CAMINHA, Pero Vaz de (1965) – A carta de Pero Vaz de Caminha. Rio de Janeiro: Agir. (original: 1500).

CARDIM, Fernão (1939) – Tratado da Terra e da gente do Brasil. São Paulo: Editora Nacional. (original: last years of the sixteen century).

DAVID, Nicholas & KRAMER, Carol (2001) – Ethnoarcheology in Action. London: Cambridge University Press.

DENEVAN, William M. (1992) – Stone versus metal axes: the ambiguity of shifting cultivation in

Prehistoric Amazonia. In: Journal of the Steward Anthropological Society. v.20, n.1/2, p.153-165.

IHERING, H. Von (1908) – Os machados de pedra do Brasil e seu emprego na derrubada do mato. In: Revista do Museu Paulista. v.12.

LAMING-EMPERAIRE, Annette; MENEZES, Maria José & ANDREATTA, Margarida (1978) – O trabalho da pedra entre índios Xetá, Serra dos Dourados, Estado do Paraná. In: Coleção Museu Paulista, *Série Ensaios*. São Paulo, USP, v. 2.

LÉRY, Jean de (1972) – Viagem à Terra do Brasil. São Paulo: Martins/EDUSP. (original: 1576).

LIMA, Â.P. (2005) – *Função dos calibradores e sua inserção na cultura material Tupiguarani.* Prous, A. (Orientador) Monographie to receive de degree of bachelor in Social Sciences. FAFICH – UFMG.

MAZIÈRE, G. & MAZIÉRE, M. (1997) – La recherche archéologique en guyane. In: L'archéologie en Guyane, p. 17-54.

KÓZAK, Vladimir; BAXTER, D.; WILLIAMSON, L. & CARNEIRO, R. (1979) – The Héta Indians: fish in a dry pound. In: Anthrop. Papers of the Am. Mus. of Nat. History, New York.

PETREQUIN & PETREQUIN (1989) – Ethnographie d´un outil de pierre: les haches polies de L'Irian Jaya.

PROUS, André (1992) – Arqueologia Brasileira. Brasília: UNB, 604 p.

PROUS, André (1986/90) – Os artefatos líticos elementos descritivos e classificatórios. In: Arquivos do Museu de História Natural/UFMG. Belo Horizonte, v. 11, p. 19-20.

PROUS, A.; ALONSO, Márcio.; PILÓ, Henrique.; XAVIER, L.A.F.; LIMA, Ângelo Pessoa & SOUZA, Gustavo Neves de (2003) – Os machados pré-históricos no Brasil – descrição de coleções brasileiras e trabalhos experimentais: fabricação de lâminas, cabos, encabamento e utilização. In: Canindé: Revista do Museu de Arqueologia de Xingó. 2, p. 161-236.

SCHIFFER, Michael B. (1999) – The material life of human beings: artifacts, behavior, and communication. London. New York, Routledge.

SALVADOR, Frei Vicente do (1627) – História do Brasil. Bahia, 1627.

SOUZA, Gabriel Soares de (1971) – Tratado descritivo do Brasil em 1587. São Paulo: EDUSP. (original: 1587).

SOUZA, Gustavo Neves de (2008) – O Material Lítico Polido do interior de Minas Gerais e São Paulo: entre a matéria e a cultura. Master tesis. Universidade de São Paulo. 148 p.

SOUZA, Gustavo Neves & FIGUEIREO, Filipe Amoreli (2003) – Experimentação de perfuração em madeira: avaliação do investimento. In: Anais do XII Congresso da Sociedade de Arqueologia Brasileira.

STADEN, Hans (1968) – Viagem ao Brasil. Rio de Janeiro: Edições de Ouro. (original: 1557).

TENÓRIO, Maria Cristina (2003) – Os amoladores-polidores fixos. In: Revista Arqueologia 16, p. 87-108.

THEVET, André (1944) – Singularidades da França Antártica. Rio de Janeiro. (original: 1558).

VILHENA – VIALOU, Águeda (1980) – Tecno-tipologia das indústrias líticas do sítio Almeida em seu quadro natural, Arqueo-etnológico e regional. São Paulo, USP, Instituto de pré-história/Museu Paulista, 170 p.

THE LITHIC TECHNOLOGY OF LARANJAL DO JARI I:
A KORIABO SITE AT SOUTH AMAPÁ

Bruno de Souza BARRETO
(IEPA)

Mariana Petry CABRAL
(Supervisor, Archaeologists – IEPA)

Abstract: *This paper will present preliminary results of a research with lithic collection in Laranjal do Jarí I, a large habitation site linked to Koriabo pottery, located in southern Amapá State, Brazil. This site was identified in 2009 and excavated in July of the same year by archaeologists of IEPA in a preventive archaeology activity. The obtained results indicate a peculiar industry of polished artifacts, especially those of passive use, produced as by-products.*

Keywords: *Lithic Technology; Polished artifacts; Koriabo Phase; Pre-colonial Archaeology; Archaeology of Guianas*

Résumé: *Dans ce document sera présenté les résultats préliminaires d'une recherche à la collecte des lithique Laranjal do Jari I, un site d'habitation important lié à la poterie Koriabo, situé au sud de l'Amapá Etat, le Brésil. Ce site a été identifié en 2009 et fouillée en Juillet de cette année pour l'équipe d'archéologie de lEPA dans une activité de l'archéologie préventive. Les résultats obtenus indiquent une industrie particulière d'artefacts polies, en particulier ceux de l'utilisation passive, où il n'y a pas intention de polir la pièce pour faire un outil spécifique.*

Mots-clés: *Technologie lithique; objets polis; Phase Koriabo; pré-coloniale archéologie; Archéologie de Guyanes*

INTRODUCTION

In the prehistory of the Guiana´s shield, one of the gaps on the archaeological data refers to the ceramic assemblages known as Koriabo, raising discussions in the academy about their origin, migration route and chronology. Some scholars have placed them in the later period of Guiana's prehistory, placing their age around 1200 AD (Meggers e Evans, 1960; Versteeg e Buberman, 1992; Rostain, 1994a; Rostain, 2008). However, some older radiocarbon datings were obtained to the sixth century of the Christian Era (Boomert, 2004). Its origin is not a consensus among researchers in the region, and several origins and migration routes have been suggested.

The first writings about sites associated to Koriabo earthenware date of early 20th century (Boomert, 2004), but a classification for this type of pottery only was made after the results of systematic researches conducted in 1950s by Clifford Evans and Betty Meggers (1960). From excavations of six strata cuts in four archaeological sites located at the basin of Barima River, in Guyana, they defined the Koriabo phase and its diagnostic features in five styles, three plain and the other two decorated, linking them to Incised-Punctate Tradition (Evans e Meggers, 1960: 144, 145).

After Koriabo sites were identified in the following years in various parts of the Guyana shield such as Suriname, Guyana, Venezuela, northwestern Pará State and, more recently, in the state of Amapá, Brazil (Versteeg and Buberman, 1992; Versteeg, 1998; Boomert, 2004; Rostain, 1994a; Rostain, 2008; Saldanha and Cabral 2009a; Saldanha and Cabral 2009b). Despite its wide dispersal at Guyana plateau, this is the only culture that has not been found outside of this area. Therefore Rostain (2008:298) attributed a particular importance for these groups, which according to him, could have come from the central Amazon basin or the center of the Guyana Shield.

Considering the controversy and wide dispersion of this ceramic complex, the case study of the lithic industry of Laranjal do Jari I, a Koriabo site located in the lower Jari river, south of Amapá, intends to be a way to contribute to this discussion about the human occupation of related to Koriabo pottery in late regional prehistory. This culture, still little known in Amapá, is embedded in networks of regional trade (Versteeg and Buberman, 1998; Rostain, 2008; Van den Bel, 2010), and thus, a detailed investigation of the local context is necessary in order to relate the data obtained here with results presented by other researches in the countries belonging to the Guyanas plateau.

Therefore, the aim of this paper is to provide a general characterization of this lithic industry, with the emphasis on chipped and polished artifacts, both active objects (those that are the result of a intended transformation for tools manufacture) and passive objects (those that are transformed due to use).

REGION OF STUDY

The Laranjal do Jari I site is placed in southern Amapá state, near the border with Pará state, which is marked by

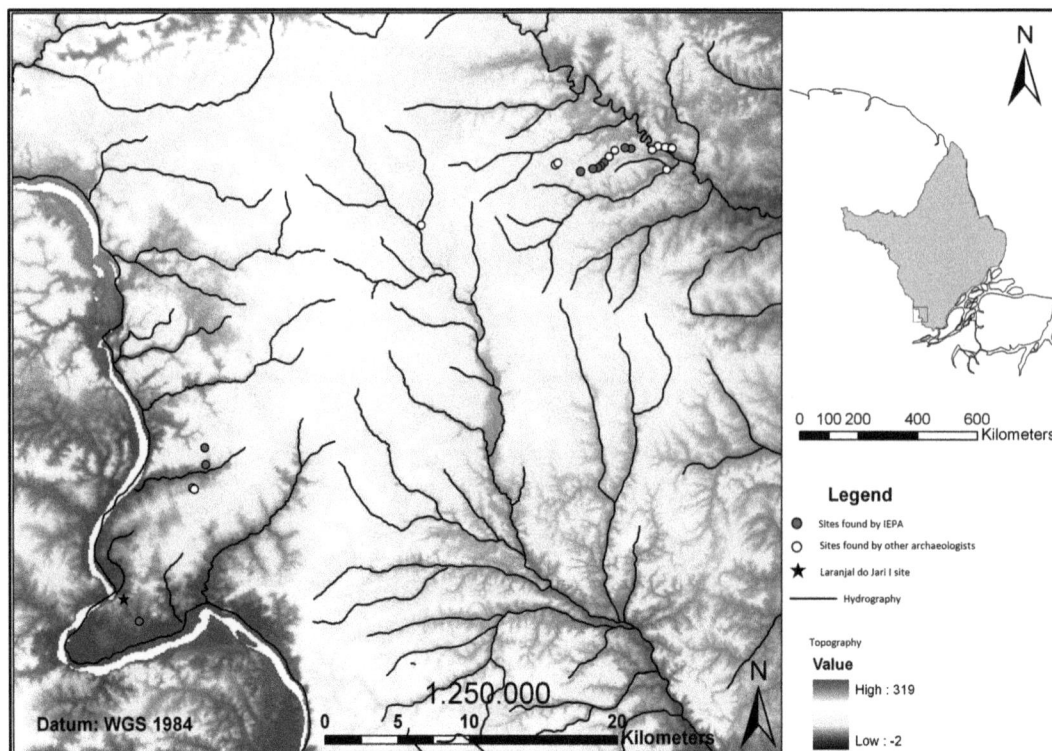

Figure 1. Map of the southern region of Amapá State, between the basins of the Jari, São Luis and Cajari rivers. It shows the dispersion of some archaeological sites in this region

the course of Jari river. Situated on the right bank of the lower Jari and close the Laranjal do Jari city, the site is located approximately 700 m from the riverbank.

About 1600 m away, other habitation site has been identified linked to Koriabo phase in a prospection conducted in July 2009, during the excavation of the site Laranjal do Jari I. It was registered as Laranjal do Jari II and was located on the top of a flat plateau area in the Buritizal neighborhood. Around it, the topography is characterized by a seasonal flooded area, composed of *buritis (mauritia flexuosa)* forest vegetation. The site was excavated by the IEPA team in January and February of 2011.

In October 2011, a prospection conducted by IEPA team at the BR-156 road led to the identification of seven sites. In this prospection, the sites identified had many bifacial lithic artifacts, as well as flakes of bifacial manufacture. In addition to these sites, in 2007 another team of archaeologists identified nine sites in the region (Fogolari, 2009:60), close to those found by IEPA, on the outskirts of Cajari river basin, near the Água Branca community. In a secondary road near the urban area of Laranjal do Jari city, IEPA team identified another three archaeological sites in the same period, and a fourth site had been identified before that (id).

In regard to the geographical characteristics of this region, the area of Laranjal do Jari city is characterized by being heavily modified by human activity. However, the vegetation where the two excavated sites are situated is representative of high-sized mainland forest associated to flat terrain or softly wavy topography (Rabelo *et al.*, 2007:14.15). Near the mouth of Arapiranga creek, a tributary of Jari river, the vegetation changes to large-sized floodplain forest with high frequency of palms (id).

The geomorphology in the site area is characterized by flat top reliefs of specific forms from southern Amapá tabular lowered plateaus (Rabelo *et al.*, 2007:16. 17), and the region's geological formation dates from Tertiary period and it is peculiar of sandy-clay deposits of the Alter do Chão formation (Radam Brazil, 1974, op. cit: 20, 21).

ARCHAEOLOGICAL FIELD METHODS

The site was identified in 2009 during the construction activities for a Technical School. In July of that year, it was excavated by the IEPA team, being identified as a large open air habitation site containing pottery associated to Koriabo and Mazagão phases, with a package of anthropogenic dark earth sometimes measuring one meter deep (Saldanha and Cabral, 2009), resulting from human occupation at the site.

The methodology used included the delineation of 10 x 10 meters squares, hand collection of archaeological material on the surface, excavation of the stratigraphic package of Amazonian Dark Earth through backhoe mechanical shovel, and manual excavation of structures.

Of all anthropogenic features identified, a total of 340 were excavated. They were characterized due to their

Figure 2. Left, panoramic photo of the excavation in Laranjal do Jari I site. On the right, piece of pottery with diagnostic features of the Koriabo phase style Koriabo Scraped

morphology and material found in archaeological context. Of these, the largest portion was interpreted as post holes, which are related to the support of huts, which leads us to believe that it is characteristic of a habitation site, resembling another Koriabo site excavated in French Guiana (Crique Sparouine), which had a similar context with funeral burials associated with households (Van den Bel, 2010). The others structures were interpreted as pits containing ceramic deposits and other features types, including funerary material.

At the end of the excavations, the spatial location of these anthropogenic structures was recorded with the topographical level, allowing the record of the spatial arrangement of all structures on the site, in order to understand the relationship between them, inferring possible areas of activity. In total, an area of 4200 m^2 was excavated.

METHODOLOGY OF LITHIC ANALYSIS

The study methodology of this collection follows two distinct but complementary steps. First, we followed a list of techno-typological analysis prepared for another research project in a context of studying the pre-ceramic and ceramic contexts in a central portion of the state of Amapá. This list seeks information on typology, technology and features of the pieces, such as the raw material and its type of processing in order to understand the process of artifact's manufacture.

This list of attributes was based on methodological proposals such as William Andrefsky's (1994), but adapted to regional context, as the lithic industries of this region are very different from those found in North America and other regions of the world. According to Andrefsky (1994: 61, 62), the techno-typology is a method by which we can make comparisons and differentiations between lithic sets, as well as facilitate the ordering of data into classes that help us understanding the technological organization. Moreover, instead of a detailed description of each individual piece, this approach is favorable because it saves time (Andrefsky, 1994: 61).

As described above, the classification of items into a techno-typological list facilitated a preliminary

characterization of lithic technology in this site, providing an overview of the pieces, so that the data can be organized systematically, inferring occurrences of technologies employed, raw materials used and types of artifacts more or less frequent. However, it should be understood that such method is part of "analytical constructions with ordinary and chronological purposes" (Mansur, 1986:118). It follows that we can select the pieces that should be prioritized for the drawing and description in order to provide a better understanding of the collection.

For the individual description of pieces, which is the second step in the analysis, we took as reference the descriptive categories of Sirlei Hoeltz (2005), as well as the illustrated glossary for description and drawing of lithic pieces by Hameister *et al.* (1997).

After drawing, pieces descriptions were performed based on the descriptive list proposed by Hoeltz (2005), in which qualitative aspects of artifacts are valued, which may have gone unnoticed by the techno-typological classification. Also, the detailed reading of gestural sequences that led each piece was important for understanding the production of the object in a synchronic and diachronic perspective.

Based on this methodology, we seek to obtain specific information, such as how much a crude block was modified to reach the its current stage (Hoeltz, 2005:) and some general information related to this industry, related to activities that were performed on the site and that involved decisions and choices which can be distinctive of cultural markers (Mansur, 1986:116).

RESULTS

In total, 540 pieces were classified on the techno-typological list, all from the Amazonian Dark Earth pack excavated with mechanical shovel. However, 376 pieces were considered as unmodified rocks in their natural state. Some of them could not be identified in regard to its raw matiral, but it is known that the majority is composed of sedimentary rocks of Alter do Chão Formation, which covers the tertiary period of geological formation at this region (Rabelo *et al.*, 2007: 16, 17). These rocks are related to the geology around the site, in the area comprising the cities of Laranjal do Jari (AP) and Monte Dourado (PA), according to the report prepared by the RADAM Brazil project (1974), which indicates the existence of fine sandstones, siltstones and mudstones with lenses of conglomerate and coarse sandstone, little consolidated and even friable, generally horizontally stratified.

The pieces which have undergone human interventions, most of the changes observed are related to polishing, which is most often unintentional, referring to those artefacts that have been modified due to the use. In order to provide clearer results, the data that will be presented here refers to the set without the natural fragments.

Polished Artifacts

We identified 85 pieces with traces of abrasion on their surface. The polished artifacts are almost entirely characterized by a passive polishing, resulted from the abrasion of other pieces on them, turning these polished surfaces into by-products of other activities.

However, there are artifacts that have intentional polishing on its surface, such as flakes and fragments of shaped polished instruments. This polishing was named active, on opposition to the passive type described above. These pieces are the minority of polished artifacts, counting only nine pieces. This list below refers to the amount of polished artifacts identified on the site by type of polishing: active and passive.

Table 1. Amount of polished artifacts identified on the site by type of polishing: active and passive

Polished artifacts by use (passive)	N° (%)
Polishing by use on iron ore with features of Hematite (red ocher)	35 (41%)
Polishing by use on another raw materials	40 (47%)
Total	**75 (88%)**
Artifacts intentionally shaped by Polishing (active)	
Flakes and fragments of polished tools	7 (8%)
Fragmented axe blades (proximal end present)	1 (1,3%)
Fragments of axes (proximal end absent)	1 (1,3%)
Fragmented spindle whorl	1 (1,3%)
Total	**10 (12%)**
General Total	**85 (100%)**

Shaped pieces (active objects)

The active polished artifacts correspond to the minority of polished instruments identified in the site, with a total of nine pieces. Among these, there are six flakes with polishing on dorsal/superior surface and instrument fragments, which were interpreted as such because of the uniformity of the polished surface, forming small edges. Moreover, five pieces were made of a greenish igneous rock, a common raw material for making polished axes in the context of Guyana pottery sites (see Rostain, 1994:298). Other pieces were a fragmented axe (edge absent), a fragment-edged axe reused as a hammer, and a spindle whorl broken in half (used in weaving).

The flakes with polishing on the dorsal/superior surface could be associated with maintenance of polished tools, such axes, possibly due to the renew of its edges. Almost all these pieces with intentional polishing (active) are related to igneous rocks of greenish color, which indicates the preference of these populations for this type of raw material in the manufacture of polished instruments.

Pieces Polished by use (passive objects)

Most of the polished pieces analyzed in our sample correspond to a type of modification by use, totalizing 75 pieces (88%). Of this total, 35 pieces correspond to modifications of the iron ore with properties of hematite (red ocher). In the case of this raw material, polishing is related to the friction of this mineral to one another rock, for the removal of pigments (see Kipfer, 2007). The use of iron oxide minerals such as hematite is widely known and quite common in the pre-history of Amazon and Brazil, as well as in other contexts in the world (Evans and Meggers, 1960; Semenov, 1982; Kipfer, 2007; Rostain, 1994a; Boomert, 2004).

All the polished hematites presented multidirectional striations macroscopically visible and better perceived with the aid of binocular lens. The morphology of these pieces varies between tabular, quadrangular and irregular. We observed three different characteristic patterns of the polishing traces present in these parts, which are: 1) concave, convex or flat surfaces covering an entire face, 2) several facets of a single-sided polishing of the piece with striations pointing in several directions and 3) scars of chipping on the edge of polished surfaces, some small and others reaching up to 2 cm in length. These three patterns of wear traces on hematite are representative of distinctive gestual operations.

We also observed in this collection other raw materials such as sandstone. These pieces are plates with concave or flat surfaces, presenting circular and multidirectional striations. One of these plates has traces of red pigment on the polished surface, following the direction of circular striations, which may indicate the use in association with red ocher.

Artifacts with these characteristics are known in the archaeological literature of Guyana as palettes. Those are small metates slabs used to grind pigments, presenting some remains on the grinded surface (Rostain, 1994a; Vacher *et al.*, 1998; Kipfer, 2007). Rostain (1994a: 319) related these artifacts to the production of pigments that are used to paint ceremonial pottery, body painting or on staining of bones for secondary burial.

Another piece polished by use, with concave surface, has the two parallel faces striated and several multidirectional cross lines. The piece is fragmented in the longitudinal and transverse axes and was reused after breaking to prepare a chipped edge that has macro wear traces of use. These concave polished rocks are also used for food processing, as grinding of vegetables (Rostain, 1994a). In total, 40 artifacts with passive polishing on other raw materials (as sandstone) were analyzed.

Chipped Artifacts

The chipped artifacts on this site have one occurrence of 13%. We identified 21 pieces so far. Most of them have bifacial and unifacial chipping on block and semilunar or trapezoidal morphology, generally fragmented on

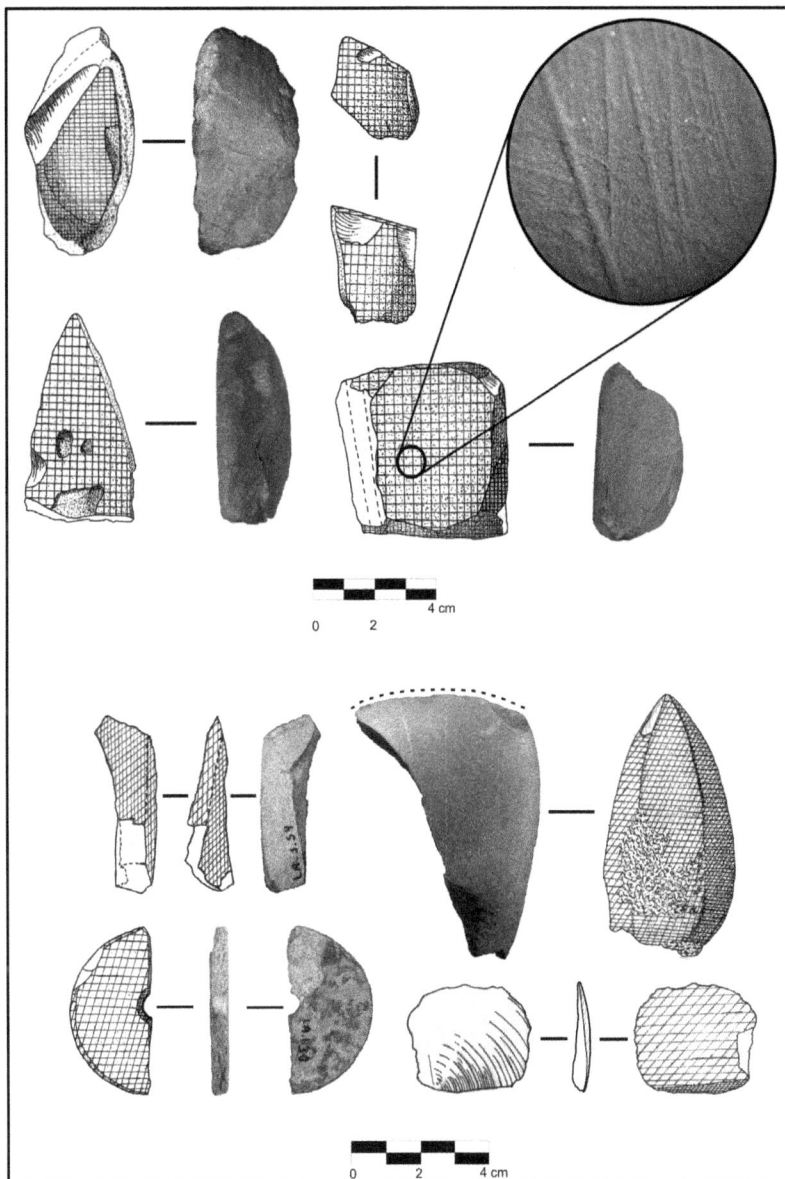

Figure 3. Above: passive polished artifacts, polished hematites by use.
Below: Active polished artifacts, flakes and fragments of tools

transverse axis, with dimensions ranging from 3 to 6 cm of lenght, 3 to 7.5 cm of width and 1.2 to 3 cm of thickness. The other chipped artifacts are retouched flakes from quartz pebbles with macro wear traces of use.

The main raw material used for the shaping of these bifacial and unifacial pieces was metamorphic rocks horizontally stratified. When looking at the fractured section of the piece is possible to notice features of the rock schistosity, as several layers juxtaposed horizontally, which when subjected to chipping tend to fracture irregularly at these sites, and the stigma left by removal of the flakes of edge shaping show stepped fracture characteristics. One of these unifaces was made on pebble of quartz, with dimensions of 10.6 x 7 x 4.8 cm and has the morphological characteristics of a chopper. The low amount of flakes on the site, related to these raw materials, indicates that these artifacts were manufactured out of the site.

Unifacial and Bifacial Artifacts with Polishing Features

The artifacts that show scars from chipping and polishing are a total of three pieces. They were made of different raw materials, identified as metamorphic rocks. Their dimensions range from 6.2 to 9.1 cm lenght, 3.9 to 6.7 cm width and 1.4 to 1.9 cm thickness. For most pieces, it is possible to see that the flakes were removed after polishing, formatting a cutting edge. While for the other two it is noted that the polishing is posterior to flaking.

DISCUSSION AND CONCLUSIONS

Based on the information presented here, we can state that the lithic technology of the site is predominantly focused on polishing, specifically regarding to unintentional transformations. In this type of pieces, the

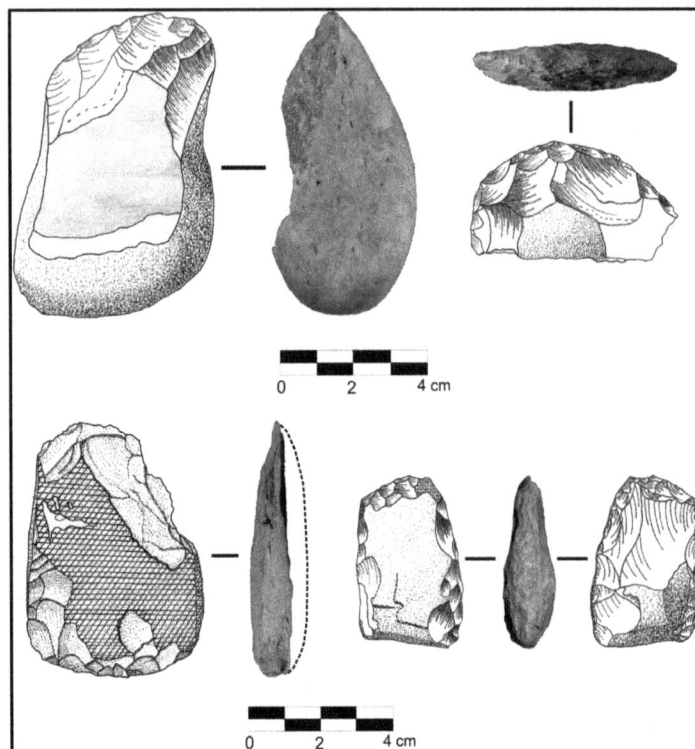

Figure 4. Above: Chipped Artifacts. Below: Chipped artifacts with traces of polishing, on the left the piece was drawn with the cutting edge to down

main raw material used (47% of cases) was sedimentary rocks of the Alter do Chão formation and metamorphic rocks, which could have been used as an abrasive surface for formatting another polished artifacts, such as axe blades and other instruments.

The iron ore with features of Hematite appear with 41% of frequence. Some pieces of this mineral show striations on the polished surface, losing a red ferruginous pigment. Barbara Kipfer (2007:152, 226) in a dictionary of artifacts, has made reference to this raw material (hematite) for the production of red coloring to be used in body painting, as well as in rock painting and vessel painting.

In the excavations realized by Evans and Meggers (1960) in the Koriabo contexts in British Guyana, there were identified several rocks with concretions of hematite which presented rounded and striated surfaces. These fragments, named by them as rubbing stones, were explained like being raw material to obtain red coloring, proposing the intention of those people in using these minerals to produce pigments. Arie Boomert (2004) also refers to polished iron oxides due to use, in Koriabo context, but with low frequency in the collection studied. In Suriname, the pottery collections studied by him have a high incidence of decorative motifs with red painting over white slip, mainly in carinated vessels.

To quote another example, in the South African prehistory, the red ocher was heavily employed by people who lived in caves and rock shelters, concerning to the use of this raw material mixed with a vegetal resin to make a glue that would be used in lithic tools hafting.

This type of application of iron oxide was proved by micro-residual analysis and experimental studies, which attest the usefulness of this mineral in hafting technology (Wadley, 2005; Lombard and Wadley, s/d).

According to these experimental works, the proceeding is done initially with the removal of red colored powder through friction, or scraping, of coarse granular sandstone, over nodules of hematite. The process leaves wear traces visible macroscopically, such as polishing and striation of scraped surface, making facets on the piece. After that, the red powder is mixed with a vegetal resin, hafted and brought to the fire (Wadley, 2005). This is one of the employments of this mineral that may be used for other purposes beyond coloring. André Prous (1986/1990:17) also refers to the usefulness of this mineral as a kind of glue: "the powder of hematite, oxidant, may be used to harden resins destined to fix lithic pieces on the haft".

In the Guyana's shield, there are occurrences of polished axes with hafting, found in river beds and creeks. Six of them were identified in French Guyana, one in Brazil (in a beach near Belém) and one in British Guyana (Versteeg and Rostain, 1999:05). However, the analysis done on adhesive material used to fix the blade to haft shows that there is no similarity with hafting technology present in South Africa (id).

A preliminary interpretation of data presented here indicate that the choice of red ocher like raw material is related to the scraping of its surface for the removal of red colored pigments. The other 40 polished pieces over diverse raw materials may be associated to their use as portable polishers to shape other polished tools, according to Vacher el al (1998) typology. It also may have been used for scraping on the red ocher (hematite), considering that some pieces of hematite have several facets of polishing in the same surface, as well as in other surfaces, suggesting that it had been scraped on another rock on the floor.

According to Semenov (1982:251), this technology of pigment removal is very frequent in the context of Superior Paleolithic in Russia, where slabs of sandstone are employed with a pestle, or mano, which is grated over it in a circular moving. The diagnostic features are polished surfaces with maximum of waste on the center of the piece and curved cross lines (id). Sometimes, the slabs of sandstone are too small and then, the use of small pieces to grind red ocher is necessary (id). These small pieces utilized to scrape on iron oxide have several facets on the same surface of the piece (id: 254).

Still about this question of mineral coloring utilization, André Prous (1986:16) emphasize that pigments of mineral source are frequently found at Brazilian archaeological sites, owing to be more resistant than vegetal ones. According to the author, these pigments are obtained out of stones rich in iron particles, generally red hematites or rocks modified by weathering which reaches to create a ferruginous carapace on them, that may be scraped off to obtain red pigments (id).

Therefore, from the analysis of polished hematite from Laranjal do Jari I, we may raise two interpretative hypothesis. The first relates to the use of red colored pigment in the *chaîné operatorie* of ceramic manufacture. In this case, the red pigment would have been added to the clay, as temper, resulting in pottery with reddish color. In the second hypothesis, red pigment would be use for other purposes, such as body painting, leaving no other on the archaeological record.

In the ceramic collection of Itabru site, another Koriabo context studied by Boomert (1979:81), pottery containing grains of hematite on the paste of sherds were identified. According to him, these minerals have been intentionally added as temper for ceramics. Those sherds are characterized with incomplete oxidation and yellow-grey to grey-brown and dark-grey colour in cross section.

Some experiments could be done to test these hypothesis. Regarding the first one, an experimental work with pottery manufacture adding red ocher to clay would elucidate its results. Allied to this, the mineralogical analysis of some ceramics from the site could tell us if the powder of hematite have been added to the paste (samples have been sent to analysis).

Regarding the red paint, some ceramic bowls on this site have red paint over white slip. However, this painting is eventual, and when present, it is almost completely eroded. Analysis of this red pigment would allow to identify whether it is of mineral or vegetable source.

Regarding to the chipped artifacts, the most significant pieces on the site are those with unifacial and bifacial edges. The raw materials seems to respond poorly to chipping, which causes the stigmas of flakes removal to exhibit a stepped fracture, and not the expected conchoidal fracture.

At the habitation site Saut Mapaou, another Koriabo context in French Guiana, chipped artifacts like these were interpreted by Rostain (1994a: 342) as pre-forms of polished axe in early stages of manufacture. According to him, these pieces were prepared using green schist as raw material, through the removal of flakes with a hard hammer.

Artifacts like these have also been identified by Vacher *et al.* (1998) on the River Basin Sinnamary, French Guiana, but are not assigned to pre-forms of polished instruments, being called just chipped blocks. In Suriname, the sites of the Brownsberg complex were interpreted as sites of specialists in the manufacture of bifacial stone tools, which were traded with other groups in the coastal region in an exchange network (Boomert & Kroonenberg, 1977).

In the particular case of this collection, we cannot say these flaked artifacts were made as pre-forms of axes, because so far there is no correlation between the raw material of these pieces and of polished instruments found at the site.

Based on case study of lithic collection, we seek to contribute with discussion about the Koriabo context in Guyanas. The lithic technology of this site is unique, if compared to other collections found in the Amapa State, which makes it interesting to a more accurate study of this region. This requires the excavation at other sites located in this region as well as the study of these lithic collections in order to compare the lithic sites present in sites containing Koriabo pottery, to ascertain their similarities and differences.

Acknowledgements

I thanks to Daiane Pereira for help me with the drawings, and Julia Paladino for correction of the english version of this text.

References

ANDREFSKY Jr.W. (1998) – Lithics: macroscopic approaches to analysis. New York: Cambridge University Press. 325 p.

BOOMERT, A. (2004) – Koriabo and the Polychrome Tradition: the Late-Prehistoric era between the Orinoco and Amazon mouths. In Late Ceramic Age Societies in the Eastern Caribbean. Paris; Oxford: BAR International Series 1273. p. 251-265.

BOOMERT, A. (1979) – An analysis of the ceramic finds from Itabru, Berbice river. Journal of archaeology and anthropology. Georgetown. 2:1, p. 77-89.

BOOMERT, A.; KROONENBERG, S.B. (1977) – Manufacture and trade of stone artifacts in prehistoric Surinam. In Ex Horreo. Amsterdam: Universiteit van Amsterdam. p. 9-46.

EVANS, C.; MEGGERS, B (1960) – Archaeological investigations in British Guiana. Washington: Smithsonian Institution. 418 p.

FOGOLARI, E. (2009) – Levantamento arqueólogico sistemático prospectivo e programa de educação patrimonial na pavimentação da BR-156/AP. Erechim: Habitus. 141 p.

HAMEISTER, M. [et. al.] (1997) – Pequeno glossário ilustrado para representação gráfica de artefatos líticos. Revista do Cepa. Santa Cruz do Sul. 21:26, p. 7-33.

HOELTZ, S. (2005) – Tecnologia lítica: uma proposta de leitura para a compreensão das indústrias líticas do Rio Grande do Sul, Brasil, em tempos remotos. Porto Alegre: PPGH-PUCRS. 460 p.

KIPFER, B.A. (2007) – Dictionary of artifacts. Oxford: Blackwell Publishing. 354 p.

LOMBARD, M.; WADLEY, L. (s/d) – The impact of micro-residue studies on south African middle stone age research. Terra australis. 30, p. 11-28.

MANSUR, M.E. (1986/1990) – Instrumentos Líticos: aspectos da análise funcional. In Arquivos do museu de história natural. Belo Horizonte: UFMG. p. 1-91.

PROJETO RADAM BRASIL (1974) – Rio de Janeiro: Folha SA.22 Belém, Departamento Nacional de Produção Mineral. 432 p.

PROUS, A. (1986/1990) – Os artefatos líticos: elementos descritivos classificatórios. In Arquivos do museu de história natural. Belo Horizonte: UFMG. p. 173-195.

ROSTAIN, S. (1994a) – L'occupation amérindienne ancienne du littoral de Guyane. Paris: Centre de recherche em archaeologie precolombienne (CRAP), Université de Paris I. 938 p.

ROSTAIN, S. (2008) – The archaeology of the Guianas: an overview. In Handbook of South American archaeology. Nova York: Springer Science. p. 279-302.

SALDANHA, J.D. de M.; CABRAL, M.P. (2009a) – Relatório Final: projeto de Levantamento e Resgate Arqueológico na Área da Mina do Projeto Ferro Amapá (MMX). Macapá: IEPA, 135 p.

SALDANHA, J.D.M.; CABRAL, M.P. (2009b) – Relatório preliminar de resgate do sítio arqueológico Laranjal do Jarí I. Macapá: IEPA, 28 p.

SEMENOV, S.A. (1981) – Tecnología prehistorica: estúdio de las hierramientas y objetos antigos a través de las huellas de uso. Madrid: Akal. 373 p.

VAN DEN BEL, M. (2010) – A koriabo site on the lower Maroni river: results of the preventive archaeological excavation at Crique Sparouine, French Guiana. In Arqueologia Amazônia 1. Belém: MPEG/IPHAN/SECULT. p. 61-94.

VERSTEEG, A.H.; BUBBERMAN, F.C. (1998) – Suriname Before Columbus. Mededelingen Surinaams Museum. Paramaribo. 49a. p. 3-65. [Consult. 25 Mai. 2012] Disponível em WWW:_URL http://home.wxs.nl/~vrstg/guianas/suriname/suriname.htm.

VERSTEEG, A.H.; ROSTAIN, S. (1999) – A hafted Amerindian stone axe recovered from the Suriname river. Mededelingen Surinaams Museum. Paramaribo. 55. [Consult. 25 Mai. 2012] Disponível em WWW:_URLhttp://home.wxs.nl/~vrstg/guianas/suriname/bijl.htm.

WADLEY, L. (2005) – Putting ocher to test: replication studies of adhesives that may have been used for hafting tools in the middle stone age. Journal of human evolution. 49, p. 587-601.

VACHER, S. [et al.] (1998) – Amérindiens du Sinnamary: archéologie en forêt équatoriale (Guyane). Paris: Editions de la Maison des sciences de l'homme. 297 p.

LES INDUSTRIES DES SITES DU HAUT RIO SÃO FRANCISCO: OUTILLLAGE "SIMPLE", OU "COMPLEXE"? LE CIMETIERE DE BURITIZEIRO ET L'ABRI BIBOCAS DE JEQUITAI

M. Jacqueline RODET

Centre d'Archéologie préhistorique et FAFICH-Université Fédérale de Minas Gerais,
et Mission Archéologique Française de Minas Gerais

A. PROUS

Centre d'Archéologie préhistorique et FAFICH-Université Fédérale de Minas Gerais,
chercheur du CNPq (Brésil) et Mission Archéologique Française de Minas Gerais

J. MACHADO

Centre d'Archéologie préhistorique-Université Fédérale de Minas Gerais;
étudiant de Master en archéologie – Paris X

L.F. BASSI

Centre d'Archéologie préhistorique-Université Fédérale de Minas Gerais;
étudiant de Master en archéologie PPGAN-UFMG, Belo Horizonte

Résumé: *Nous analysons les industries lithiques de l'Holocène de deux sites (abri et site à ciel ouvert) du Brésil central. Nous montrons que l'apparente simplicité de la plupart des artefacts (éclats utilisés bruts débité sur galets ou blocs d'origine locale) et de leur débitage cache en réalité des procédés différenciés et précis, adaptés àux diverses morphologie des galets et aux caractéristiques des matières premières. La présence dans les sites de quelques outils façonné et retouchés avec soin fabriqués sur certaines matières plus rares et d'excellente qualité montre que l'absence de modification des tranchants de la plupart des instruments n'est pas due à un manque de technique, mais au fait que les débitages apparemment "simples" fournissaient des outils standardisés parfaitement adaptés aux nécessités courantes.*

Abstract: *We examine the Holocene lithic industry of two archaeological sites (a shelter and an open air one) of central Brazil. We show that the apparent simplicity of most of the artifacts (unretouched flakes from pebbles or blocks of local origin) and debitage processes covers differential and specific ways, adapted to the morphology and to the characteristics of the worked stones. The present of scarse fashioned and carefully retouched instruments (made with excellent and rare raw materials) shows that the absence of retouching on most instruments is not due to the lack of technical knowledge. On the contrary, the apparently simple debitages provide standardized tools perfectly adapted to current necessities.*

LES SITES DE BURITIZEIRO ET JEQUITAI

Le fleuve São Francisco traverse tout le Brésil Central et le nord-est du pays. Les *municípios* (circonscriptions administratives) voisins de Buritizeiro et Jequitaí se trouvent à la limite entre son cours supérieur et son cours inférieur, au niveau des derniers rapides qui y rendent la navigation difficile. C'est peu em aval des rapide que se trouve la confluence avec le rio Jequitai, qui descend des montagnes de l'Espinhaço. (Fig. 1: carte).

Le site à ciel ouvert « Caixa d'Agua » de Buritizeiro a été occupé épisodiquement à partir de 10.500 BP. Il se trouve à quelques dizaines de mètres des rapides – exceptionnellement riches en poissons de grande taille – et occupe le haut d'un petit escarpement qui le met à l'abri des crues. Certaines occupations (particulièrement entre 6.100 et 5.000 BP) se sont étendues sur plusieurs hectares, mais ont été détruites par les aménagements urbains. Nous avons fouillé une centaine de mètre carrés de la partie préservée.

Dans la commune de Jequitaí, l'abri-sous-roche de Bibocas s'ouvre sur une vingtaine de mètres à proximité d'une petite rivière torrentueuse et non loin d'un gisement de cristal de roche, au pied de la Serra do Espinhaço. La profondeur de la zone abritée ne dépasse pas quatre mètres. Les travaux en cours ont permis d'en fouiller 15 m^2, montrant que l'abri a été occupé depuis 10.470 BP. Les parois présentent des peintures rupestres, peut-être associées aux pigments retouvés em fouille dans les niveaux de l'Holocène moyen. Les deux sites de Bibocas et Caixa d'Agua pourraient avoir fait partie d'um même territoire qui comporterait une partie de la plaine alluviale et la zone de piedmont. A partir de 6.100 BP le site de Buritizeiro se transforma en cimetière, alors que l'utilisation du quartz s'intensifiait à Bibocas. Les orpailleurs et chercheurs de cristal utilisent encore cet

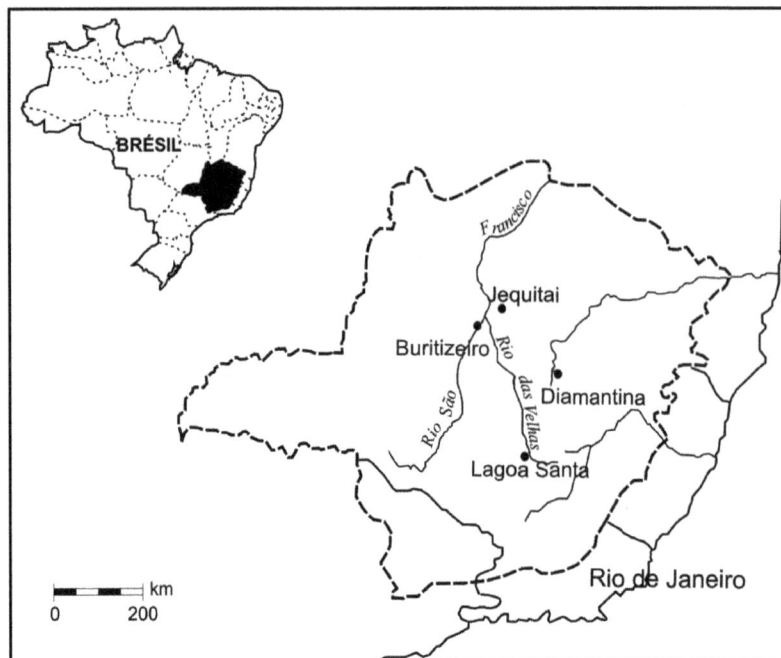

Figure 1. Carte

abri, où ils retirent le córtex des cristaux avant de les vendre aux industriels.

LES MATIERES PREMIERES

Alors que les industries lithiques taillées des autres régions du Brésil Central utilisaient presque exclusivement la matière la plus abondante localement (quartz à Lagoa Santa; silexite dans la vallée du Peruaçu, etc.), la vallée du rio São Francisco facilitait l'accès à une plus grande variété de roches. Certaines sont d'origine locale, tandis que d'autres pouvaient être facilement transportées em pirogue. On exploita principalement les grès silicifiés de grain moyen qui forment les parois des abris (dont Bibocas) qui s'ouvrent dans la Serra do Espinhaço, ou ceux, de grain moyen ou grossier, de qualité variable et toujours assez tenaces, que l'on trouve sous forme de galets dans les rivières et dans quelques dépôts terrestres. On trouve d'excellentes quartzites vers le sommet de la Serra. Des cristaux de roche (qui atteignent de très grandes dimensions) abondent dans tout la montagne depuis le píedmont (près de Jequitaí) jusqu'aux très hautes vallées (région de de Diamantina). Des gisements de sílexite et de calcédoine d'excellente qualité se trouvent dans les formations qui longent le rio São Francisco (formation Mata da Corda); on trouve ces matières premières sous forme de petits galets dans le cours inférieur de plusieurs affluents du rio São Francisco. Dans le lit même du grand fleuve on trouve des affleurements d'arkose; cette roche se taille assez bien, fournissant des tranchants efficaces – mais peu durables – pour l'écaillage des poissons (les pêcheurs utilisent encore des éclats à l'occqsion, quand ils ont oublié leur couteau), ainsi qu'une matière première facilement travaillée par piquetage et polissage pour la fabrication de récipients, de meules et d'enclumes. Le grès friable, utilisé comme polissoir, était probablement amené depuis le cours supérieur du São Francisco. On ne sait pas encore l'origne (probablement lointaine) des roches vertes et de la sillimanite (fibrolite) utilisée pour la fabrication des lames polies que l'on trouve dès la toute première occupation. Le calcaire, disponible à Lagoa Santa sur le cours supérieur du rio das Velhas (principal affluent du São Francisco dans la région qui nous intéresse) ne semble pas avoir été recherché par les riverains du São Francisco.

LE DEBITAGE DES GALETS DE GRES SILICIFIE ET D'ARKOSE

Une grande partie de l'industrie des deux sites, tout au long de la séquence, est formée par des produits de taille de galet; il fallut d'abord déterminer s'il s'agissait d'outils sur galet (*choppers* et *chopping-tools*) ou d'éclats débités à partir de galets-nucléus. Le grand nombre d'éclats retirés, jusqu'à épuisement des galets, a montré que l'objectif principal était bien d'obtenir des éclats. Les galets nucleus mesurent environ 10 à 12 cm de long et présentent des formes diverses (aplatis, sub-sphériques, cylindriques ou ovales). Ils furent débités jusqu'à exhaustion et les éclats sont fréquemment fracturés accidentiellement en Siret. On doit souligner que leur néo-cortex offre des surfaces excellentes comme plan de percussion, tandis que la rencontre d'une face corticale et d'une face d'éclatement et des tranchants fournit des tranchants particulièrement aigüs (Fig. 2). Notons que presque tous les galets débités paraissent avoir été également utilisés comme percuteurs (en general de manière peu intensive, pour ne pas créer des fissures gênantes au moment de les débiter). Leur débitage a toujours été fait par percussion dure; les tailleurs ont utilisé plusieurs méthodes, chacune d'elles adaptée à la

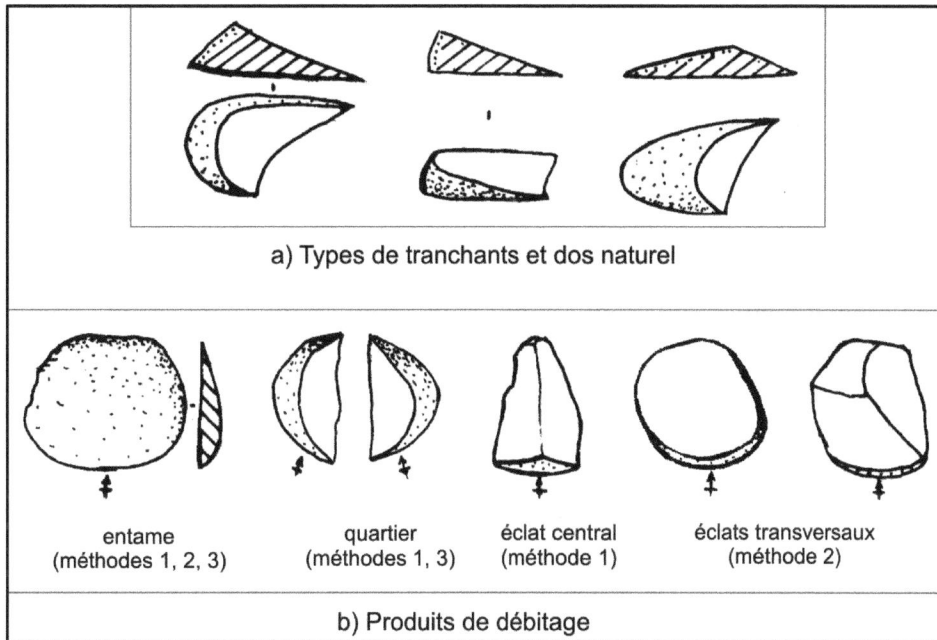

Figure 2. Tranchants et Produits

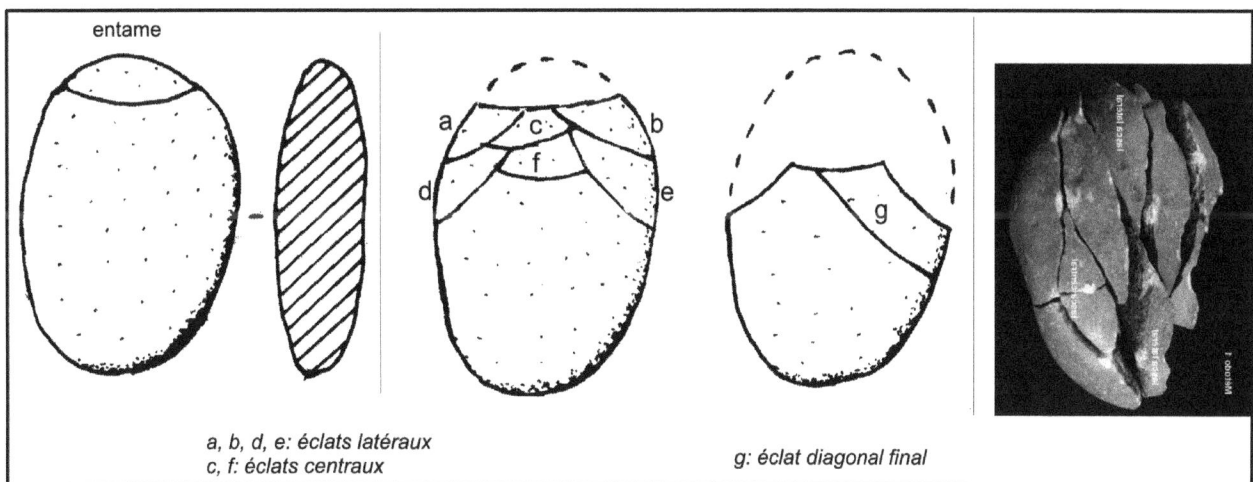

Figure 3. Méthode 1

morphologie du galet travaillé. Nous présenterons les trois méthodes les plus fréquentes, qui ont produit des éclats en forme de tranche ou de quartier d'orange – presque toujours utilisé sans retouche.

1° méthode

La première méthode (Prous 1995/1996; Prous 2004; Rodet *et al.* 2007) s'applique à des galets aplatis eu peu épais (Fig. 3). Elle consiste à retirer um éclat inicial d'une des extrémités, puis de deux éclats latéraux immédiatement derrière le négatif laissé par cet éclat d'entame. Um quatrième éclat est alors retiré entre les deux nouveaux négatifs; on obtient ainsi successivement um éclat cortical eliptique, deux éclats latéraux em forme de quartier d'orange (un gauche et l'autre droit) à neo-córtex proximal-latéral et un éclat central triangulaire ou trapezoidal de talon néo-cortical à tranchant sans neo-

córtex. L'angle formé par le plan de percussion et la surface corticale est relativement incliné; on peut ensuite retirer du front de taille une ou deux nouvelles séries d'éclats latéraux et d'éclats centraux, mais l'angle devent rapidement plus abrupt, rendant l'extraction plus difficile. Souvent, le tailleur progresse davantage sur un des deux côtés du galet, ce qui permet d'obtenir en son milieu de grands éclats qui le traversent obliquement et sont donc plus larges que le diamètre du nucleus. Ils présentent alors un tranchant formé par la rencontre d'une surface neo-corticale avec une surface d'éclatement. Le nucleus abandonné rappelle morphologiquement un *chopper* (galet taillé unifacialement).

2° méthode

Elle s'applique surtout aux galets épais et de section plutôt elliptique ou circulaire (Fig. 4). Le tailleur frappait

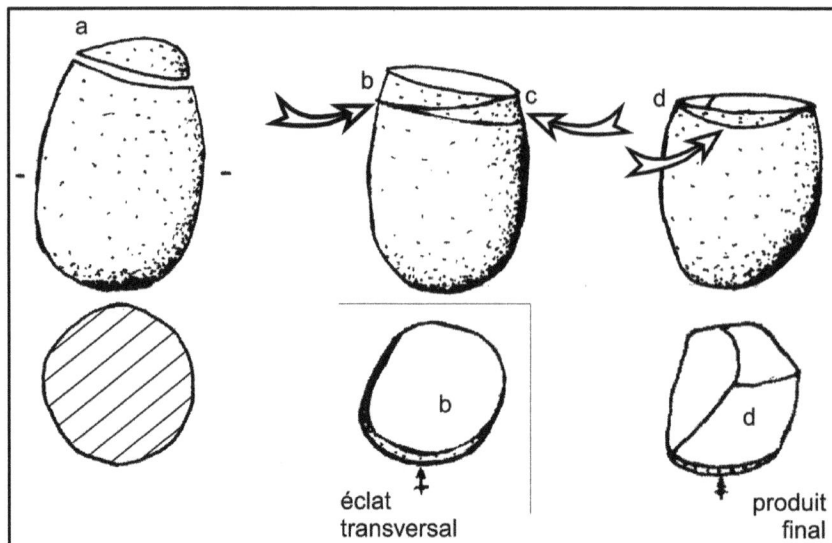

Figure 4. Méthode 2

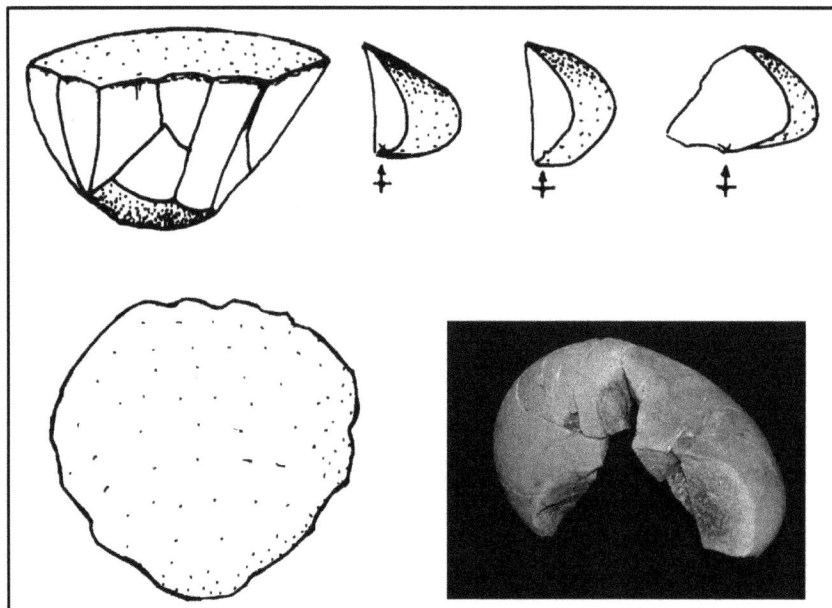

Figure 5. Méthode 3

alternativement deux points diamétralement opposées, retirant des éclats transversaux par rapport à la longueur du galet (Rodet 2006; Rodet *et al.* 2007). Les éclats provenant de ce débitage bidirectionnel sont souvent plus larges que longs et ont un dessin semi-circulaire; ils présentent un neo-cortex limité à un large talon arrondi qui forme un dos naturel, tandis que le tranchant est défini par la rencontre de deux surfaces sans néo-cortex. La face supérieure présente les négatifs de deux éclats d'origine opposée. Cette méthode paraît avoir été surtout destinée à obtenir des couteaux à dos naturel mais avec um grand risque de réfléchissement des éclats. On doit souligner que, dans tous les cas, les nucleus étaient abandonnés après un ultime retrait pour extraire un éclat perpendiculaire aux deux séries antérieures. Il s'agirait donc, là encore, d'un produit préférentiel "reconnaissable par le croisement des negatives sur sa face superieur".

3° méthode

Cette méthode est préférée pour le débitage des galets dissymétriques qui possèdent une face plane opposée à une face plus convexe, ou de galets à deux faces planes, mais épais (Fig. 5). Le nucleus est exploité à partir de la surface la plus aplatie du galet, qui est utilisée comme plan de frappe unique (Prous 1995/1996; Rodet *et al.* 2007). Après le retrait d'un éclat d'entame on continue l'exploitation du galet par débitage centripète, en progressant toujours dans le même sens sur le pourtour du galet, qui est tourné progressivement par le tailleur. En général, les éclats affectent toute l'épaisseur du galet. Les produits ainsi obtenus sont en forme de quartiers d'orange. Selon l'arrondi plus ou moins prononcé du galet à l'endroit d'extraction, l'éclat présente un tranchant aigü semi cortical mais pas de dos naturel, ou un tranchant sans cortex et un dos cortical. La quantité de cortex diminue au fur-et-à-mesure que le débitage avance et que les éclats sont plus distants de l'éclat d'entame. Le nucléus abandonné présente une forme sub-pyramidale, et le plan de frappe est encore totalement neocortical. Quant il est allongé, le nucleus résiduel ressemble à um outil plano-convexe avec lequel il peut être confondu; ce nucléus peut d'ailleurs être réutilisé comme outil (dans d'autres sites du Brésil Central, on a pu vérifier para étude au microscope métallogaphique que ces outils épais totalement façonnés étaient utilisé pour le travail du bois (Alonso & Mansur 1986/90).

LE DEBITAGE DES BLOCS DE GRES SILICIFIE ET D'ARKOSE

Les grands éclats retouvés dans les deux sites (d'arkose à Buritizeiro; de grès dans l'abri de Bibocas) ont été extrait de matières locales de qualité medíocre provenant de la paroi de l'abri, ou des blocs qui affleurent dans la zone des rapides. Ce sont des pièces qui peuvent mesurer une dizaine de centimètres, débitées par percussion dure directe (talon épais, point d'impact et bulbe très marqués). La forme généralement parallélépipédique des blocs exploités a facilité l'extraction d'éclats à talon et à dos cortical, qui présentent des convergences avec les produits de débitage des galets. Certains de ces éclats ont eu leur tranchant aménagé par des retouches limitées (courtes et larges, généralement directes) qui ne modifient pas la morphologie initiale du support, et très peu l'angle et la forme du tranchant. Il n'est pas toujours facile différencier les retouches vraies de marques d'utilisation ou de piétinement.

L'UTILISATION DES PRODUITS TAILLES EN QUARTZITE ET ARKOSE

L'analyse tracéologique réalisée à la loupe et au microscope métallographique par M. Alonso n'a montré aucune trace d'utilisation diagnostique sur les dizaines d'éclats de galets qui ont été observés. On n'y trouve que des micropolis indifférenciés. Indépendemment du fait que le grès très granuleux rend difficile l'observation, on doit considérer que l'usage probable de ces éclats coupants était surtout d'écailler les poissons, ce qui ne développe pas de traces d'utilisation prononcées. Les tranchants des plus grands éclats de grès silicifié présentent parfois des micro-fracture et des écaillements qui pourraient être dûs à des travaux sur des matières plus résisitantes, mais nous n'em n'avons pas encore fait l'étude tracéologique. Les bords de nucleus de grés silicifié présentent souvent um égrisement qui suggère une réutilisation comme instrument. Nos expérimentations montrent cependant que ces traces proviennent probablement du débitage de ce matériau très tenace.

Quant aux grands éclats d'arkose, leur altération est telle que leurs tranchant ne permettent plus l'observation de traces d'usage.

LE DEBITAGE DU QUARTZ

Dans le site de Buritizeiro, où on ne le trouve que sous forme de petits galets, le quartz fut débité essentiellement sur enclume. Eclats et nucléus présentent des talons écrasés ou concaves en raison de la perte de matière, très prononcée aux points d'impact dans le cas du débitage du quartz par ce procédé. Les produits y furent utilisés bruts ou très peu retouchés. Dans l'abri de Bibocas, proche de riches gisements, les cristaux de quartz de qualité moyenne ou médíocre, ainsi que les blocs de quartz de filon furent également taillé sur enclume; les petits et moyens cristaux de meilleure qualité furent débités en tranche par extraction d'éclats perpendiculaires à l'axe morphologique du cristal – soit à partir de la couronne, soit à partir de la racine – souvent jusqu'à épuisement (Bassi e Rodet 2011). Ces produits ne presentaient pas des retouches ou sont très peu modifiés. Les très grands cristaux de roche (plusieurs dizaines de centimètres) furent traité de manière totalement diferente. Débités hors de l'abri ou de la zone fouillés (sur les gisements?) on en extrayait de grands supports; ils étaient ensuite amenés et parfois façonnés et retouchés dans l'abri. On trouve en effet dans ce site des fragments de pointes bifaciales et des outils plano-convexes, ainsi que quelques éclats compatibles avec le travail d'amincissement et de retouche de pièces bifaciales, et de façonnage de flanc d'outils plano-convexes. Alors que le débitage est toujours réalisé par percussion dure, le façonnage l'est parfois par percussion organique (Fig. 6).

LE DEBITAGE DES SILEXITES ET DE LA CALCEDOINE

Dans les deux sites, la présence de ces matières allogènes est discrète, bien que constante tout au long de l'occupation. Elles étaient destinées principalement à l'obtention de petits outils retouchés sur éclat. Les galets de faible dimensions étaient débités au percuteur dur, de forme peu organisée, sans plan de percussion préférentiel. Les éclats ne dépassent guère 2 à 3 cm de longueur et ont été retouchés en perçoir ou en unifacial sur éclat allongé. Ces petits éclats ont eu leurs tranchants utilisés de forme exhaustive: la somme de bord retouché et/ou utilisée peut atteindre 8 à 10 cm pour um éclat de approximativement 4 cm de long (Machado *et al.* 2009). On n'a pas retrouvé de nucleus ou de supports de grandes dimensions, mais la présence de quelques outils d'une dizaine de centimètres – particulièrement à Buritizeiro, où furent retrouvées des pointes bifaciales et de très belles pièces unifaces – montrent que de grands objets étaient fabriqués ailleurs, et parfois transportés jusqu'aux sites étudiés. On note que l'une des pointes de silexite a été taillée à froid, puis soumise à une préparation thermique et finalement retouchée avant d'être abandonnée fragmentée. Notons qu'il ne semble pas s'agir d'une chauffe accidentelle – alors que beaucoup d'autres pièces présentent effectivement des traces d'étonnement. Les éclats de silexite et de calcédoine présentent des talons lisses, souvent préparés par abrasion; ont n'observe que très peu d'accidents de taille.

Figure 6. Façonnage et Retouche

CONCLUSION

Efficacité et simplicité caractérisent l'ensemble de l'outillage et les procédés de débitage dans les sites de Buritizeiro et de Jequitaí. Les tailleurs préhistoriques ont profité de manière consciente et raisonnée des caractéristiques de galets, et particulièrement de la bonne qualité des tranchants à face neo-corticale. Il n'était pas nécessaire de décortiquer au préalable les nucléus. Le débitage n'est jamais 'opportuniste' – dans le sens où il serait inorganisé. Il utilise des méthode simples, mais jamais "simplistes", car elles sont choisies en fonction de la morphologie du galet et de la forme des produits désirés; celle-ci est aussi standardisée que celles des lames ou des éclats Levallois du Paléolithique européen. Le fait que la plupart des outils soient de simples éclats bruts ne signifie pas un manque de capacité à produire des outils "complexes", car la présence de quelques pointes bifaciales et d'unifaces totalement façonnés, y compris en cristal de roche – une matière très sensible et délicate à travailler – montre bien que certains tailleurs au moins dominaient parfaitement les techniques et les méthodes nécessaires à la fabrication de bifaces amincis. Les petits outils de précision étaient fait em sílexite et normalement retouchés; leur analyse tracéologique, qui n'a pas encore eté faite, dira peut-être s'ils ont travaillé à la préparation des nombreuses pointes de projectile en os retrouvés dans les sépultures de Burtizeiro. Les innombrables couteaux probablement utilisés pour la préparation de la viande et des poissons étaient faits en éclats à dos naturel extraits des galets. Les grands éclats retirés des blocs de roche locale étaient probablement destinés aux travaux plus lourds, comme la préparation d'outils en bois.

Il n'en reste pas moins que l'on note une certaine évolution des habitudes tout au long de la séquence chronologique. Les niveaux les plus profonds montrent une choix plus sélectif des meilleures matières premières, une meilleure préparation des nucleus avant l'extraction des éclats (talons égrisés); ils sont peut-etre les seuls dans lesquels on observe l'utilisation de la preparation thermique. Cet investissement plus poussé dans le travail de la pierre au début de l'Holocène est semblable à celui que l'on a décrit pour d'autres industries du Brésil Central et du nord-est, qui sont caractérisées par l'abondance des outils façonnés plano-convexes. La difference apparente entre les industries anciennes de Buritizeiro et de Jequitaí et celle des abris d'aval vient sans doute de l'utilisation préférentielle d'autres formes de matières-premières et, particulièrement de galets dans les sites que nous venons de présenter. Finalement, il n'est pas nécessaire d'imaginer que la taille des galets aurait été réservée aux non spécialistes alors que celle du silexite et du cristal de roche aurait été le privilège de bons tailleurs. Ces roches fournissaient des outils destinés à des fins différentes; les couteaux sur éclats de galet étaient obtenus d'une forme parfaitement consciente et contrôlée, par des tailleurs qui savaient comment profiter au maximum des caracéristiques de la matière-première.

Bibliographie

BASSI, L. & RODET M.J. (2011) – Análise Tecnológica do Lascamento de Cristal de Quartzo: o Estudo do Sítio Bibocas II, Jequitaí – Minas Gerais, Brasil. Caderno de Resumos. XIV Congresso da Sociedade de Arqueologia Brasileira.

LIMA, M. Alonso & MANSUR, M.E. (1986/90) – Estudo traceológico de instrumentos em quarto e quartzito de Santana do Richo, MG. Arquivos do Museu de História Natural UFMG, Belo Horizonte. 11, p. 173-194.

LIMA, M. Alonso & MANSUR, M.E. (1992) – Análise funcioal de instrumentos em sílex da Lapa do Boquete (período entre 12.200 e 11.000BP). In Souza, A.; Gaspar, M. & Seda, P. Eds. Anais da 6° reunião científica da SAB, Rio de Janeiro.. 2, p. 738-744.

MACHADO, J.; DINIZ, L.; BASSI, L-F.; RODET, M.J. (2009) – As indústrias líticas lascadas em silexito e calcedônia de dois sítios arqueológicos do vale do rio São Francisco: estudo inter-sítios (Bibocas II, Jequitaí e Caixa d`Agua, Buritizeiro, Minas Gerais). SAB. Belém. Caderno de Resumos. p. 16.

PROUS, A. (1992) – Arqueologia Brasileira. Brasilia: Editora UnB 613 p.

PROUS, A. (1996) – Algumas características das indústrias lascadas sobre seixos no Brasil central e nordestino In Kern, A. org. *Anais* da 8° Reunião da Sociedade de Arqueologia Brasileira, EDIPUC-RS, Coleção Arqueologia, Porto Alegre. 1:1, p. 131-150.

PROUS, A. (2004) – Apuntes para análisis de industrias líticas. Ortegalia. Ortigueira: Fundación Federico Maciñeira. Monografia 2, 171 p.

PROUS, A.; RODET, J. & LIMA, A. (2011) – Les vivants et leurs morts: évocation des rites funéraires dans le préhistoire brésilienne (12.000-500 BP). In Vialou, D. ed. Peuplements et Préhistoire en Amérique. Paris: CTHS, pp. 394-406.

RODET, M.J.; DUARTE, D.; CUNHA, A.N.C.; DINIZ, L.R.; BAGGIO, H. (2007) – Os métodos de "fatiagem" sobre seixo de arenito/quartzito do Brasil Central: exemplo do sítio arqueológico de Buritizeiro, Minas Gerais. In Anais do XIV Congresso da Sociedade de Arqueologia Brasileira. Florianópolis. (CD).

METHODOLOGY FOR INTEGRATED RESEARCH FLINT PRODUCTS OF THE NEOLITHIC SITE STARYE VOITKOVICHI 1 IN BELARUS*

Galina N. POPLEVKO

Institute for the History of material culture RAS, 191181, St.-Petersburg, Dvorzovaia nab., d. 18, Russia
poplevko@yandex.ru

Abstract: *The paper offers a methodology of complex analysis of the flint industry from the peat-bog site of Starye Voitkovichi 1 in Belarus. The study is based on the traceological evidence. The technology of primary flaking characteristic of the industry under consideration was mainly oriented at the production of flakes. The 2004-2005 collection consists of over 5 thousand items, and only 328 of them are blades and blade fragments. The primary flaking was based on the hard hammer technique, since many striking platforms bear circular and semi-circular fissures, as well as tiny pits and dents. Traces of using antler hammers are rare. The traceological study of a sample consisting of 411 objects revealed 350 working edges, that were used in different operations. The most numerous are the tools that served to process animal products. They are followed by bone and antler working tools, which, in turn, are followed by tools for working wood and, finally, stone. The tool set is characteristic of the Mesolithic or transitional (Mesolithic to Neolithic) sites. The comparison of the typological and traceological results leads to the conclusion, that the study of stone industries must be complex and include typological, technological and traceological methods. The key role in this approach is played by the traceological method.*

Keywords: *Neolithic of Belarus, peat-bog sites, traceological analysis, complex study of flint artifacts*

The peat-bog site of Starye Voitkovichi 1 was discovered by V.K. Polikarpov. The first archaeological excavations were conducted by M.M. Chernyavsky in 1988 (Chernyavsky, 2002, c. 91-99). Later, the works were continued by A.A. Razlutskaya in 2004 (Razlutskaya, 2005, c. 258-260) and 2005 (Razlutskaya, 2005 field report, Archive of the Institute of History, National Academy of Sciences of Belarus, file № 2267). The excavations of 2004-2005 yielded a great number (over 5 thousand items) of flint objects and ceramic fragments. According to A.A. Razlutskaya, the stone raw materials are dominated by local high quality flint of different shades of blue-grey color

The objectives of the present work can be formulated as follows: 1) the study of the surfaces of flint tools aimed at the identification of microscopic use wear traces on their working edges; 2) identification of use wear traces associated with different operations; 3) technological, typological, and traceological (use-wear) analysis of the materials; 4) comparative analysis of the typological and traceological data.

The sample under study consisted of 411 items, including complete blades and blade fragments, 5 intact or broken arrowheads, several tens end-scrapers, big retouched flakes, and cores. All the objects, except several blades and end-scrapers, lack secondary retouch. At the first glance, one may suppose that here we have to deal with a workshop oriented at the production of blades and flakes with the purpose of their subsequent transportation or exchange. However, the traceological study of a small sample has shown that it was not the case. Despite the absence of intentional or use retouch, nearly all of the studied artifacts have well expressed micro-traces of

utilization in diverse operations. The study was carried out with the help of a stereoscopic microscope MC-2CR-ZOOM and a metallographic microscope LaboMet-И-2 with magnifications ranging from 10x to 600x. The typologically distinct artifacts included into the sample consisted of 5 arrowheads, several end-scrapers, push-planes, and retouched flakes, 7 cores, 3 core rejuvenation flakes, and 33 blade fragments.

TECHNOLOGICAL CHARACTERISTIC

The technology of primary flaking characteristic of the industry under consideration was mainly oriented at the production of flakes, which constitute the overwhelming majority of finds. While the whole 2004-2005 collection consists of more than 5000 items, there are just 328 blades and their fragments. The technological analysis of blades necessarily includes the study of heir metric parameters (Poplevko, 2003a). The overwhelming majority of blades are represented by fragments. According to their length, they can be divided into three groups. The first and most numerous (174 items) group comprises blades and blade fragments, the length of which varies from 2,0 cm to 3,0 cm. The blades and fragments included into the second group are 3,5-5,0 cm long (92 items). The third group consists of 49 blade fragments, measuring 1,0-1,5 cm long.

The results of the traceological study of the given sample of flint tools testify to a wide usage of hard hammer percussion of nodules and large flakes, since many striking platforms bear circular and semi-circular fissures, as well as tiny pits and dents, usually resulting from the use of stone indenters (Poplevko, 2003b, c; 2007). For the time being it is possible to assert, that flint was knapped by means of the percussion technique with the use of stone or, much less frequently, antler.

As to antler hammers and punches (intermediate tools), it is still impossible to say how widely they were employed. To answer this question a statistical analysis of both technical and metrical parameters of blade removals is needed, as well as a traceological analysis of their striking platforms. Such an analysis is planned for the future.

The cases of abrasive preparation of the exterior platform edges are rare. Arrowheads are made by small sharpening bipolar retouch (Razlutskaya, 2005, рис. 1). One of them has distinct lateral wings and is bifacially worked over the whole surface. The other is retouched along the perimeter, with the retouch forming sharp points and flat bases. The end-scrapers are formed by two- and multi-row steep retouch. As distinct of the arrowheads, the retouch here is neither regular nor parallel, which is indicative of frequent resharpening. The working edges of end-scrapers can be sub-rectangular, rounded, or oblique with respect to the long axis of the tools. The shape of the working edge depended on the shape of the original blank. Most end-scrapers were made of big or mid-sized blade flakes. Several objects are made on blades. Only few of them can be classified as morphologically standardized types of end-scrapers.

MICROWEAR CHARACTERISTICS

A randomly chosen sample of traceologically analyzed objects consisted of 411 objects. They included a number of typologically distinct tools such as arrowheads, several end-scrapers, blades and flakes of different size. The use-wear study allowed identification of numerous working edges, and, as some of the artifacts had 2 working edges, the total number of tools exceeded the number of respective blanks. Of 411 objects 126 lacked any traces of wear, while the remaining 285 items had 350 working edges. At the same time, the number of morphologically identified tools was much less, just 83 items (table 1).

All the traceologically identified tools were classified into a number of groups according to the characteristics of worked materials (table 2). The studied sample is dominated by tools used to process meat and other animal products (42,6%). They are followed by tools for working bone and antler (38%), tools used to work wood (17,1%), and, finally, stone working tools (2,3%).

The groups of tools associated with processing animal products (products of hunting) and working osseous materials make altogether 80,6% of the studied objects (42,6% + 38%).

The most numerous are meat knives, represented by 115 items. The tools with well expressed micro-traces of wear, seen under 30x to 60x magnification (Figure. 1), include harpoon insets (25 items), arrowheads (5), end-

Table 1. Comparison of the typological and traceological data

Categories of tools	Identified typologically	Identified traceologically
points	6	5
tools for chopping	3	
miniature axe	1	
adzes and adze-like objects	9	
burins	14	
end-scrapers	12	47
flakes	2	
lancet	3	
perforators	13	1
reamer	1	
push-planes	7	77
insets	12	
meat knives		115
harpoon insets		25
borers		15
plane knive insets		44
cutters		11
chisel		5
retoucher		5
Total:	**83**	**350**

scrapers for working hides (3), and a perforator. The bone and antler working tools are represented by 133 objects, including 28 end-scrapers, 60 push-planes, 11 borers, 23 plane knives, 10 cutters, and 1 chisel (Figure 2). The assemblage of wood-working tools consists of just 60 items, including 16 end-scrapers, 14 push planes, 21 plane knives, 4 borers, 4 chisels, 1 cutter (Figure 2).

The group of tools related to stone working contains 3 push planes for working soft stone or shells, and 5 retouchers. The importance of traceological analysis is obvious not only because of the numerousness of the identified tools, but also because it permits to distinguish new categories of tools, to identify some of the materials they were applied to, to reconstruct the economic specialization of the site. The results of the use-wear analyses have shown, that the inhabitants of Starye Voitkovichi 1 widely used osseous and, somewhat less frequently, wooden artifacts, though none of these are preserved in the cultural layer. The traceological evidence can also serve as a basis for paleoeconomic reconstructions. The subsistence economy of the site's inhabitants was based on hunting and processing products of hunting and fishing, which is reflected in the tool set. It is dominated by meat knives (115), followed by end-scrapers and push-planes (124). Much less numerous are plane knives (44), borers (15), and perforators (1). Tools used for other functions are represented by single items.

Table 2. Distribution of the traceologically identified tools from Starye Voitkovichi 1 according to the types of worked materials

№.	Traceologically identified tools	Working of hunting products	Bone and antler working	Wood working	Stone working
1.	arrowheads	5			
2.	knives for meat	115			
3.	harpoon insets	25			
4.	perforator	1			
5.	end-scrapers	3	28	16	
6.	push-planes		60	14	3
7.	borers		11	4	
8.	plane knive insets		23	21	
9.	cutters		10	1	
10.	chisel		1	4	
11.	retoucher				5
	Altogeher: 350 copies	**149**	**133**	**60**	**8**
	%	42,6%	38%	17,1%	2,3%

This tool set is characteristic of the Mesolithic assemblages, dominated by implements associated with processing animal tissues and working bone and antler. All the end-scrapers are made of small or mid-sized flakes and generally weakly retouched. The tools assemblage contains 1 complete Yanislovitsy type point and two distal fragments of analogous points, characteristic of the Mesolithic period. In addition, there are several crescents, and a fragment of a microblade with obliquely retouched edge. Worthy of special note is also a microblade with both ends slightly rounded by retouch. The presence of mictoliths additionally testifies to the early age of the site. The technology of blade production, their intentional fragmentation, the rarity of big tools, the presence of microliths, and the character of the subsistence economy are indicative of the Final Mesolithic or transitional (Mesolithic to Neolithic) age of the site.

It is for the first time that the traceological analysis has been applied to the flint tools from Belarus. This study is supposed to set the beginning to further systematic research.

Acknowledgements

The research was supported by the Russian Foundation for Humanities, project № 10-01-00553a/B, and the Russian Foundation for Basic Research, project № 10-06-00096a.

I express my deep appreciation to the author of excavations 2004-2005 the site Starye Voykovichi 1 A.A. Razlutskoy, for the opportunity to work with the materials.

Bibliography

CHERNYAVSKIY M.M. (2002) – New Neolithic materials from the upper reaches of the Shchara in western Belarus. In: Badania archeologiezne w Polsce pyinocno-wschodniej I na zachodniej Biaiorusi w Latach 2000-2001. Bialystok. p. 91-99 (in Poland).

POPLEVKO, Galina (2011) – Results of the microwear study materials Neolithic site Starye Voitkovichi 1. In: *Na rubiezy kultur. Badania nad okresem neolitu I wczesna epoka brazu.* Bialystok, p. 305-320 (in Poland)..

POPLEVKO, G.N. (2003a) – Methodical aspect of a complex study on blade industries (with special reference to the materials of Kremennaya III). In: Arkheologicheskie zapiski, vol. 3 "Stone age". Rostov-upon-Donu, p. 143-162 (in Russian).

POPLEVKO, G.N. (2003b) – To the methodology of identification of percussion techniques in the study of stone industries (with special reference to the materials of the Mesolithic site of Vyshegora I). In: Kontaktnye zony Evrazii na rubezhe epokh. Conference abstracts. Samara. p. 73-80 (in Russian).

POPLEVKO, G.N. (2003c) – Criteria of determination of stone flaking techniques. In: Mezhdunarodnoe (XVI Uralskoe) arkheologicheskoe soveshchanie. Conference abstracts. Perm'. p. 53-55 (in Russian).

POPLEVKO, G.N. (2007) – The metodics of integrated research into stones industry. St-Petersburg, Russia, 388 p.

RAZLUTSKAA, A.A. (2005) – Report on field research on the territory of Baranovichi district in 2005- Archive of the Institute of History, National Academy of Sciences of Belarus, case No. 2267. Minsk (in Belarus).

RAZLUTSKAA, A.A. (2005) – Report on field research on the territory of Baranovichi district in 2005- Archive of the Institute of History, National Academy of Sciences of Belarus, case No. 2267. Minsk (in Belarus).

RAZLUTSKAA, A.A. (2005) – Excavations of the peat-bog site Voitcovichi-1 on Lake Koldychevskoe. In: Gistarychna-arkhealagichny zbornik, No. 20. Minsk. p. 258-260 (in Belarus).

CHERNYAVSKIY, M.M. (2002) – New nealityčnyâ matèryâly w vârhouâu Ščary do Zahodnâj Birds. In: Badania archeologiezne w Polsce pyinocno-wschodniej I na zachodniej w Latach Bialorusi 2000-2001. Bialystok. p. 91-99.

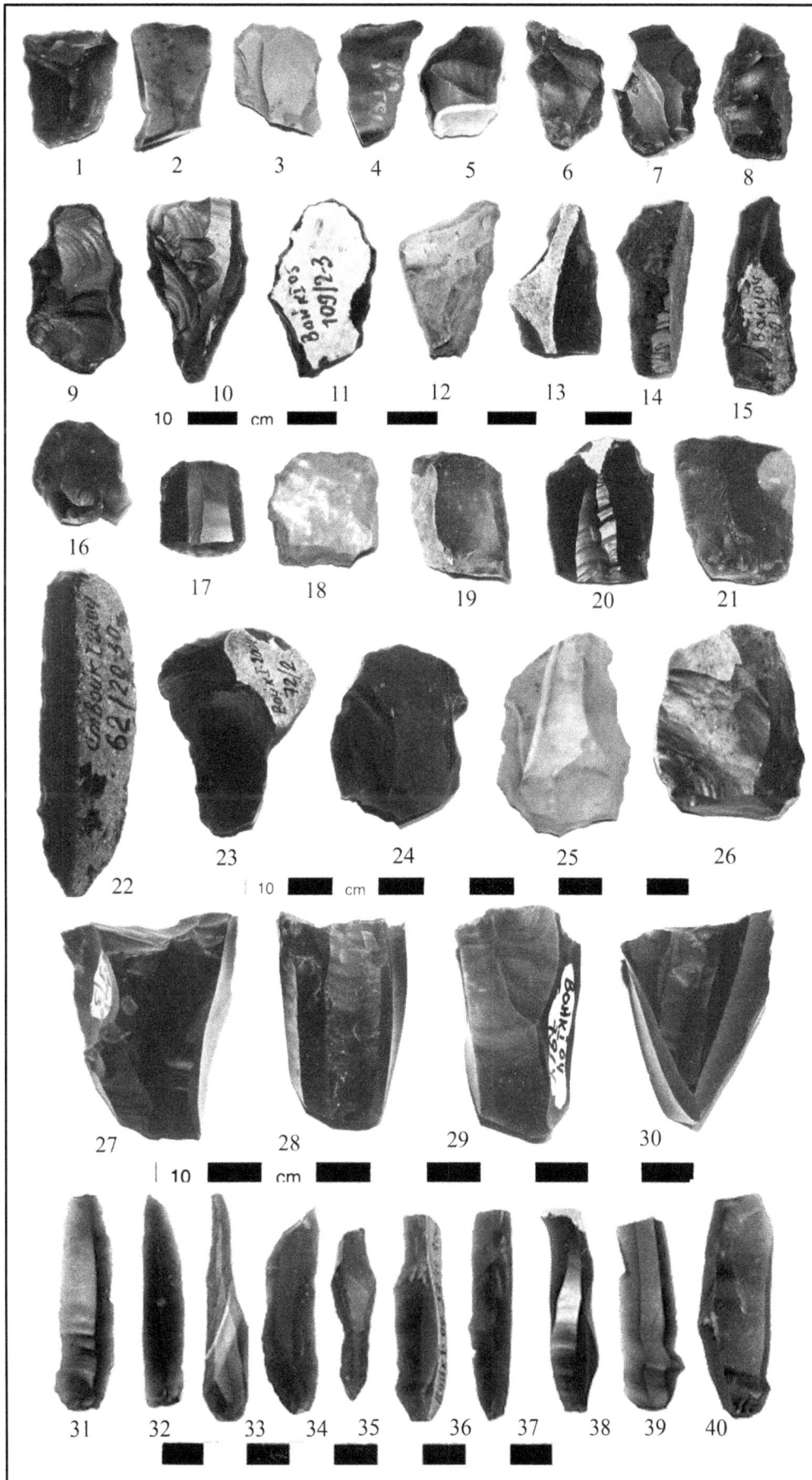

*Figure 1. The peat-bog Neolithic site of StaryeVoitkovichi 1. 1 – Plane knife insets for wood.
Magnification: Ax80; Bx160; Cx240; Dx320; Ex400; Fx560. 2 – Meat knives.
Magnification: C1x30; D1x40; E1x60; F1x80; G1x120; H1x160*

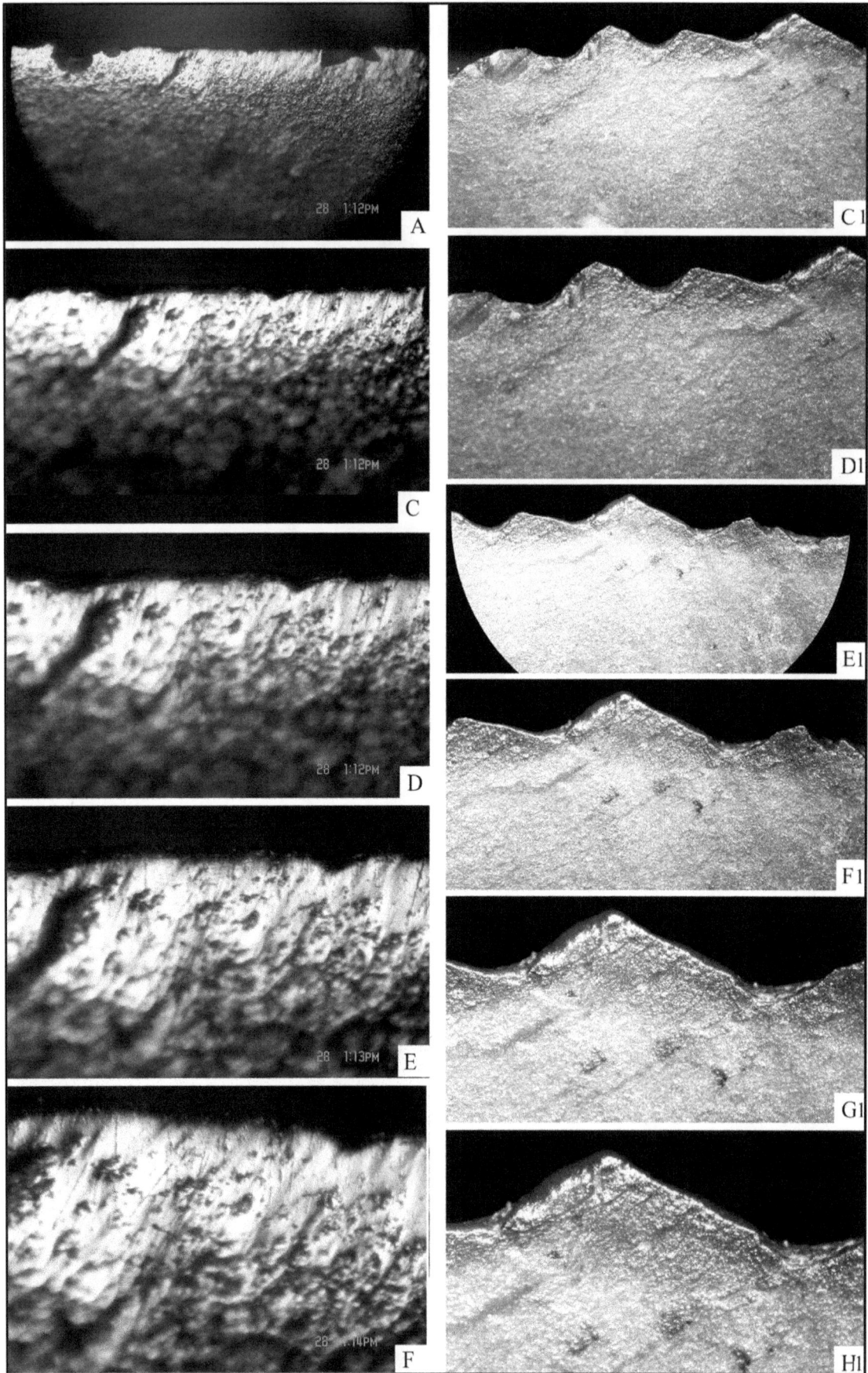

Figure 2. The peat-bog Neolithic site of StaryeVoitkovichi 1. Flint. Tools for bones, horns:
1-2, 5, 7, 9.11, 17, 23-24 – scrapers; 3, 6, 12, 14-16, 26 – push-planes; 4, 10 – borers.
Tools for wood: 8, 18, 19, 21, 25 – scrapers. Tools for hide: 22 – scraper.
Without a trace – 13, 16, 20. Cores – 27-30. Tools on the blades – 31-40

EXPERIMENTAL APPROACH TO PREHISTORIC DRILLING AND BEAD MANUFACTURING

Maria GUROVA, Elka ANASTASSOVA
National Institute of Archaeology and Museum, BAS, Sofia, BG

Clive BONSALL
School of History, Classics and Archaeology, University of Edinburgh, UK

Bruce BRADLEY
Department of Archaeology, University of Exeter, UK

Pedro CURA
Museum of prehistoric art, Mação, Portugal

Abstract: *From the very Early Neolithic in the Balkans two categories of objects are recognized as having been involved in prehistoric drilling activities. The first are beads and other decorative and prestigious items made of bone, shell, pottery and various minerals. The second comprises toolkits of micro-perforators/borers found among the flint assemblages of several sites.*

This paper presents experiments in drilling different materials with the aim of testing several practical issues. A series of micro-borers were produced and used for manual and mechanical drilling (with a pump drill). Various samples (mainly prepared thin plates) of minerals and rocks were used, ranging in hardness (on Mohs scale) from 3 (marble, limestone, calcite) to 6.5 (amazonite, nephrite). Biominerals were also used: aragonite (shells) and apatite (bones). Actual bead production was approached by manufacturing 16 delicate beads of 5 different materials using fine sand and water abrasion. Though not conclusive, the experimental work was instructive in many of the parameters, procedures and technical details of prehistoric drilling.

Key words: *Drilling, micro perforators/borers, beads, experiments*

Résumé: *Dès le début du Néolithique ancien dans les Balkans, la perforation est reconnue en préhistoire grâce à deux catégories d'objets qui peuvent s'inscrire dans le contexte technique de la perforation. La première est constituée de perles ou d'autres objets décoratifs et prestigieux faits d'os, de coquillage, de céramique et de différentes matières minérales. La deuxième catégorie d'objets est constituée d'outillage – de micro-perçoirs et de forets découverts au sein des assemblages en silex de certains sites.*

Nous présentons ici une expérimentation de forage de différents matériaux afin de vérifier certaines pratiques de gestion de l'outillage. Une série de micro-perçoirs ont été produits et utilisés pour le forage manuel et mécanique à l'aide d'un foret à pompe. Des plaques de roches de natures différentes et de duretés variables ont été perforées: des duretés de 3 sur l'échelle de Mohs avec le marbre, le calcaire et la calcite à 6.5 avec l'amazonite et la néphrite. Des biominéraux étaient inclus également: de l'aragonite (coquillage) et de l'apatite (os). La production de perles au sens propre a été approchée en façonnant 16 perles fines faites de 5 matériaux différents. Elles ont été abrasées à l'aide de sable fin et d'eau. Loin d'être définitifs, les résultats de l'expérimentation ont permis d'identifier des paramètres, des procédures et des détails techniques utiles à la compréhension des forages préhistoriques.

Mots clés: *Forage, micro-perçoirs/forets, perles, expérimentation*

PREHISTORIC BACKGROUND

From the very Early Neolithic in the Balkans two categories of objects are recognized as having been involved in prehistoric drilling activities. The first category is represented by beads and other decorative and prestigious items made of bone, shell, pottery and various minerals such as marble, serpentinite, malachite, nephrite and jadeitite. The second comprises toolkits of micro-perforators/borers found in the flint assemblages of several sites. There are some notable examples, as follows:

– A toolkit of 'micro-points' (borers) was recovered from Neolithic contexts at Franchthi Cave (Argolid, Greece).

The association with cockle shell beads led C. Perlès to suggest the existence of a workshop for shell bead manufacturing at Franchthi during the Early Neolithic (Perlès 2001, 223-224, and fig. 10.5). In a later publication she argued that the abundance of the 'micro-points' and borers in conjunction with the careful raw material selection, the evident standardization in their form and technique (representing a homogeneous techno-morphological toolkit), and the large quantity of shell beads support the hypothesis of bead making as craft production beyond the needs of the local community (Perlès 2004, 153). It should be stressed that C. Perlès' conclusions about the Franchthi workshop were influenced by the results of a detailed experimental study of shell beads that were mass produced using a pump drill equipped with flint drill bits, which were fixed in position with a mixture of pine resin and beeswax. The efficiency of this technique of mechanical drilling permitted the replication of about 3000 cockle shell beads. This experimental approach represents one of the most exhaustive and efficient reconstructions of a 'chaîne opératoire' of craft specialization ever undertaken (Ricou, Esnard 2000).

– Excavations at the site of Schela Cladovei in Romania (Iron Gates region) have revealed a similar association of micro-perforators/borers with beads in various stages of preparation and made of different materials (mainly stones).[1] The assemblage of toolkits and beads are under study, the results of which will hopefully elucidate the challenging problem of prehistoric mineral bead manufacturing.

– The Early Neolithic site of Kovačevo in south-west Bulgaria represents a particularly interesting case study of abundance of micro-perforators/borers; more than 100 examples were found, made of local flint and showing a broader range of morpho-metrical characteristics. The tips of the tools are from short to medium, not always clearly separated from the body, sometimes asymmetrical, and fashioned by semi-steep to abrupt bilateral retouch. The morphological characteristics of the micro-perforators suggest they were used for making perforations, but there is no clear contextual association between this toolkit and the perforated objects from the site.[2] Use-wear analysis of the large series of micro-perforators from Kovačevo reveals used implements (with more-or-less well developed microtraces), broken pieces (possibly through utilisation) and unused tools. Further study focusing on comparative correlative observations on micro-perforators and drilled objects is needed to clarify many of the interpretive issues associated with these two categories of artefacts. Here, it is worth recalling the analysis of drill bits and beads from Mezra Teleilat (southeast Turkey) by Güner Coşkunsu (2008), which is an example of the integrated study of a toolkit and its products and their functional and processual interpretation.

– A particularly interesting case of incomparable prehistoric necklaces comes from the Early Neolithic site of Galabnik (western Bulgaria).[3] The length of the necklaces exceeds **8m!** X-ray analysis revealed the mineral composition of the beads as white carbonate (*Gastropoda, Dentalium*), green illite (possible

serpentinite), limestone, volcanic rock (?) and nephrite for the particular three-section element of the necklaces (Kostov 2007; Kostov, Bakamska 2004). The most remarkable feature is that the holes/perforations consistently have a diameter of 1.2 mm.

Against this background, one of us (MG) initiated an experimental programme[4] that was designed to approach the skills involved in prehistoric drilling activities, the archaeological remains of which inevitably arouse the interest and curiosity of prehistorians.

THE EXPERIMENTAL PROGRAMME

The best way to understand these beautiful and sophisticated objects and the narratives embodied within them is to reconstruct the range of abilities and skills that had been developed by the people who produced them. A series of experiments on drilling different materials were undertaken with the aim of testing several practical issues relating to tool efficiency for drilling and optimal parameters for bead fashioning. The experimental work was done passing different stages at different places: in Exeter and Edinburgh (UK); Sofia and Bulgarian countryside (Bulgaria); Mação (Portugal).

Various samples (mainly prepared thin bifacially polished plates from 2 to 4 mm in thickness) and some mineral and rock blanks (debris) from Russian jewellery production, which were obtained by MG some years ago in St. Petersburg, were prepared for use. These ranged in hardness (on Mohs scale) from 3 (marble, limestone, calcite) to 6-7 (nephrite, jasper, aventurine).[5] Biominerals were also used: aragonite (from shells of the bivalves, *Anodonta cygnea* and *Mytilus galloprovincialis spp – class Bivavlia*) and apatite (pieces from long bones of pig and calf).[6] Information about the minerals used in the experiments is presented in table 1.

A series of perforators/borers were fashioned by E. Anastassova and M. Gurova using debitage pieces from the Kovačevo site, which had been discarded because they lacked contextual information. Their morphometric parameters were more suitable for manual than mechanical drilling. Another series of perfectly shaped micro-borers with elongated abruptly retouched bits pronouncedly separated from the body of the tool were prepared by B. Bradley. The blanks came from improvised cores of high quality black flint (available in the Experimental Archaeology Laboratory at Exeter University), Balkan Flint (a nodule collected by CB from the Danube floodplain in southern Romania) and bicoloured jasper from the Rhodope Mountains in

[1] Bonsal, C.; Boroneanţ, A. Balkan flint in the Romanian Iron Gates. Paper presented at the 15th Annual Meeting of the European Association of Archaeologists, Riva del Garda (Trento, Italy), 15-20 September 2009.

[2] The jewellery and prestigious objects from the site are still under study. The artefacts from the site are not yet fully published and one of the authors (M. Gurova), who is studying the flint can only share some preliminary observations on her typological and functional study.

[3] Excavated by M. Chohadziev. Information about the necklaces was provided by Dr A. Bakamska to whom the authors express their gratitude.

[4] This programme started during the tenure of a European Research Fellowship awarded to M. Gurova by the Caledonian Research Foundation and the Royal Society of Edinburgh, with nominator of the project – Prof. Clive Bonsall.

[5] The plates of mineral samples were prepared by Prof. R.I. Kostov and made available along with information about the hardness of the samples and their provenance.

[6] The bone samples were obtained with the help of Dr K. Dimitrov.

Table 1.

Mineral/Rock (Variety)	Transparency/Colour	Hardness on the Mohs scale	Thickness	Time of drilling one hole	Source
Minerals					
Tremolite (nephrite)	semitransparent; yellow-green	6-6.5	3 mm	2 h 40 min (No hole produced)	Russia
Feldspar (microcline - amazonite)	non-transparent; pale green	6-6.5	3 mm; 4 mm	2 h 10 min (No hole produced)	Brazil
Lazurite	non-transparent; dark blue	5.5	3 mm	3 h 22 min	Russia
Malachite	non-transparent; green	3.5-4.5	4 mm	10 min	Russia
Rocks (mineral aggregates)					
Serpentinite (antigorite)	pale to dark green	4	3 mm	7-8 min	Bulgaria
Limestone (calcite)	biogenic; yellow	3	3 mm	3 min	Bulgaria
Marble (calcite)	coarse-grained; pale gray	3	2.5-3 mm	12 min	Bulgaria
Biominerals					
Bones		5	2 mm	12 min	Bulgaria
Shells		4	2-3 mm	10 min	?

southern Bulgaria. This series of drill bits were of an appropriate shape and size to be used for mechanical drilling with a pump drill. Two pump drills were made available by Katharine Verkooijen (Exeter University). There is no incontrovertible evidence for the use of the pump drill at any of the Early Neolithic sites mentioned above, but this type of drill was successfully used for experimental studies of the drills from Çayönü in Anatolia (Altinbilek *et al.* 2001), as well as for making replicas of shell beads from the Artenacien sites in SW France (Ricou, Esnard 2000). No attempt was made to use a bow drill in our experiments. Nor did we attempt to use the 'piquetage' (pecking) and additional percussion technique for making holes in bead roughouts, as was suggested for the manufacture of carnelian beads from Iraq (Tixier *et al.* 1982), or the rather sophisticated knapping technique attested for the manufacture of barrel-cylinder carnelian beads in Harrapan times (for experimentation and description of this last-mentioned technique, see Roux *et al.* 1995).

The bead production *sensu stricto* was approached by manufacturing several delicate discoid beads of serpentinite, limestone, bone, shell and marble using fine sand and water for abrading each bead individually on a grinding slab of metamorphic schist.[7] A detailed photographic record (still images and videos) was made by M. Gurova using a Canon Power Shot A610 digital camera. Micro-photographic documentation of the artefacts and beads was made using a Keyence VHX-100 digital microscope (at magnification x 20 to x 100) belonging to the Conservation Laboratory of NIAM-BAS. The detailed results of a use-wear analysis of the experimental artifacts, and comparison with the archaeological implements, will be the subject of separate paper.

The descriptions and observations presented below relate to the initial stages of our experiments, their challenges, impediments, empirical knowledge and ability acquired, and our ideas for improvements in future work.

Biomineral processing

– As mentioned above two species of shell (hardness 4 on Mohs scale) were used in the experiments – *Anodonta cygnea* drilled mechanically and *Mytilus galloprovincialis* with both mechanical and handmade holes; the results do not differ significantly under microscopic observation. It should be stressed, however, that about 10 min of work with the pump drill produces a rather regular hole with pronounced rotational striations and there is no need for drilling from the opposite side of the shell (fig. 1 – A). A shell of *Mytilus galloprovincialis* with a manual hole made for 10 min was chosen for cutting and bead shaping. The shell blank broke accidentally (through lateral splitting) into 2 pieces, which individually proved very fragile for friction and other shaping procedures. In all, 2 small beads were produced from this blank, which took 35 min in total.

– Drilling of bone (5 on Mohs scale) produced some surprising observations regarding the frequency of fragmentation of flint tools, as well as the efficiency of hand drilling; bone beads were easy to shape after sawing with an untretouched flint blade, followed by abrasion/grinding on metamorphic rock (schist) slabs with fine sand and water. Three holes (1 mechanical and 2 handmade – the latter more conical in profile) were made in 38 min; the sawing of the bone took 30 min and a similar amount of time (35 min) was taken up by the shaping of the 3 beads. The total time consumed by the fashioning of the bone beads was 1 h and 43 min (fig. 1 – B).

---

[7] The bead fashioning was undertaken by M. Gurova in Bulgaria, assisted in the serpentinite processing by E. Anastassova.

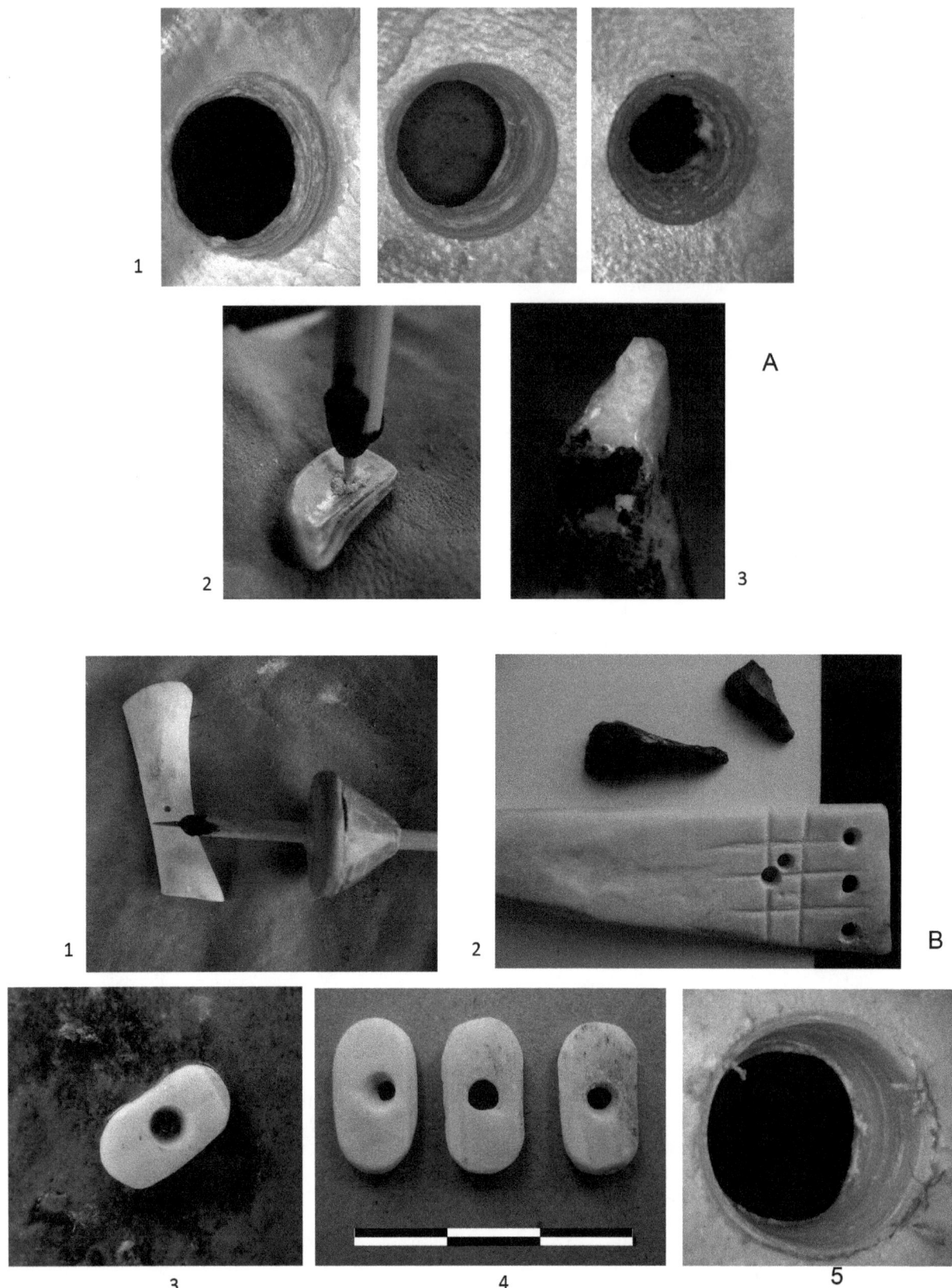

Figure 1. Illustration of various processing: A – shell processing (mechanically drilled holes – 1, 2; torsion fracture of a drill-tip – 3); B: bone processing (mechanical and manual boring – 1, 2; fashioning the elongated beads – 3, 4; mechanical hole – 5). Photos and microphotos (x 25) by M. Gurova

Rock / mineral processing

Seven rock/minerals were used in drilling experiments with a pump drill: marble and limestone (3 on Mohs scale); serpentinite (4 on Mohs scale); malachite (3.5-4.5 on Mohs scale); lazurite (5.5 on Mohs scale); amazonite (6-6.5 on Mohs scale) and nephrite (tremolite) with the hardness of amazonite. The latest 3 minerals were very difficult for work and after the first unsuccessful attempt made in Edinburgh and Sofia, the experiment was abandon. Later on, because of the fact that these mineral were very important for our experimental programme, their working was continued in 2012 in Mação (Portugal) with the energetic and creative help of Pedro Cura.

– quite instructive was an experiment with a button-like piece (jewellery blank) of **lazurite** (fig. 2 – A, 1)**,** which was made narrower by sand and water abrasion, but 20 min drilling produced almost no visible cavity in the material. The next stage of drilling this piece in Mação consisted in 62 min mechanical drilling with water and sand additives on the side with old small hole from Sofia. Subsequently was effectuated a drilling on the other side for making bipolar hole. In total 115 min were needed till the hole is made (fig. 2 – A, 2). Five additional min took an enlarging the hole with another borer with suitable fine tip (fig. 2 – A, 3), because the borer tip which was use in the pump drill was already too rounded. Thus this lazurite 3 mm thick piece was perforated for 3 h 22 min in total without subsequent fashioning for obtaining a finished bead parameters.

– **the piece of amazonite** (fig. 2 – B, 1) was shaped for 40 min and drilled for 15 min without visible results, a second piece without any modification by abrasion was drilled for 30 min with 2 borers (one of which was quickly broken) and again the result was a less than 2 mm cavity in the material with no prospect of creating a complete perforation; rounding and a polish spot was observable on the tip of the flint drill bit. The shaped piece was additionally worked in Mação with 50 min mechanical drilling on the side previously worked; 60 min drilling on the opposite side for bipolar approach. The borer in the pump drill got too rounded and not efficient and the last 5 min manual boring was performed with an unused perforator made by E. Gyria. Finally the piece was halved after 2 h 5 min mechanical and 5 min handhold perforation ....and thus the intention to use it as bead failed (fig. 2 – B, 2).

– one of the best challenge consisted in re-starting to work a piece of **tremolite (nephrite)** after the complete fiasco of the initial attempt to drill this material in Sofia. The re-established process took place in in Mação and was performed by P. Cura (fig. 2 – C). He manufactured suitable borer and used a variation of a pump drill entirely made of wood. The drilling was done alongside with some details as facilities for reliable fixing of the mineral piece and available toolkit for regular resharpening of the borers. In a whole P. Cure made, used and resharpened 5 borers during the drilling operation (fig. 2 – C, 1-3). Flint borers broken systematically with different resistance: from 15 to 43 min. Finally after 2 h and 40 min energetic mechanical drilling there was a symptomatic hole (cavity) 2 mm deep with no chance for affective advancment of the work and with an unavoidable need for rethinking the drilling strategy (fig. 2 – C, 4). This unachieved experiment will undoubtedly be prolonged till some promising results occur.

– **malachite** processing consisted of a very nice bipolar cylindrical hole made by BB for 10 min with water added as a lubricant to speed up the process; noticeable rounding of the borer was produced with many mineral residues on the flint tool and many microchips of flint in the hole created. No subsequent alteration was made to this malachite piece (the experiment will be continued at a later date);

– drilling of a plate of grey **marble** started in Exeter with a hole made for 8 min by BB, but the plate was accidentally crushed when later on MG tried to separate a piece for bead shaping. Subsequently a small button-like bead blank was produced in 5 min by sand and water abrasion, with drilling taking 12 min: thus the bead was made in only 17 min. It is worth noting that use of a flint drill-bit on marble produced the most significant micro features of use: rounding, smoothing and bright spotted polish with transverse striations.

– a series **of 6 limestone** beads were manufactured, starting with cutting the limestone for 35 min with a bifacial point (made by BB) which served as a very efficient knife. Thus 6 rectangular pieces were produced, which were subjected to fine abrasion with sand and water resulting in 6 disc-shaped blanks after another 35 min. The drilling of a hole in each bead with a pump drill took about 3 min, the manufacture of all 6 beads taking altogether 1h and 28 min of working time;

– the most successful of the experiments in bead manufacturing was the work on **serpentinite** – a beautiful and relatively easy to work greenish mineral. The *'chaîne opératoire'* started with the use of a nice plate in which 4 holes were made with a pump drill in 30 min with noticeable rounding and smoothing of the flint borer (fig. 3; 1–3); sawing and separating of the perforated pieces took 13 min with a further 60 min of abrading of each bead on the grinding slab using fine sand and water, resulting in 3 disc-shaped beads (fig. 3: 4-7). Technological traces of bead manufacturing (abrasion) are easily observable on the perimeters of the items, although no rolling of the beads on slabs (as described by Wright *et al.* 2008) was performed for additional smoothing and faceting of their edges. The best example of a serpentinite bead, less than 1 cm in diameter and with a very regular shape and smooth periphery was made by EA in 1 h with a delicate and careful fashioning approach, including treatment with a small hand held abrader and short individual rolling of the piece into a schist slab (fig. 3: 8, 9). These, undoubtedly the most beautiful of the beads produced in our experiments, were produced in 2 h and 43 min.

CONCLUDING NOTES

At this stage of the experimentation programme no definitive conclusions can be drawn. Nevertheless, some observations can be put forward on the basis of empirical data and detailed documentation of the experimental procedure, as follows:

Figure 2. Illustration of various processing: A – lazurite working (1 – stages of shaping; 2 – the hole after 3 h 10 min drilling; 3 – the borer for manual finishing of the hole); B – amazonite processing (1 – pump drill and piece of amazonite; 2 – the final breakage after 2 h 10 min drilling) and C – nephrite processing (1 – 5 borers used and broken during the drilling; 2 – borer resharpening and use; 3 – drilling by P. Cura; 4 – the small cavity after 2 h 40 min unsuccessful mechanical drilling). Photos by M. Gurova

– there is a relation between the morphology of the perforators/borers and their potential/actual use: the pieces inserted into a pump drill must have pronounced pointed parts, i.e. must be 'drill bits/borers' (in French, 'forets à mèche'), and not simple perforators with short amorphous tips;

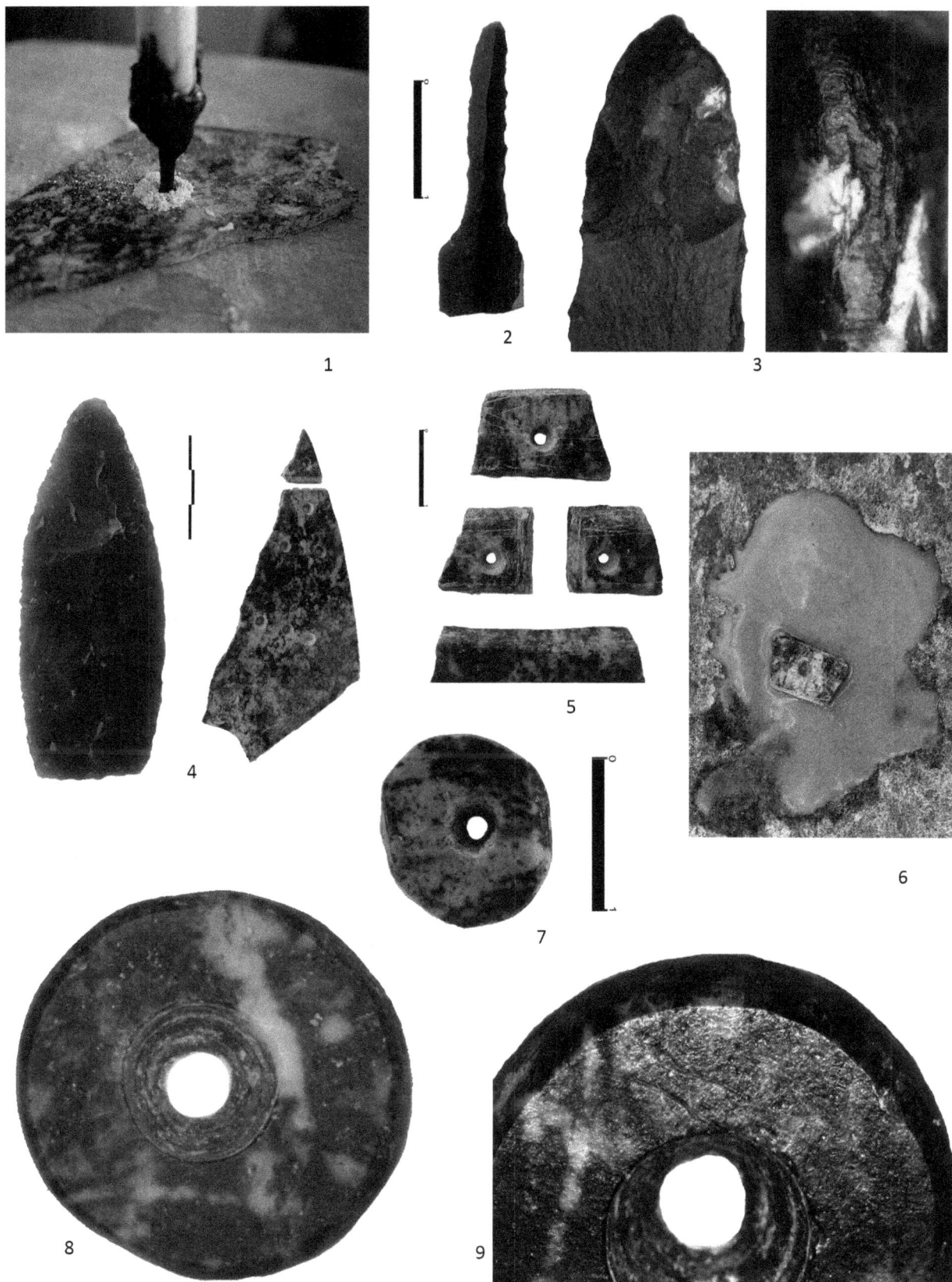

Figure 3. Serpentinite processing: drilling with pump-drill (1); drill-bit and detailed aspect of the ventral scars and smoothing of tip edges (2, 3); cutting raw material blanks (4, 5); shaping bead with abrasion on a slab (6); finished beads (7-9). Photos and microphotos (x 25) by M. Gurova

– there is no evidence to link the breakages/torsion fractures of the borers with the manner of perforating (manual or mechanical) and/or the hardness of the worked material. Some borers break very easily and quickly after perforating begins (i.e. within the first minute);

– the rounding and matt smoothing are typical micro-wear features appearing on borers after prolonged friction with the worked material. Bright polish appeared in 3 cases: in drilling marble, amazonite and lazurite;

– apart from the hardness of the working material (from 3 to 6.5 on Mohs scale), the appearance of microwear traces depends also on the raw material of the drills – the polish resulting from drilling marble for a short time appeared on a jasper borer, while the drilling of amazonite and lazurite was done using flint drill bits with much slower development of micro-polish on their edges and tips.

– in general the perforators used in the experiments can serve as preliminary indicators and comparative examples when considering archaeological collections of similar items; in this respect the assemblage/toolkit from Kovačevo is more likely to have been used in hand processing activity;

– holes produced with a pump drill and by manual boring, respectively, are easier to distinguish on biominerals (bone, shell) than on fine-grained minerals. The distinction is more recognizable in the case of conical vs bi-conical/bipolar holes;

– the hardest materials that were drilled successfully were bones and malachite – 4-5 on Mohs scale. In this respect, prehistoric beads made from carnelian, turquoise, tremolite (nephrite) and other minerals harder than 5 on Mohs scale still represent something of an enigma and a challenge to reproduce;

– the experiments suggest that serpentinite and limestones are suitable (and aesthetically valuable) materials for bead manufacturing;

– both drilling and bead shaping are more efficient with the addition of water; water and fine sand were essential additives for bead abrasion and shaping in the case of both mineral and biomineral beads;

– as a final note – the small heterogeneous necklace shown in fig. 4 comprises 6 limestone, 4 serpentinite, 3 bone, 2 shell and 1 marble beads: the total time required for its preparation was 6 h and 46 min, but the fact must be kept in mind that pre-prepared mineral plates were used, which facilitated the bead manufacturing process enormously.

FURTHER PERSPECTIVE

Apart from the acquisition of valuable empirical knowledge, the experiments prompted new questions, which would not have arisen outside the context of our research into prehistoric skills and techniques. Different questions arise on the level of a concrete experimentation programme, when compared to that of more general reasoning based on experimentation and the extrapolation

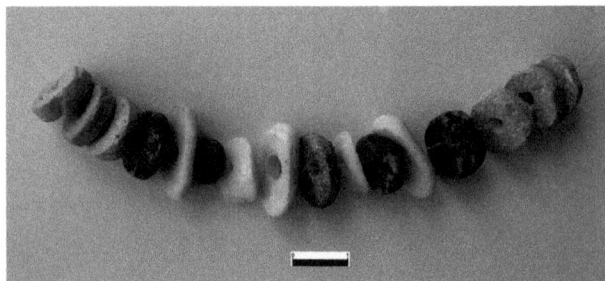

Figure 4. Necklace consisting of 16 individually prepared beads (15 made by MG and 1 – by EA)

of its results to archaeological remains from different contexts.

On the first level many challenging issues are envisaged for further work, building on our initial research. These we were only able to take into consideration in connection with the complexity and obvious infeasibility of the many of skills involved in the production of a necklace such as that from Galabnik in Bulgaria (*vide supra*). Our further and more detailed experimental programme will include the following variations on our preliminary work: a series of mechanical drillings by different types of borers in the same material in order to reveal differences in efficiency due to the morphometrical and technological characteristics of the tools; successive drillings using one type of borer on different materials in order to reveal the effect of the raw material on the tool's resistance; a series of drillings on roughouts of varying dimensions versus drilling of shaped beads, in order to gain a more comprehensive understanding of the chaîne opératoire.

On the level of fashioning beads there are also variations of challenging opportunities/procedures to be tested and observed (see below). One of the crucial objectives of further experimentation will be to produce a significant number of used tools and undertake their careful use-wear analysis, assuring sufficiently reliable results for comparison with archaeological toolkits. One of the ambitions of the research team is to succeed in drilling and manufacturing beads of nephrite, replicating as closely as possible the archaeological examples in terms of manufacturing sophistication and aesthetical perfection.

At the second more general level of consideration, other issues may be listed. One question is to what degree the manufacture of varying toolkits for perforating/drilling is due to functional anticipation or decision making based on practical experience. When the association between toolkits and drilled products is not obvious, then doubts arise about the efficiency of the toolkits presumed to have been for perforation. For example, the fragility of the extremely fine drill bits from the late PPNB site of al-Basît (Jordan) led Rollefson to doubt their mechanical use (Rollefson, 2002; Rollefson, Parker 2002); moreover the differences in morphology among the various micro-drills recovered from sites in the Mississippi River valley were confusing with respect to their functional interpretation, and only use-wear analysis resolved the problem (Yerkes 1983).

Experimental bead manufacturing *sensu stricto* should balance between examples already done and illustrated in the specialized literature, and taken as a matrix for subsequent reproduction of the know-how, and the spontaneous decisions and ad hoc approaches during the experimental manufacturing. However, very few real innovations are expected in this field, which already contains many detailed descriptions of *'chaîne opératoires'* and analytical technological approaches (e.g. Kenoyer *et al.* 1991; Roux *et al.* 1995; Wright *et al.* 2008).

The only relevant approach seems to be one that requires a combination of the experience gained through experimentation and detailed artefactual analysis of the archaeological remains (both toolkits and beads) in order to formulate (and hopefully answer) the right questions coming from and belonging to a specific context. This will be the objective of a further programme of experimentation and cognitive quest based on the initial study presented above.

Other questions we hope to investigate as our research into bead manufacturing in the Early Neolithic of SE Europe continues concern the acquisition and use of raw materials, for the production of both the beads and bead making equipment. Were materials obtained locally or from distant sources? What characteristics other than hardness influenced the choice of raw materials for bead making? Why did some communities make extensive use of mollusc shells for bead making, while others (who had access to shells) hardly used them at all and focused instead on lithic materials? Although our initial experiments have shown that relatively soft stones like limestone and serpentinite can be perforated quite easily using flint drills, how did Early Neolithic people manage to drill through harder materials like jadeite and nephrite?

Acknowledgments

The authors would like to express their gratitude to several institutions and individuals for their help in the experimentation programme. The Caledonian Research Foundation and the Royal Society of Edinburgh awarded a European Research Fellowship to M. Gurova and thus initiated the experimentation.

We also thank Katharine Verkooijen (Exeter University) for preparing the two pump drills used during the experiments in Edinburgh, Bulgaria and Portugal, Prof. Ruslan Kostov (University of Geology and Mining, Sofia) for providing the mineral samples and associated information, Dr E. Gyria (Institute of history of the material culture, St.-Petersburg), Aneta Bakamska (Historical Museum, Pernik) for the photograph and information of the necklace from Galabnik, and Dr Kalin Dimitrov (NIAM-BAS, Sofia) for providing the bone samples used in our drilling experiments.

References

ALTINBILEK, Ç.; COŞKUNSU, G.; DEDE, Y.; LOVINO, M-R.; LEMORINI, C.; ÖZDOGAN, A. (2001) – Drills from Çayönü. A combination of ethnographic, experimental and use-wear analysis. In Caneva, I.; Lemorini, C.; Zampetti, D.; Biagi, P. eds. – Beyond Tools. Redefining the PPN Lithic Assemblages of the Levant. Studies in Early Near Eastern Production, Subsistence, and Environment 9, 137-144. Berlin, ex oriente.

COŞKUNSU, G. (2008) – Hole-making Tools of Mezraa Teleilat with Special Attention to Micro-borers and Cylindrical Polished Drills and Bead Production. Neo-Lithics, 1/08, 25-36.

KENOYER, J.M.; VIDALE, M.; BHAN, K.K. (1991) – Contemporary stone beadmaking in Khambhat, India: patterns of craft specialization and organization of production as reflected in the archaeological record. World Archaeology 23/1, 44-63.

KOSTOV, R. (2007) – Archaeomineralogy of Neolithic and Chalcolithic artifacts from Bulgaria and their significance to gemmology. Sofia: "Sv. Ivan Rilski".

KOSTOV, R.I.; BAKAMSKS, A. (2004) – Nefritovi artefakti ot rannoneolitnoto selishte Galabnik, Pernishko. Geologia i mineralni resursi, 11/4, 38-43 (in Bulgarian).

PERLÈS, C. (2001) – The Early Neolithic in Greece. The first farming communities in Europe. Cambridge World Archaeology. Cambridge: Cambridge University Press.

PERLÈS, C. (2004) – Les industries lithiques taillées de Franchthi (Argolide, Grèce). T. III. Du Néolithique ancien au Néolithique final. Bloomington & Indianapolis: Indiana University Press.

RICOU, C.; ESNARD, T. (2000) – Etude expérimentale concernant la fabrication de perles en coquillage de deux sites artenaciens oléronais. Bulletin de la Société Préhistorique Française, 97/1, 83-93.

ROLLEFSON, G. (2002) – Bead-Making Tools from LPPNB al-Basît, Jordan. Neo-Lithics, 2/02, 5-7.

ROLLEFSON, G.; PARKER, M. (2002) – Craft Specialization at al-Basît, Wadi Musa, Southern Jordan. Neo-Lithics, 1/02, 21-23.

ROUX, V.; BRIL, B.; DIETRIH, G. (1995) – Skills and learning difficulties involved in stone knapping: the case of stone-bead knapping in Khambhat, India. World Archaeology, 27/1, 63-87.

TIXIER, J.; INIZAN, M.-L.; CHEVALLIER, J. (1982) – Une technique de perforation par percussion de perles en cornaline Larsa, Iraq. Paléorient, 8/2, 55-65.

WRIGHT, K..; CRITCHLEY, P.; GARRARD, A. (2008) – Stone Bead Technologies and Early Craft Specialization: Insights from Two Neolithic Sites in Eastern Jordan. Levant, vol. 40/2, 131-165.

YERKES, R. (1983) – Microwear, Microdrills and Mississippian Craft Specialization American Antiquity, vol. 48/3, 499-518.

CERAMIC TECHNOLOGY: FRAGMENTS OF
AN EXPERIMENTAL PROCESS

Jedson Francisco CEREZER

Trás-os-Montes e Alto Douro University – UTAD; Cience and Technology Institution – FCT- project:
SFRH/BD/74394/2010;Quaternary and Prehistory group of GeoSciences Center Unit (uID73 – FCT);
Instituto Terra e Memória; Portugal
jcpithi@gmail.com

Abstract: *The technological process for obtaining a ceramic material capable of resisting the use requires, in essence, the domain of a broader process which is divided into several chains of operations. In this logic the study of experimental archaeology used to ceramic technology, allows us to understand various stages of the production process and advance into new studies ranging from the behavior of the material during the use to the analysis of the fragments, and all the associate forms, composition of the paste and surface finishes with the function of the piece.*

This article is based on experimentation in Guarani ceramic from the southern Brazil with real possibilities of application in any context involving ceramics within what is known as earthwear, as is the case in progress, the Iberian Neolithic ceramics. On this base, it is built technological parallel by applying a common methodology.

Keywords: *Ceramic technology, Experimental Archaeology, Guarani Ceramic, Neolithic Ceramic*

Résumé: *Le processus technologique d'obtention d'un matériau céramique, capable de résister à l'utilisation exige, par essence, le domaine d'un processus plus vaste qui est divisé en plusieurs chaînes d'opérations. Dans cette étude, la logique de l'archéologie expérimentale appliquée à la technologie céramique, nous permet de comprendre les différentes étapes du processus de production et d'avancer sur des nouvelles études allant du comportement de la matière lors de l'utilisation jusqu'à l'analyse des fragments et, ainsi, associer formes, composition de pâte et finitions de surface à la fonction de la pièce.*

Cette communication est basée sur l'expérimentation en céramique Guarani du sud du Brésil avec un réel potentiel pour une application sur tous les contextes impliquant la céramique au sein de ce qui est connu comme earthwear, comme c'est le cas en cours, de la céramique du néolithique ibérique. Sur cette base, nous construisons parallèles technologies grâce à l'application d'une méthodologie commune.

Mots clés: *Technologie ceramique; Archeologie experimentale; céramique Guarini, céramique neolithique*

INTRODUCTION

This article is a sample of the results obtained during the process of archaeological trial (Cerezer, 2009) and other results found during the research activities at the ceramic technology investigation department of the Museum of Mação, Portugal, from 2010 to mid 2011.

The ceramic technology which we refer to in this article is, to classify, the one that includes the low-temperature baked ceramics, terracotta or earthenware with firing temperatures at around 850 to 1000° C. In this context it is possible to classify the prehistoric ceramic as equivalent to the European Neolithic period.

Although it is a research that can be used in several contexts, our study shows, in particular, Guarani ceramic of southern Brazil compared to the neolithic ceramic of the Upper Ribatejo, Portugal. Even though they are distinct contexts in time and space, both represent agricultural societies, or as in Guarani case, horticulture. The variation of the forms in the analyzed sets using the same methodology, allows us to observe the preferences and technological options that can, in our view, determine regional patterns or even cultural tradition.

CERAMIC TECHNOLOGY AND ARCHAEOLOGICAL EXPERIMENTATION

The way chosen to the development of our research goes through a strict relation between the "Artifact" with the Production – Utilization – Economy – Territory. This way to conduct the research and the experimental works allows us to look at the piece as a result of human work, capable of supplying their needs in different territories with different geomorphologic contexts.

To obtain a ceramic artifact in conditions that it is able to be used, it is necessary to follow a "production process" which involves a series of distributed operations in at least four "operative chains" considered all sort of complex, that can be described as: Composition of **Paste, Manufacturing and Surface Treatment, Decoration and Firing.**

The **paste** composition involves the selection of some types of clay or one clay according to the preference or the availability that the ceramist has. The process of cleaning and preparation of it can vary intensively with more or less degrees of intensity for both dry or wet clay.

After having selected the type of clay, it can be used pure or with the addition of some non-clay element, this last one can be used to increase or decrease the clay's plasticity.

In case of adding non-plastic elements, these can be found in nature in a condition of use without any previous treatment or in other cases, as for the "grog" – milled ceramic shard – an intensive process of preparation is needed with the assistance of other instruments, until it reaches the desired particle size. The thickness of the non-plastic grain can vary, on a distinct macroscopic scale that can be defined as – the small: less than 2 mm; the medium: more than 2 mm to 4 mm; large: more than 4 mm.

We know that when preparing the non-plastic we produce a significant amount of dust, that are very small grains – smaller than 0.5 mm, and this process makes it difficult to find a precise macroscopic classification of how much is the concentration of these elements in a ceramic paste. The maximum size of non-plastic elements normally follows the purpose of the part to be manufactured, having a logical relationship between wall thickness and extent of the no-plastic.

This way we can see that, depending on the type of paste that is used when making a ceramic artifact, we can have a lot of chains of operations, that can increase if we consider the process of sifting and kneading, the latter being very important to avoid air bubbles on the vessels walls – if the bubbles remains they can cause extensive damage to the artifact during the firing process.

About the kneading of the paste, this is a process that can also be done during the time of the manufacturing of the piece, in a specific action to conduct the particles that compose the paste, improving this way the physical structure of the same.

The manufacturing process is, undoubtedly a creative process that requires a lot of skill. Sometimes the creative freedom of the artisan has to be suppressed, even though it maintains the characteristic and particular traits of his individuality, the strict rules of a social process of learning and/or keeping of the identity can represent unquestioned values. These rules can be seen at different times of the production process; however it is in the "morfotipology" of the pieces that we can see this characteristic in a more explicit way.

There are many ways to produce a ceramic object, the most common in the artifacts we are referring to, is the technique of "Colombino", in other words, the coils overlap. This is the most suitable technique for the production of large artifact. Other techniques are also used, such as is the molded, shaped, and overlapping plates. This distinction can be noted with some training in the fragments where the negative appear or in a vertical analysis of the of the center parts of the artifacts walls.

It is also during the manufacturing process that the **surface treatment** happens, which in some cases can also have a decorative function. The distinction from a productive surface treatment and decorative one is directly linked to its character and the role it develops in the production process. As an example of a surface treatments we can use the plain style, considered productive by its nature, for its function in a container, especially on the inside surface of the vessels used as "domestic stuff." On the other side we have other styles as the corrugated, brushed, striatum etc that even having a decorative aesthetic, they are considered part of a production process, improving their use specially because of the decreasing of time spent when finishing these type of pieces. Although the same cannot be said for the styles that are burnished, ungulate, incisive, ribbed or painted.

It is important to make distinction between the decorations and the steps that are performed during the production process. Highlighting the ones made with the wet paste, in state of leather or dry paste, before firing and the ones made while or after firing.

The production requires a large knowledge of the steps of making the artifact that goes from making of the base, walls, keels, bulges and bottlenecks, as well as the edges and the lips. This nomenclature can vary from school or country, but they are actually segments that form a bowl as it can be seen in Sheppard (1956) and La Salvia and Paperback (2nd ed. 1989: 117). This sequence that runs from the base to the edge requires, depending on the size of the bowls, production times that can vary depending on weather conditions of the production place.

The hours of production are very important to the processes of **Decoration**, where the drying time of the artifact directly influences the quality of the results. In this process we will disconsider any type of "fixtures" because they are not common or even absent in morphotypologies we are discussing about. We will use as examples the incised or ungulated decorations styles even though there are many more of them.

We can see incised decorations in the Neolithic ceramic forming a sequence of drawings with plain lines or curved lines, usually in the upper part of the artifact. These decorations are made with fresh paste or paste in a state of leather, if they were made in dry parts we would notice the difference in the furrows, while in the former situation they are made by pressure leaving a groove with a smooth mark, in the second case they are made by the incision remaining marks of "crackle" that is a synonymous for scraping.

On the Guarani ceramic, the ungulate is only possible in fresh paste because it is only in this state of paste that the artisan can mark the surface of the artifact with a fingernail. Sometimes the ungulate is associated with other decoration or other kind of surface treatment. Most of the times however, it is present in small artifacts or small parts of large artifacts, obviously because this is a long time consuming activity.

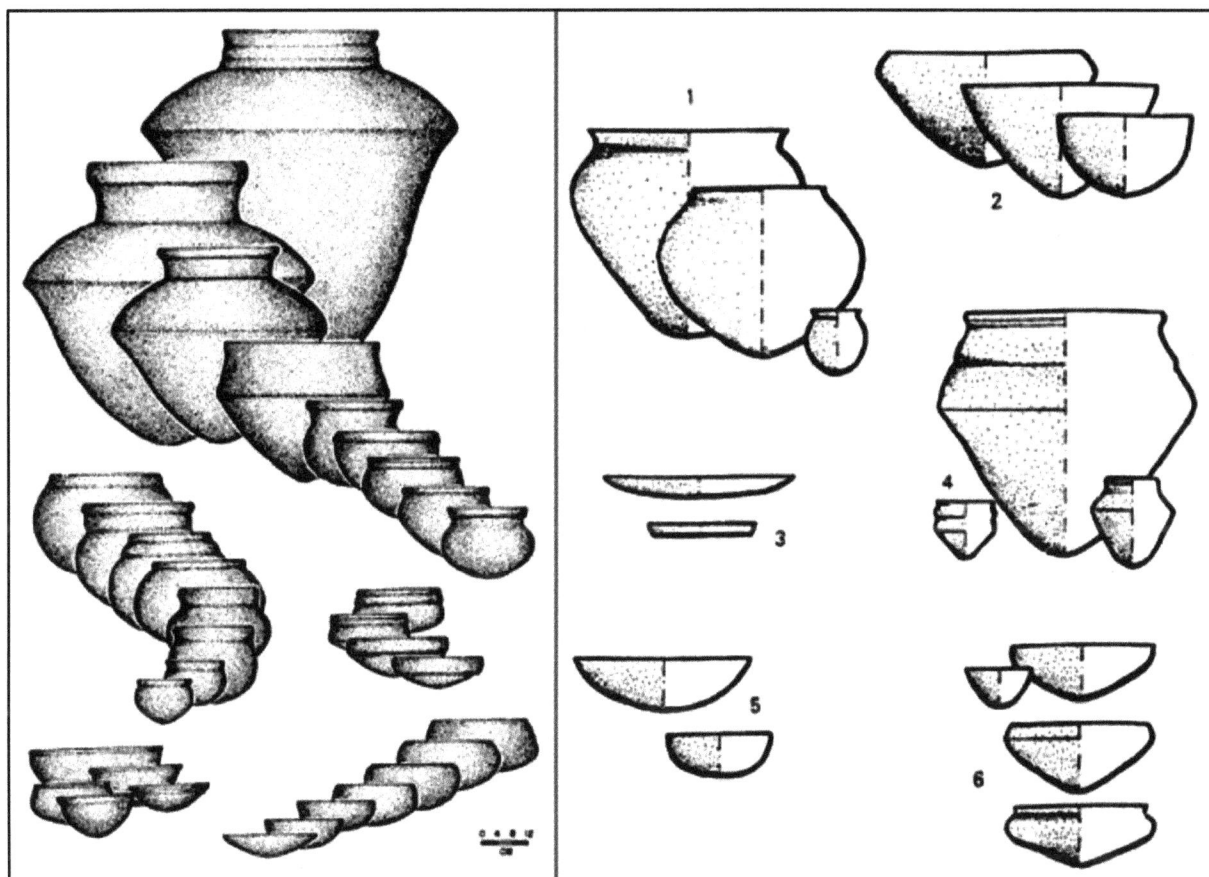

Figure 1 A. serial forms of ceramic of "Tupiguarani Tradition" (Schmits, 1991)
still have nowadays a strong presence in academic discussions. Figure 1 B.
Guarani artifacts classes (Brochado and Monticelli, 1994)

The **painted decoration** is not a present element in the Neolithic ceramics we are discussing about, however it is a common feature in Guarani ceramic, presenting colors in shades of white, red and black.

The painting started to be used by some researchers to determine an archaeological tradition as we can see in Meggers and Evans (1970). With inheritance of the decades of 60/70, the painting assumed a crucial role to determine time inside the system of "steps and traditions" by the system of ranking (Fig. 1 A) – serial forms of ceramic of "Tupiguarani Tradition" (Schmits, 1991) still have nowadays a strong presence in academic discussions.

On the opposite side of this model there is the use of form and function (Fig 1 B) – Guarani artifacts classes, (Brochado and Monticelli, 1994), with their name in Guarani and English: 1) *Yapepó* – pot; 2) *ñaetá* – casserole; 3) ñamopyú – roaster; 4) cambuchí – hoist or pitcher; 5) ñaé, nãembé – dishes; 6) cambuchí caguabã – cup or bowl. In each class we have a specific surface treatment, in this case the painting is only present in certain forms with a specific function (see summary on Noelle, 2008 p. 38). We confirmed this fact with the use of the artifacts, because during our research to reproduce the forms of Guarani ceramic we also used the artifacts in food preparation and storage of liquids.

It is important to say that each of the analyzed models raise a big discussion and will deeply determine the type of approach given to the artifact and consequently to entire context that concerns the society and the surrounding territory.

In technical terms the painting is "cold", or in other words, made after firing. The little information that exist up to the present indicates the use of oxides for the reds and blacks and to the white is used the "*caulin*" (Jacome, 2006). These information help us strengthen our observations about the use of oxides during the firing process, proving that it is not possible for this type of technology, to obtain or maintain the red color during the cooking of an artifact. Another fact that contributes in this situation is the disappearance of the painting by leaching effects, showing that the material is not molten with the ceramic during the cooking, concluding this way, that this is an after cooking painting.

The **firing** process, also called **burning** is another step in the production process, requiring a large knowledge by the artisan. We can say that this step is a complex operational chain, because to have the artifacts correctly dry it is necessary fuel and a combustion structure, besides a large mastery of the temperature phases and burning.

We know that the special ovens to cook ceramics are only associated to more recent periods of the European prehistory and for the Guarani ceramic there is no information of its existence. The absence of traces of these structures suggests the use of a technique known as "open fire" where the pile of artifacts is covered with a flammable vegetal material and fired to make the burning of the artifacts.

We decided to eliminate variables in our research in order to have greater control of the various stages of the production process. Because of this decision we used a combustion structure like an "oven", this kind of structure allowed us to cook the artifact with a reduced risk of breaking them, which contributes to the analysis of so-called "manufacturing errors" that we know now ours are very similar to those found in the archaeological records. As we can seen in Fig. 2, where we have negative of the coils, on the top we can see the picture of an experimental piece and at the bottom a picture of an archaeological piece.

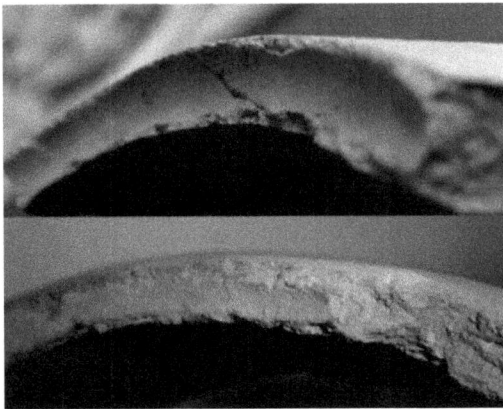

Figure 2. Negative rolls in archaeological and experimental piece

In our experiment we could also reproduce the same color effects found on archaeological pieces, demonstrating this way, that the changes in the colors of the artifact's walls are mainly, effects caused by the atmosphere while cooking them. Darker tones are produced in reduced environments, with the least amount of oxygen. Yet the red tones are the result of oxidizing environments with more oxygen.

It was only possible to achieve many of the results in our research deciding to break some of the pieces. The logic of this experimental process came from a searching problem, where we felt the need to study the ceramic fragment in an opposite process of what the archaeologist makes. This way we needed whole parts that could become fragments. To obtain the artifacts we developed a rigorous methodology, with written records of all stages of the productive process as we described in summary above or in full at Cerezer, (2011).

To break the pieces we chose a method where we had a progressive pressing force from the base to the board. To make it possible we used a hydraulic press, putting the base of the pieces on a flat surface as shown in Fig. 3.

As soon as we had the fragments in hands we started to compare the same with archaeological fragments. These comparisons allowed us to discuss about the assumptions "taken as truth," showing that, they were mainly just mistakes, that attributed to bad cooking the effects such as the "black heart" – the core of the wall in dark shades – negative of the rollers, a straight segment of the fracture lines, etc..

The analysis of the fragments allows us with some experience to contribute a lot in the study of the productive process by the observations related to the sequence of *colombinos* and the particles orientation, the

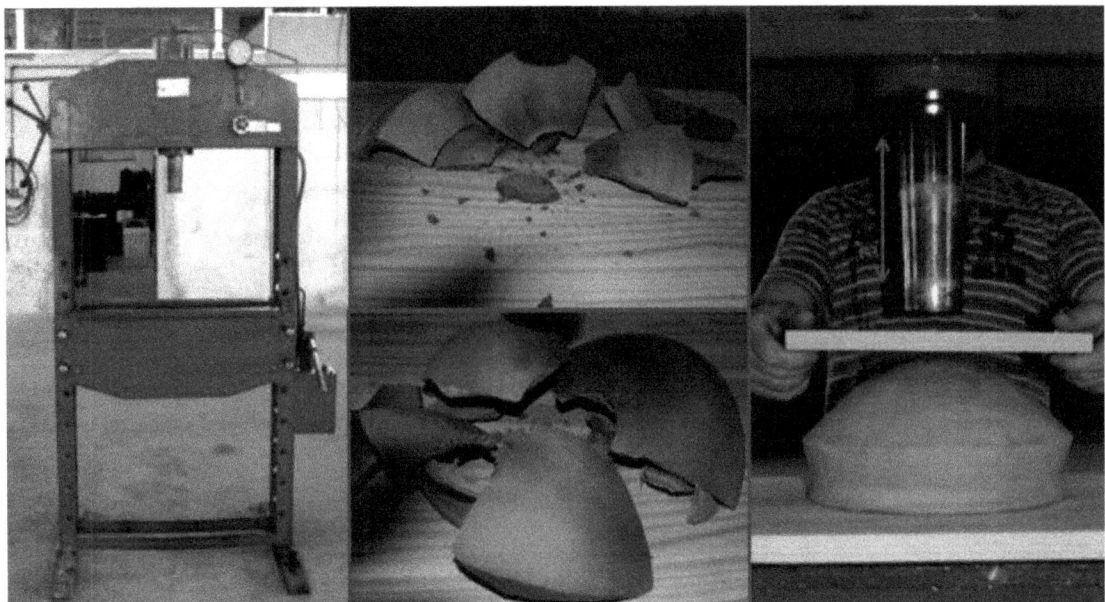

Figure 3. System hydraulic press to break pots

characteristics of the non-plastic elements present in the extremity, the core coloration of the walls, the fails at the junction of the rollers, the oxidation and reduction shades besides the direction of the surface treatment, as shown in Fig. 4.

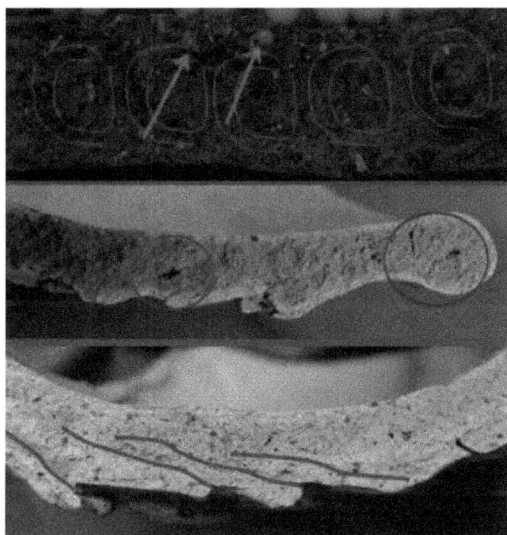

Figure 4. Macroscopic observations from the core of a ceramic fragment

To increase the number of analogies we used some of our vessels on a "heuristics" perspective to achieve more data. We used them in various activities, including those that would be called a collective group meal for 25 to 60 individuals. For each shape, we applied its function such as: for liquid storage we used the *Cambuchis* (bowls); to serve drinks we used the cups or bowls *Cambuchi caguabã* and for food preparation and boils we used *Yapepó*- pans and so on.

The results helped to confirm the hypotheses that come from the historical data that can be seen in La Salvia and Brochado (1989 2nd ed. 1989), Brochado, Monticelli and Neuman (1990), Brochado and Monticelli, (1996), Noelli and Brochado (1998) and synthesized in Noelle (2008: 17-47) and was reaffirmed by us, in Cerezer (2009), with technological data about the facility of manufacturing and reaffirming in this article with experimental data on its use.

The functional application of each artifact form allows us to observe, for example, the reasons of certain "production rules", such as: the *Cambuchis* differ from *Yapepós* as seen in Fig. 5, especially in the opening diameter and degree of openness on the board, as well as on the shoulders and keels. They also bring in most of the cases an enhanced lip suggesting the function of a holder to tie some sort of rope, both to help in the transport of liquids or for a cover fastening. The difference in the degree of openness and diameter of the mouth of the artifact facilitates the use of it in the function for which it was conceived as we can see in our hypotheses presented in the picture below.

Figure 5. Functional hypothesis, from the form and surface treatment

We could also notice in the pans that went to fire, used by us in food preparation, the appearance of lighter patches on the bottom, they are spots that arise through the process of re-oxidation of the walls of the artifact, they occur when the part is submitted to higher temperatures than those of burning, and they normally are in very specific points of the parts, especially in the part where they come into contact with the most intense heat of the fire, empirically where the fire is between the "yellow and white" color.

The re-oxidation is visible in archaeological parts and fragments of the Guarani ceramics, mostly with a corrugated surface treatment, on the Neolithic ones we see this in parts that are not decorated. Suggesting to the Neolithic case what we proved to Guarani ceramic: the existence of different functions for each type of vessel.

About the painted artifacts we can contribute with some data. Besides presenting a plain surface treatment painted from the bigger bulge up to the mouth of the piece, in the case of the hoists, its morphology difficult to use them in food preparation, especially to mix the ingredients inside the piece. Adding this fact to the soot that permeates the walls of the piece and the excessive heat of a cooking process, capable of destroying the painting, we can safely say that the painted parts did not go to fire for preparing food.

This way we could follow our discourse about the inexistence of painted ceramic in certain archaeological sites, or the higher frequency of fragments with certain types of surface treatment and enter the field of social organization using the articles of André Soares (1997, 1998), and infer information about the Guarani territory in an extension to the article of Noelli (1993). However, the data we have, on a larger scale for Guarani ceramic, contribute to a better understanding of the vessels, also helping in the understanding of their land and space distribution and consequently making it possible to discuss the individuals who made them and their needs.

Therefore, we can say that an experimentation research must follow rigorous measures of control in its various stages in order to know at the end of the process, as in our case, either with whole vessels or just fragments of them, how to create a data frame of analogies capable to facilitate the reading of an archaeological artifact. This reading should be built first with information regarding the technology of what is related to the operative chains that make up the production process of the ceramics.

On a second moment we can make use of data from the "marks of use," whether they are constructed by means of laboratory tests or results from empirical observations in experimental procedures. The important thing is to get as much information as possible to answer questions. Because sometimes we use very complex studies to answer simple or not so important questions if we consider all the elements that compose the large complex of a ceramic vessel.

We consider important and necessary to think about the study of a ceramic material, to see an artifact as something designed for individuals who are part of a society with rules and specific limits and that have a territory on their domain.

Therefore the study should be thought in a logic of **Production** – where the productive process is composed by several operative chains that allows to make an artifact in a condition to be used that meets the needs for which it was designed for; **Utilization** – to consider forms and functions of the vessels in a society, although they may fulfill more than one function, such as the reuse of the vessels as urns, where there are pre-established rules that justify a temporary permanence of some morfotipologies; **Economy** – the existence of economic needs reflects in the material culture and this is possible to restore, food waste and signs of the usage may indicate economic activities as well as laboratory studies of clays origins or "rare land" for trade network, can, in macro and micro contexts infer data to more or less dynamic economies and their respective complexity; **Territory** – using spatial analysis of archaeological sites and geomorphologic contexts, added to morfotipologic studies of the vessels or their fragments it is possible to discuss about areas of territorial domination, circulation networks, preferred domination spaces, regional hierarchies.

In this logic we consider appropriate to conclude with a quote from Fernando La Salvia and José Proença Brochado:

"Being the ceramic a determinant technologic element of a behavior, our preposition is to see the man who developed a technology as a satisfaction of his needs and lives inside an ecologic context, where niches occur with different geologic, pedology and vegetable characteristics, determining distinct behaviors inside the same cultural tradition". (La Salvia, Brochado, 2ª ed. 1989: 8).

This work was financed by the Portuguese Government FCT – Foundation for Science and Technology under the project SFRH/BD/74394/2010.

References

BROCHADO, J.P. (1973) – Migraciones que difundierón la tradición alfarera tupiguarani. Relaciones. Buenos Aires. N. S., VII, p. 7-39.

BROCHADO, J.P. (1989) – A expansão dos Tupi e da cerâmica da tradição policrômica amazônica. Dédalo: revista do Museu de Arqueologia e Etnologia. São Paulo. 27, p. 65-82.

BROCHADO, J.P.; MONTICELLI, G. (1994) – Regras práticas na reconstrução gráfica das vasilhas de cerâmica guarani a partir dos fragmentos. Estudos Ibero-Americanos. Porto Alegre. 20:2, p. 107-118.

BROCHADO, J.P.; MONTICELLI, G.; NEUMANN, E.S. (1990) – Analogia etnográfica na reconstrução gráfica das vasilhas guarani arqueológicas. Veritas. Porto Alegre. 35:140, p. 727-743.

BONA, I.A.T. (2006) – Estudo de assinaturas químicas em cerâmica da tradição tupiguarani na região centra do estado do Rio Grande do Sul. [Tese de doutoramento em Ciências na área de Tecnologia Nuclear, apresentada ao Instituto de Pesquisas Energéticas Nucleares].

CEREZER, J.F. (2005) – A cultura Depositada em Acervo, Proposta de Catálogo para o Acervo Arqueológico do Museu Comunitário de Itapiranga. [Dissertação de Pós Graduação apresentada para o programa de Pós-Graduação Processos Interdisciplinares, URI Campus de Erechim.]

CEREZER, J.F. (2009) – Revendo problemáticas, traçando perspectivas: contributo da arqueologia experimental para a cerâmica guarani. [Tese de mestrado apresentada para o programa de mestrado em Arqueologia Pré-histórica e Arte Rupestre do IPT/UTAD].

CEREZER, J.F. (2011) – Cerâmica Guarani: Manual de experimentação arqueológica. Herechim: Habilis.

CRUZ, A.R.; OOSTERBEEK, L. coord. (2000) – Territórios, Mobilidade e povoamento no Alto Ribatejo I – indústrias e ambientes. Série ARKEOS, 9. Centro Europeu de Investigação da Pré-História do Alto Ribatejo.

DINIZ, M. (2001) – Neolitização e Megalitismo: Arquitecturas do Tempo no Espaço. In: Gonçalves, V.S., ed. – Muitas antas, pouca gente – Actas do I Colóquio Internacional sobre Megalitismo. Lisboa. Instituto Português de Arqueologia. p. 105-116.

GUILAINE, J. (2000/2001) – La Difúsion de la Agricultura en Europa: una difúsion aritmética. In: ZEPHYRUS, Revista de Prehistoria y Arqueología. Ediciones Universidad de Salamanca. 53-54, p. 267-272.

FORD, J. (1962) – Método cuantitativo para estabelecer cronologías culturales. Washington: Union Panamericana (Manuales Técnicos; 3).

JÁCOME, C.P. (2006) – Ayquatiá da Yapepó: Estudos dos materiais utilizados na cerâmica pintada Tupiguarani de Minas Gerais. [Dissertação apresentada ao Curso de Mestrado em Artes Visuais da Escola de Belas Artes da Universidade Federal de Minas Gerais].

LA SALVIA, F.; BROCHADO, J.P. (1989^2) – Cerâmica guarani. Porto Alegre: Posenato Arte e Cultura.

MEGGERS, B.J.; EVANS, C. (1970) – Como interpretar a linguagem da cerâmica – manual para arqueólogos. Washington: Smithsonian Institution.

MEGGERS, B.J.; EVANS, C. (1985) – A utilização de seqüências cerâmicas seriadas para inferir comportamento social. Boletim. do Instituto de Arqueologia Brasileira. Série Ensaios. Rio de Janeiro. 3, p. 38-48.

NOELLI, F.S. (1993) – Sem tekohá não há tekó: em busca de um modelo etnoarqueológico da aldeia e da subsistência Guarani e sua aplicação a uma área de domínio no delta do Jacuí, Rio Grande do Sul. Porto Alegre: PUCRS. [Origalmente apresentada como tese de mestrado).

NOELLI, F.S. (1996) – As hipóteses sobre o centro de origem e rotas de expansão dos Tupi. Revista de Antropologia. São Paulo. 39:2, p. 7-53.

NOELLI, F.S. (2000) – A ocupação humana na região sul do Brasil: arqueologia, debates e perspectivas: 1872-2000. Revista USP, São Paulo. 44:2, p. 218-269.

NOELLI, F.S. (2004) – La distribución geográfica de las evidencias arqueológicas guarani. Revista de Indias. Madrid. 64:230, p. 17-34.

NOELLI, F.S. (2008) – José Proenza Brochado: vida acadêmica e arqueologia tupi. In Prous, A.; Lima, T.A., orgs. – Os ceramistas tupiguarani. Sínteses regionais. Belo Horizonte: Sigma-Sociedade de Arqueologia Brasileira; IPHAN, p. 17-47.

NOELLI, F.S.; BROCHADO, J.P. (1998) – O cauim e as beberagens dos Guarani e Tupinambá: equipamentos, técnicas de preparação e consumo. Revista do Museu de Arqueologia e Etnologia: São Paulo. 8, p. 117-128.

NOELLI, F.S.; SOARES, A.L.R. (1994) – Epidemias e o etnocídio dos Guarani causados pela presença européia na bacia Platina. In Resumos dos Trabalhos Apresentados no Encontro de História e Geografia do Prata. Porto Alegre: Instituto Histórico e Geográfico do Rio Grande do Sul, p. 11.

NOELLI, F.S.; SOARES, A.L.R. (1996) – Tentando pensar modelos sociais na arqueologia guarani. Porto Alegre. [Trabalho realizado para apresentação no 3° Encontro Estadual de História, realizado em 1996].

ORTON, C.; TYERS, P.; VINCE, A. (1993) – Pottery in archaeology. Cambridge. Cambridge University Press (Manuals in Archaeology).

OOSTERBEEK, L. (1994) – O Alto Ribatejo e o Mediterrâneo. Espaço Contínuo ou Hierarquizado? In: Actas do 1° Congresso de Arqueologia Peninsular. Porto: Sociedade Portuguesa de Antropologia e Etnologia. III: 119-132.

OOSTERBEEK, L. (2004) – Archaeographic and Conceptual Advances in Interpreting Iberian Neolithisation. In: Documenta Praehistorica, (Porocilo o raziskovanju paleolitika, neolitika in eneolitika v Sloveniji). 34, p. 83-87.

SCATAMACHIA, M.C.M. (2004) – Proposta de terminologia para a descrição e classificação da cerâmica arqueológica dos grupos pertencentes à família lingüística tupi-guarani. Revista do Museu de Arqueologia e Etnologia. São Paulo. 14, p. 291-307.

SCHMITS, P.I. (1991) – Pré-História do Rio Grande do Sul. São Leopoldo. Unisinos.

SOARES, A.L.R. (1997) – Guarani: organização social e arqueologia. Porto Alegre. PUCRS.

SOARES, A.L.R. (1998) – Revisitando a organização socio-política guarani: pode-se fazer Etnohistória e Arqueologia? In Anais das VII Jornadas Internacionais sobre as Missões Jesuíticas. Chaco: Instituto de Investigaciones Geohistóricas, p. 569-582.

SOARES, A.L.R. (1999) – Os horticultores guaranis: problemáticas, perspectivas e modelos. In Quevedo, J., org. – Rio Grande do Sul: quatro séculos de História. Porto Alegre: Martins Livreiro, p. 61-101.

SOARES, A.L.R. (2002) – Arqueologia, História e Etnografia: o denominador guarani. Revista de Arqueologia Sociedade de Arqueologia Brasileira. São Paulo. 14-15, p. 97-114.

SOARES, A.L.R. (2005) – Contribuição à arqueologia guarani: estudo do sítio Röpke. Santa Cruz do Sul: EDUNISC (Teses e dissertações. Série Conhecimento; 30).

SOARES, A.L.R.; NOELLI, F.S. (1996) – Tentando pensar modelos sociais na arqueologia guarani. Porto Alegre. [Trabalho realizado para apresentação no 3° Encontro Estadual de História, realizado em 1996].

SHEPARD, A.O. (1956) – Ceramics for the Archaeologist. Washington: Carnegie Institution of Washington.

A SCULPTURE AS AN INTERFACE FOR AN ARCHAEOLOGICAL SPACE

Rosana Tagliari BORTOLIN
DAV CEART UDESC (Brazil)

Virgínia FRÓIS
CIEBA FBA UL (Portugal)

Abstract: *The communication concerns the interface between contemporary art and archaeology through the reading of the sculpture O Ninho de João do Barro (João do Barro's Nest) by Rosana Tagliari Bortolin, built in the ruins of the castle of Montemor-o-Novo, in Portugal, during the III Simpósio Internacional de Escultura em Terra Cota – Habitar 2001 (3rd International Symposium of Terracotta Sculpture – Habitar 2001), directed by Virgínia Fróis.*

We will start from a dialog with the archaeological traces of the surrounding environment: the museological place, as an historical, artistic and cultural heritage, and as a creative possibility in the field of sculpture. Its vandalization and erosion have reduced it to a state of ruin banishing it to the initial "anthropological place". As a way to integrate and reference the existing construction, we propose a revitalization of the sculpture, using similar bricks to the ones found in the pavements of the dwellings raised during excavations.

Keywords: *Sculpture, archaeology, ceramics, ludus*

The 3° Simpósio de escultura em terra(cota) *was a reflection about the place; the man-made dwellings and the regathering of the relation of belonging to that place; man as modeller of its space; sculpture inhabited by ideas; dwelling and living of that idea.*

In the game of hide and seek we learn to be near and far of the "coitus". The body exercises the ability to resist without shelter, without, however, ceasing to look for it.

We live the time of the possibility to go to all places. We still feed the desire of paradise. Virtually and physically, we have all places at our reach and a single body. (Fróis, Habitar, 2001)

DWELLING IS QUESTIONING, CREATING A PLACE

We begin by quoting the introduction text of the contest for ideas of the *3° Simpósio Habitar 2001*. This text was accompanied by the photograph of a swallow's nest built under the *Anta Grande da Comenda* in Montemor-o-Novo.

Back then, we talked about connecting, about time, we proposed the articulation of the senses to find new ideas. We asked for sculptures to be used, inhabited.

The Brazilian sculptor Rosana Bortolin sent a model of an earth nest to this contest, made by the bird João do Barro, which stood idle in her backyard. Her proposal was to enlarge it, inhabit it and build it with her body, copying the gestures of the building birds. After it was concluded in the castle, this *house sculpture* became a place of fun for children and adults that tried its inside squatting over the bench rocks with which its interior was decorated. At the best, three children could fit inside this small house where the only thing one could only see was the sky and through where the zenith light would come in enlightening their faces. The experiencing of the

piece was simultaneously outside the *world* and inside *oneself*.

In 2009, at new year's eve, a group of young people vandalized the piece leaving it in ruins.

It's now important to clarify some of the principles that presided the symposium: a) sensitize the community towards the construction heritage and to the return to traditional techniques; b) contemporary art as mediation and participation; c) the exchange of experiences with mason bricklayers and with masters who make mud-wall and the experimentation of ancient technologies; d) the reflection about the subject "Dwelling", proposed by the artists during the constructive process of the 6 pieces made out of raw and cooked earth; e) the interaction with the population during and after the construction; f) the highlight of several points in the city.

The castle area was one of the spaces chosen to embrace a sculpture. It was an historical place, where the excavations of the old town had begun, as well as place of attraction for visitors. The most adequate piece for this space was *Ninho de João do Barro* because of the

Figures 1 and 2. Archaeological structures

conceptual and formal relations, questioning and potentiating what already existed in the place.

HISTORICAL AND ARCHAEOLOGICAL CONTEXT

Memories and speculations

It is believed that the castle of Montemor-o-Novo has a quite old foundation, in spite of the fact that the first written document referring to it is dated from 1181, in the reign of King D. Sancho I. It was this king that gave this town its first register dated from 1203 (Pereira, 2004). Also mentioned are several regal residences and the realization of courts, where the Vasco da Gama's trip is said to have been decided, in the place called Paço dos Alcaides. In this area is the church of S. João Baptista, already quoted in a document from 1303, and one of the town's urban parishes town until the end of the 18th century (Lopes, 2007).

The excavations occurred in several phases: the first one occurred between 1983 and 1987, during which period several probings were conducted in different points of the castle under the direction of the archaeologist Tatiana Resende (Almansor nr. 3). In a second phase, between 1991 and 1993, archaeologist Ana Gonçalves has coordinated the study inside the church of S. Tiago and on the grounds of the Convento de Nª Sª da Saudação (Almansor nº 11), but it was only in 1997 that the Recovery and Revitalization Program of the Castle has allowed a regular activity from which resulted the recovery of the church of S. Tiago as an Interpretative Centre of the Castle. Since 2002, regular excavations occur coordinated by the archaeologist Manuela Pereira. These works conducted by a permanent team have allowed the support to investigators and the publication of several studies related to the analysis of the pieces collected in the old town.

It is in this context/path, where a significant area of the urban structures, streets and buildings is visible (Figs. 1

and 2), that the sculpture *Ninho* is situated, and where we can constantly discover new relations, whether because of the ceramic materials of the pavements or because of the silos/tanks or because of the common pottery, that can be timely connected, freeing the space and making it a place to be used, recovering and building the memory and the culture and potentiating the present (Barrento, 2007). We also find the reason for the rehabilitation of the ancient technologies, like the value of life.

Rehabilitate to give back recreating

The use of earth to build dwellings and the discovery of ceramic accompany the entire human history and the fabrication of adobes and bricks represents a huge step forward, always renewed because one can use all the innovations provided by technology (Campbell, 2005).

The use of ceramic materials, complementary to the constructive techniques using earth, has been generalizing in the civil and popular architecture because it is based on low cost construction materials of easy access, being the historical centre of Montemor-o-novo a good example of that. The rehabilitation of the old buildings and the valorisation of the environmental qualities of earth architecture have justified the recovery of the activity of the *Telheiro da Encosta do Castelo* (Castle's Slope Tiler), one of the manufactures whose activity ceased around 1960.

Following a survey about the region's tilers and its traditional production, a proposal was made to the municipality of Montemor-o-Novo for the buy-in of the *Telheiro da Encosta do Castelo* in order to recover it, because at the time it was an old and degraded structure.

The *Telheiro* restarts its activity in 1997, as a project of local valorisation, economical development and maintenance of traditional techniques, as well as being a sort of museum for the activity. The project intents to be self-sustaining, in a market more an more sensitive to the usage of artisanal materials for the recovery and rehabilitation of constructed heritage.

Figures 3, 4, 5 and 6. Building and locations of the sculpture nest

Thus, the *Telheiro* has available in its structure resources and equipments for the realization of actions in the fields of Sculpture, Ceramics, Design, Architecture and Archaeology through which it is intended that the techniques and the materials of artisanal construction, regarding the places, are used as a base for the development of innovating artistic projects. As an example, we highlight the three *Simpósios Internacionais de Escultura em Terracota* (1996, 1998 and 2001) (9), organized by the *Associação Cultural Oficinas do Convento* (created in 1996, www.oficinasdoconvento.com), that have allowed to move towards the making of big ceramic pieces. Currently, we foresee the development of the production of copies of utilitarian objects based on the archaeological remains, as well as the creation of new pieces, which allows widening the existing potentialities.

SCULPTURE NEST

Beyond history, life

The work was conceived based on thoughts about the questions of the post-modern man, in what displacement is referred. Removed from one place and reproduced in another, the nest has become a differential in the implanted place (Figs. 3, 4, 5 and 6). It was built at the scale of a house, *in situ*, causing a change on the visual routine of the castle's ruins. The intervention has caused a discontinuity, a discomfort in the visuality of the place. The nest has showed another side, another possibility for the occupation of the place. We think that the intervention wouldn't have had the same impact in Brazil as it did in Portugal, given that this bird is a typically Brazilian bird and its nest is common. In our perspective, this work questions, causes in the viewer a questioning look, because it is a strange element to the space taken by it, as it occurs with the archaeological excavations inside modern cities. Strange elements to the present context come forth as impotent, having an historical charge of displacement of the past, causing a strangeness in the context of the surroundings.

Because of its matter, terracotta, and because of its form, a bird's nest at a human scale, this sculpture has caused questionings about its time and its relation to the body.

The artist's poetics happens through the way she communicates with the world, through that what her life has of articulation, by the way in which her current body understands and feels, connects with things and with nature. That is the conscious body that Merleau-Ponty (1989) speaks about and it is that way that her conscious body, in contact with nature, has created the work *O Ninho de João do Barro* that was based on the observation of the construction of a nest, made by a couple of birds. Her aesthetical experience made her admire the purity of the lines, the quality present in the creation of the textures, in the employment of the materials and in the different tones of the used clays. This fact relates her to a ceramist modelling a piece with detailed technique and formal domain.

In contact with the original nest, she touched it and watched its constructive details carefully. Her conscious body understood that the shape was self-structuring and that the walls that sustained the dome grew from inside a spiral that was born at the base of the nest. A spiral line grew from the centre of the nest, passed the door sideways and ended on the other side of the span. The artist enjoyed the visual and tactile qualities present in the shape, with her hand, exploited the inside, finding a rounded chamber, wide and cosy, sharpening her wish to penetrate it and inhabit it. She realized that the organicity of the lines – rounded and spiralled – pleased her and interested her deeply. This experience that her current body had through her feeling eyes was crucial for the choice of the sculptoric shape that resulted in the intervention of the Complex of the Castle's Ruins. We believe that the archaeologist understands old ceramic fragments the same way that then allows him to unite and rebuild them so that they can be recognized later on.

On the horizon of all of these visions is the world itself that inhabits, the natural world and the historical world, with all the human traces of which it is made of, and it is with this vision, the vision of Merleau-Ponty (1989), that the artist relates the nests and cocoons with her body and with architecture. The proposal of the construction of the nest at a human scale led to the idea of a house, the desire to penetrate a place and to metaphorically elect it as a place of protection. A place like home as a poetic space, that Bachelard (1998) talks about, the nest house that is never new, that naturally is the place that has the function of being inhabited, the place to which we return, to which we dream to return like the bird that returns to the nest. The place to which we return so that all of our needs are satisfied, because, according to the philosopher Gastón Bachelard (1998), the human returns occur according to the rhythm of human life that crosses the years and fights for the dream against absences and the image that refers to the house and the nest reflects an intimate component of fidelity.

The sculpture, however, operates with a double sense, with opposing narrative relations: the relation nest-intimacy and the relation nest-public space. Thus, the works reflects the questions of the post-modern, since the house-nest isn't untouchable, it is a monument and there is a displacement of this private-untouchable place to the public space that is accessible to all. The private space turns public and vice-versa, given that the post-modern

man became a kind of urban nomad, where any place that he elects may become "home" (we talk about home as the place where we allow more intimate questions to occur and that we elect as a private place of protection, either a hotel room, a car, an office, an atelier or an archaeological place to be researched. The investigator, with his operating and conscious body, the body that Merleau-Ponty (2000) talks about, may understand the environment of the past and rebuild it in its imaginary, because, according to the philosopher, we are made of the same stuff as the stuff of the world.

Thus, the recognition done at the place before the execution of the work has led the artist to understand the displacement with which the sculpture of the nest operates. Its construction inside a medieval castle led her to reflect about the questions of the art that, since the 1960's, also suffers this characteristic displacement of the post modern. Artists leave the confinement of their studios searching for nature to work *in situ* with the elements that they have available there.

The operating body of the artist makes her see, feel, touch, measure the time of the path between constructions, walk away, walk between the ruins and measure its distances. It makes her realize that the ruptures and discontinuities in the space are the ones that represent the continuity of time. The sculpture in the form of a nest is built at human scale where it can be penetrated or inhabited – like the house. The sculpture breaks the continuity of the space of the ruins, because it was built in its interior, near a small chapel that had been partly restored and near Paço dos Alcaides. The round dome of the church of S. João Baptista and the piece established a group of rounded shapes.

The intervention of the nest turns into a small monument that interferes with the routine of the big monument that are the ruins that refer to the past while the *Ninho*, in its displacement, becomes the present or a nearer future. In a first moment, the displacement present in the sculpture changes time continuity. A strangeness is created in the sense that it disorganizes the usual reading that one has of the local landscape. In a second moment, we realize that the intervention on the local landscape creates a new poetic image for the space where it is inserted and the environment is now a part of the work. Thus, we also understand the archaeological excavations that are held at that place today.

Shape up with the matter of the place

Like in archaeology, during the rebuilding of architectonical complexes or object restorations, the preparations that occur for the construction of the sculpture cause gradative changes in space and landscape, starting with the cleaning of the place, with the cut of the vegetation and with the levelling of the ground. In the case of the sculpture, the gestures used for this process modelled, in a way, the surface of the ground and made possible a special experience of the place. The cleaning of the surroundings was made for safety reasons, given that the burning of the sculpture was done during the dry season and any sparkle could cause a fire. The remaining of the grass was piled up in a big pile that was used for the sculpture's dome during the construction and for fuel for its burning. After the cleaning of the land, the ground was levelled by hand by a cut of approx. 5 cm on the highest part of the slope. This was a thorough and delicate work because it was an archeologically place where at any depth traces of other buildings could appear.

Once the ground was levelled, a layer of stone and one of sand was added, a procedure that eased the draining and the placement of refractory bricks to make the oven grid. The space of *Paço dos Alcaides* was slowly being appropriated and a sort of camp appeared. Under the few trees lined up on the side of the road that led to the castle's tower tables were improvised that were used to knead the clay as well as a small plastic tent that was used to store the clay prepared at the old *Telheiro da Encosta do Castelo*, as well as to protect it from the sun.

The materials used in the composition of its paste were plastic clay, feldspathic rock gravel (regional materials), industrial talc and grog. This paste included flammable materials to ease the burning like sawing and local fennel straw.

The walls were built using big roles of overlapped and flattened paste, forming a wall with approx. 20 cm of base that got thinner as it reached the upper part.

After drying, the sculpture was burned using the paper oven method: an oven that self consumes built around the shape. A metallic structure with approx. 80 cm of distance of the piece was created and over this structure were assembled a canvas wall and a chimney. Inside the piece and in the span between the piece and the canvas was placed coal, sawing and wood. Over the canvas were overlaid successive layers of paper dipped in slurry (almost liquid clay). Four feeders were made for the fire that burnt during approx. 2 and a half hours consuming all the material inside, which resulted in a big fire.

REMEMBERING WITHOUT CONCLUDING

The space altered by the construction of the sculpture was socially experienced in a very intense way, by all people present. The same way that it occurs in archaeological places located in dry places, the participants in the constructive process suffered from the exposure to solar beams that easily left everyone exhausted. The heat and the wind dried not only people's skins but also the clay that was being processed. The walls of the nest sculpture were covered with plastic canvas in an attempt to keep the humidity of the clay and ease the corrections that would fixate the next layers. The experienced process was a learning process, of exchange with the social and with the collective and we think that the audience became a co-author of the work since the moment of the ceramic making. We believe that there

was an inter-relation between the public space, the viewers/collaborators of the building act and the artist herself in the condition of participating sculptor of the event. Many times, the work was gradually modified without losing its conscious initial conception, like an improvisation in a theatrical scene. These modifications were based on discussions and questionings that arose during the social togetherness with the collaborative audience that participated in the game of the making, interacting during the process. We believe that these exchanges of opinions and suggestions also occur in the archaeological discoveries altering the courses of the investigations, contributions that many times are a result from the intuitions or experiences of the individual.

The social existence is, before all, theatrical and, according to Maffesoli (1982, p. 19) in his book *The shadow of Dionysus*, places are defined as a role and not as a function, being each scene particularly important. The feeling of participating, voluntary or involuntarily, is what commands the scene, capturing its totality. In this sense, we feel that the executed work, in spite of its intimate character due to its symbolic questions – related to the archetype of the nest – also moves forward towards the universe of the collective that, in our understanding, can refer to the subjects related to dwelling and to the common togetherness, besides the effective presence of the collective during the ritual of building and burning. We believe that the feeling of exchange was present in the thoughts of the participants in the symposium and the need of solidarity spread to the group as a whole, combining the individual with the collective.

The artist, with her conscious body, understood the dimension, the appearance and the feeling of being inside the sculpture as if she was inside a small house. Her feeling eyes understood that the game of lights and shadows that penetrated inside through the holes that cross its walls and through the soft cut in its dome allowing the zenith light to enter. Right there we understand that the house is the shelter of the body and that, according to Valery (apud Romeiro, Renata, 2003, in Bortolin, Rosana, 2006), it is in the house that blossoms what is in consonance with the physical body like feelings, actions and desires. In the house, the body can rest, feed and be comfortable with its own nudity and physiological needs and it is in the house that it can recompose from the actions lived in the world. In such a situation of intimacy with oneself, it becomes possible to structure ones subjectivity in order to exchange experiences with other bodies, in the streets and in other collective situations. The actions and sensations experienced by the body inside its shelter have a reflection in the perception of the surrounding world. Thus, the experienced space of the sculpture of the nest is analogous to the house where the participants of the constructive process had the possibility to share their angst, their unsettlements and other problems related to being together that occur in the intimacy of a limited space in the presence of a collective body. We also believe that archaeologists imagine and prove the way of life of the people that lived in the town and in the houses that are being revealed in the castle's complex with their researches and hypotheses.

A decay after its construction and after it has been vandalized, the sculpture currently looks like the ruins around it. It is integrated in the environment, a small ruin inside a bigger ruin. The museological complex of the castle's ruins is a regional touristic point and the number of people that walk through its spaces is big. A certain time, visitors that didn't know the history of the sculpture and saw its ruins claimed that those were the remains of an old ceramic oven.

Reformulate to connect

We propose to make a revitalization of the sculpture, almost in the same way as its initial construction process. We will start by cleaning its surroundings, we will remove the vegetation over its remains, the earth layers and the filling inside. We imagine and project to preserve what remained intact over the years, the central part shaped as a spiral. We will leave a circulation space that will also be used to access the traces of the initial sculpture. Around it we will form a circle with empty walls, which we will build from the intercalated piling of bricks, handmade in the *Telheiro da Encosta do Castelo*.

We are considering the possibility of contextualizing the bricks made in the traditional space that is the *Telheiro* and create a metalanguage through the engraving of words in some of the surfaces that will be exposed on the walls that will be built around the traces of the sculpture. We intend to make the artisanal and traditional production of the *Telheiro* contemporary by introducing words that refer to the sculpture regarding its conception, its relation with the surroundings, the feelings experienced by the artist and by the participants in the building process, the feelings and aesthetical experiences when meeting with the sculpture again. Words about the modified space, about the findings in the ruins of the old town, scenes that weren't there previously because they were covered in earth. Descriptions and drawings of the ceramic pieces rescued during the excavations and that today are stored in Museu de Arqueologia.

We conclude that the execution of our ideas, with which we mean the action of revitalizing the sculpture *O Ninho de João do Barro*, will work like an interface, a meeting possibility between contemporary art and archaeology. During this process, the attempt is to understand, with the conscious and operating body, the body that the philosopher Maurice Merleau-Ponty (2000) talks about, the possibilities of aesthetical experiences that will come during the rescue of the artistic field – experiencing the ruins of the sculpture itself will be like the phoenix that arises from its own ashes. Just like the action of the archaeologist that makes us remember a time that we didn't consciously experience.

References

AUGÉ, Marc (2003) – *Não-Lugares Introdução a uma antropologia da supermodernidade* [Non-Places: Introduction to an Anthropology of Supermodernity]. 3rd ed, Campinas: Papirus.

BARRENTO, João (2007) – "O Jardim Devastado e o Perfil da Esperança" [The devastated garden and the profile of hope] in *O estado do mundo* [The state of the world] *2nd edition*, FCG, Ed Tinta da china, Lisboa.

BACHELARD, Gaston (1998) – *A Poética do Espaço* [The Poetics of Space]. *3rd ed,* São Paulo: Martins Fontes.

BACHELARD, Gaston (1991) – *A Terra e os Devaneios da Vontade* [The Land and the Musing of the Will]. 1ª ed, São Paulo: Martins Fontes.

BACHELARD, Gaston (1994) – *A Psicanálise do Fogo* [The Psychoanalysis of Fire]. 1st ed, São Paulo: Martins Fontes.

BORTOLIN, Rosana Tagliari (2006) – *Ninho, Casa e Corpo* [Nest, House and Body]. Masters Dissertation Defended at the Escola de Comunicação e Artes – ECA da Universidade de São Paulo – USP.

LOPES, Gonçalo (2007) – *A igreja de S. João Baptista de Montemor-o-Novo: uma arqueologia do monumento* [The church of S. João Baptista of Montemor-o-Novo: an archaeology of the monument], *Almansor,* Culture Journal nr. 6 CMMM, Montemor-o-Novo.

MAFFESOLI, Michel (1985) – *A Sombra de Dionísio contribuição a uma sociologia da orgia* [The Shadow of Dionysus: A Contribution to the Sociology of the Orgy]. 1st ed, Rio de Janeiro: Graal.

MERLEAU-PONTY, Maurice (2000) – *O Visível e o Invisível* [The Visible and the Invisible]. São Paulo: Perspectiva.

MERLEAU-PONTY, Maurice (1996) – *Fenomenologia da Percepção* [Phenomenology of Perception]. São Paulo: Martins Fontes.

MERLEAU-PONTY, Maurice (1989) – *Textos Escolhidos* [Chosen Texts]. Florianópolis: Victor Civita.

PEREIRA, Manuela (2004) – *Intervenção arqueológica no castelo de Montemor-o-Novo, Almansor* [Archaeological Intervention in Montemor-o-Novo's Castle], Culture Journal nr. 3 ed CMMM, Montemor-o-Novo.

FRÓIS, Virgínia, *Habitar 2001* [Inhabitate 2011] – Montemor -o-Novo, 2001, RB / VF – August-2011.

THE USE OF EXPERIMENTAL ARCHAEOLOGY IN THE HYPOTHESIS TESTING. THE CASE OF THE BONE TECHNOLOGY OF TULAN-54 (NORTHERN CHILE)

Boris SANTANDER

Instituto Terra e Memoria, Mação, Grupo "Quaternário e Pré-História" do Centro de Geociências,
uID73 – FCT, Portugal
boris.santander@gmail.com

Abstract: *For a long time the study of bone artifacts recovered from archaeological sites has been relegated to an overview primarily based on artifacts morphology. While technologies such as lithics and ceramics have been lavish in establishing the criteria to define the functionality of the artifacts, the impulse seems to decay at the time of analyze bone tools.*

This communication focuses on the analysis of bone artifacts from the site early formative Tu-54 in northern Chile, where, from use-wear analysis of a particular artifact morphology and the use of experimental strategies for analyzing their characteristics, it was possible to test hypotheses about the possible role that these tools played in the production of textiles within the archaeological site.

Keyword: *Bone Technology, Use-Wear Analysis, Experimental Archaeology*

Résumé: *Pendant longtemps, l'étude des artefacts osseux récupérés des sites archéologiques a été relégué à une vue d'ensemble fondés principalement sur leur morphologie. Tant que les technologies comme la lithique et la céramique ont été prodigue en établissant les critères pour définir la fonctionnalité des objets, l'impulsion/l'élan semble s'afflaiblir au moment de l'analyse des outils en os.*

Cette communication se centre sur l'analyse des artefacts osseux à partir du site formative Tu-54 au nord du Chili, où, de l'analyse tracéologique d'une morphologie particulière et l'utilisation de stratégies expérimentales pour l'analyse de leurs caractéristiques, il est possible de tester les hypothèses sur le rôle éventuel que ces outils ont joué dans la production de textiles à l'intérieur du site archéologique.

Mots clés: *Industrie osseuse, Tracéologie, Archéologie expérimentale*

INTRODUCTION

Since 2006, and due the recovery of several bone tools within the archaeofaunal remains of Tulan-54, it was decided to initiate a work program in order to understand the characteristics of bone technology and their functionality within the social dynamics of the systemic context that originated the site. Thus, after a detailed morphological analysis of the remains, an use-wear analysis of artifacts was projected, including experimental studies that allow to define the production conditions of the use-wear on bone micro-topography. To allow the rising of hypothesis, was necessary to define the range of raw materials worked and use characteristics in which bone artifacts were involved. From the archaeological record, we delimited three kinds of materials which likely involve bone technology, as lithic artifacts (through edge retouching), basketry, and soft raw materials of animal origin as skin and wool. In this paper we present the results associated with work specifically on wool.

THE ARCHAEOLOGICAL SITE, TULAN-54

Located at 2.950 MASL, on the southern sector of the Tulan creek in the southeastern corner of the Atacama's Salt Lake. (Fig. 1) The site corresponds to an Early Formative occupation dated through C14 between 3080 ± 70 and 2380 ± 70 BP (Núñez, Cartajena, Carrasco, De Souza, & Grosjean, 2006). The architecture is characterized by different sectors that demonstrate a complex spatial arrangement with a central temple composed of several sub-circular structures surrounded by a perimeter wall, presenting 24 newborn human inhumations, buried with offerings at the base of the occupation. Tulan-54 constitutes a milestone in the research of the process of social complexification in this area of the Andean region, characterized by the intensification and consolidation of productive practices mainly related with the management of camelid herds (*Lama glama*) and the surplus production of beads, the emphasys in certain ritual expressions, and the use of ceramics (Núñez, Cartajena, Carrasco, & De Souza, 2006; Núñez, Mcrostie, & Cartajena, 2009; Núñez & Santoro, 2011; Núñez, 1999).

Considering the abundant presence of wool threads, fleeces of camelid fibers and abundant loop fabrics, along with the presence of artifacts morphologically similar to those defined by Benavente (1981) as part of the instrumental dedicated to textile production, was decided to formulate hypotheses related with this kind of ativities. In that sense, our working hypothesis is defined as "The Tulan-54 site presents evidence of loom textile

Figure 1. Site location.
(Modified from Cartajena 2011:271)

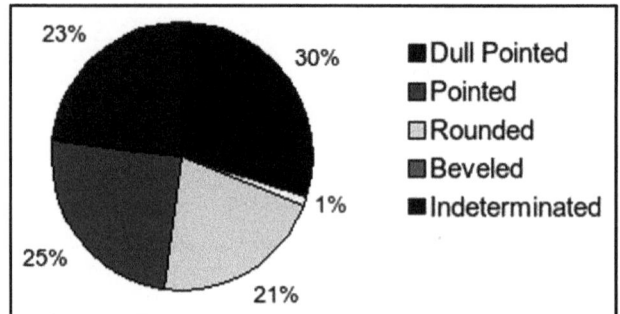

Figure 2. Morphological requences of Tu-54 Bone Tools

observed at different magnifications between 10 and 500 magnifications, (preferably between 40x and 150x), using an 20x Eschenbach® loupe, an Olympus® stereomicroscope at 60x, to subsequently being analyzed in a metallographic microscope Olympus®, with a special mount to support a camera 5.4 megapixel digital, and video output to a dedicated monitor of 17". These observations were performed at the Department of Geology, University of Chile.

In relation with the striations, the collected data includes those concerning length, depth and width of the polishing on edge and top; as also striae bottom characteristics (smooth / rough). Their location and intrinsic and extrinsic disposition (relative to the axis of the workpiece) was also detailed. In addition, the presence or absence of polishes and rounded edges was included in the database. All data was registered in a Calc database (version 2.0 for Linux), and statistically processed in order to stablish use-wear patterns.

production, which can be identified through the analysis of use-wear in the recovered bone tools".

BONE TECHNOLOGY IN TULAN-54

During successive fieldwork seasons, 97 archaeological bone tools were recovered from Tulan-54. These artifacts were cleaned and analyzed under strictly morphological criteria, based on the active portion and the cross-section morphology. Acording to Scheinsohn (1997:122), the artifacts were classified under three main categories (with exception of one single beveled artifact): **A) Pointed**, in which "the convergence of the borders of the tool at one end, configurating an active tip", **B) Dull Pointed,** where the tip has been blunted, reducing its potentiality as awl or drill; and **C) Rounded**, tools with an extreme completely blunted, with a curvature close to the circumference (Fig. 2).

Once anatomic and taxonomical analyses were performed, the artifacts were separated, measured, weighed and registered in a special database. As part of two previous works developed by the author, the artifacts were analyzed in order to establish sequential production models (Santander, 2009), and use-wear characteristics as an exploratory research (Santander, 2011).

In the framework of the use-wear analysis, the pieces were cleaned mechanically with a soft brush, and

THE EXPERIMENTAL MODELING IN ARCHAEOLOGY

Several authors observe how experimentation in archeology acquires multiple connotations (Baena, 1997; Griffitts, 1993, 2006; Vergès, 2002). This views, results on a wide range of possibilities about what is considered "experimental archaeology", which tends to make hard the delimitation and strictly definition of what corresponds to a "trully" archaeological experimentation.

We can distinguish also several kinds of experimental programs, from those interested in the replica of artifacts or processes of work (Griffitts, 2006; Osborne, 1965) to those long-term projects, such as the classic work of Keeley (Keeley, 1980) about lithic raw materials.

Griffitts (2006), details three kinds of experimental programs, primarily based on their proposed objectives. The first type is conformed by those works that seek to control as many variables involved in a particular activity, in order to better understand the dependent and independent variables involved in the formation of traces.

A second group of experimentation model, are those related to the use wear replication through the replication of supposed activities. Such studies are the most common in order to make comparisons between the experimental artifacts and the archaeological record. However, they are less useful if the goal of the experiment is oriented to understand the process of generation and intrinsic properties of use-wear. In bone technology, studies such as those developed by Buc & Loponte (Buc & Loponte, 2007; Buc & Silvestre, 2006; Buc, 2011; Santander, 2010), are included in this category.

Finally, there is a third kind of experimental programs, primarily related to the contributions of ethnographic comparison in the experimental program design, namely, the use of this information in the development of the experiments, allowing the observation of gestures, working angles, prehension of artifacts, and raw materials used. However, this kind of work can only grow up in dependence of the existence of an ethnographic context at least similar to that supposed to create the archaeological record. The Griffith's research (2006), even when it combines different strategies to approach the experimental work, is largely integrated into these programs.

In any case, experimental archeology, obey to a double epistemological process, combining both empirical and logical process, providing data to build interpretative criteria for the archaeological record, and to evaluate evidence to rise further new hypotheses (Vergès, 2002), or, as noted by González Urquijo & Ibáñez Estévez (1994:16), "This establishes an inductive-deductive system with a first phase in which the keys are constructed from interpretation of observed experimental reality, and a second phase on which the recognition of the same alterations in prehistoric remains allows an equiparation of the causes through an analogy of the consequences"[1] Grimaldi (2003), by the other hand, reflects on the nature of experimental archeology, which rests on modern epistemological pillars, in which the notions of objectivity and subjectivity should be extremely considered in the inferences production. Even if experimental archeology not exactly replicates work processes, neither the intentions of the manufacturer, is no less valid as a tool for hypotheses production and verification of these. Experimental archeology must be seen then, as a tool that moves, as science itself does, between objective and subjective fields.

THE EXPERIMENTAL DESIGN FOR TULAN-54 SITE

The bones were taken from three different animals: *Ovis aries, Capra hircus* and *Cervus elaphus*. *Ovis aries* bones were stored for two months prior to its manufacture, in a cool dry area. After that period, were cleaned by removing attached periosteum portions. *Capra hircus* bones, however, were worked within the first three days after the death of the individual, following the same procedure developed with the remains of sheep. The

artifacts produced in bones of *Cervus elaphus*, on the other hand, were prepared from residues obtained in 2009, during deer butchering activities, by the team of the Catalan Institute of Human Palaeoecology and Social Evolution (IPHES) and the Universitat Rovira i Virgili (URV, Spain), and were provided in a raw state, with exception of two pieces that had been manufactured previously. These last, were reactivated by abrasion with sandstone, in order to revive the edges, obliterating potential traces left by previous activities.

After cleaning, the artifacts were manufactured combining different techniques, which included direct and indirect percussion (with and without anvil) and longitudinal marking in order to collect information about possible manufacture processes and to control their appearance in the micro wear observations. After obtaining the preforms of the tools, the final morphology was obtained through the finish by abrasion using industrial abrasive paper (wood sandpaper .220) or sandstone rocks. In some cases, and to evaluate the role of the work process itself in polishes and rounding, the artifacts were not regularized. In total, 20 artifacts were elaborated, of which 10 were prepared with pointed morphologies and 8 with blunt tapered morphologies. Finally, in two of them, the distal end was left unprepared, but with particular emphasis on the regularization of an edge, for the work on cleaning of skins, and weft tight in loom weaving. The artifacts were described in metric terms and photographed. The artefacts, task performed and motion characteristics included in the present paper are described in the Tab. 1.

After use, the pieces were cleaned in ultrasonic bath with acetone for 5 minutes, to remove fat, and other abrasive particles which may have adhered during use. Each of the manufacturing techniques used and the task performed were transferred to a database in .ods format (OpenOffice Calc 3.2, Linux version).

The analysis of experimental bone tools was developed mainly in an stereomicroscope in a range of magnifications between 18x to 110x, and registered with a dedicated Deltapix® model "InfinityX" camera connected to a computer with an image processing software. As external illumination equipment an optic fiber lamp Olympus® was used. This observations were supported by an Olympus® metalographic microscope up to 500x, and some of the artifacts were also observed in an Electronic Scanning Microscope JEOL®, model JSM-6400.

RESULTS ON EXPERIMENTAL MATERIALS

At microscopical level, the experimental artifacts that were used for textile work reveal the low invasiveness of wool working. Of the 8 tools made and used on wool, in three of them were indistinguishable, even under an electron microscope, obvious signs of striation. The low visibility of the striations, undoubtedly lies on the low abrasiveness of wool, since in different kinematic, and

---

[1] Translation is ours, original in spanish.

Table 1. Experimental artifacts. Description of morfology and activities performed

ID	Anatomical unit	Taxa	Active Point	Section	Category	Angle	Cinematics	Time of use	Strokes
Ex-6	Metatarsal	*Ovis aries*	Pointed	Ovoidal	Batten	90°	Compressing	30'	2000
Ex-8	Radius	*Capra hircus*	Pointed	Circular	Needle	90°	Needlework	12'15"	360
Ex-9	Femur	*Ovis aries*	Dull Pointed	Semicircular	Batten	90°	Sliding Compressing	25'	1000
Ex-10	Radius	*Capra hircus*	Dull Pointed	Triangular	Batten	90°	Sliding Compressing	11'20"	1000
Ex-11	Metapodial	*Cervus elaphus*	Straight (border)	Ovoidal	Batten	90°	Sliding Compressing	50'	1000
Ex-13	Metacarpal	*Cervus elaphus*	Dull Pointed	Ovoidal	Shuttle	<35°	Thread transport on loom	+24 hours	+ 2000
Ex-14	Metapodial	*Cervus elaphus*	Straight (border)	Ovoidal	Batten	90°	Sliding Compressing	+24 hours	1000
Ex-19	Tibia	*Bos taurus*	Dull Pointed	Rectangular	Batten	90°	Sliding Compressing	+24 hours	1000

different numbers of strokes, was impossible to develop more than very fine striations, usually isolated, but oriented consistently with the respective kinematic of the work. One of the pieces, however, exhibited transverse to the axis traces of the work piece, even when the direction of the motion was clearly longitudinal. Seems fairly clear that the most useful criteria for distinguishing bone artifacts involved in wool related work, is a smooth polish, extended and which tends to obliterate the traces of manufacture attacking both the bone surface as the bottom, edges and cusps of the manufacture micro-wear (Fig. 3). An interesting and unexpected observation could be made during the work with one of the artifacts, used as shuttle in a loom with wool. Even with a detailed elaboration, some small portions of the artifact were not enough polished, and the *Lama pacos* wool remained sucked in the artifact during the weaving process, making impossible the work. Then, the tool was detailed polished with fine sandpaper, removing any kind of irregularity. Once corrected the issue, the artifact became an extremely useful tool. Same situation happened with the battens used.

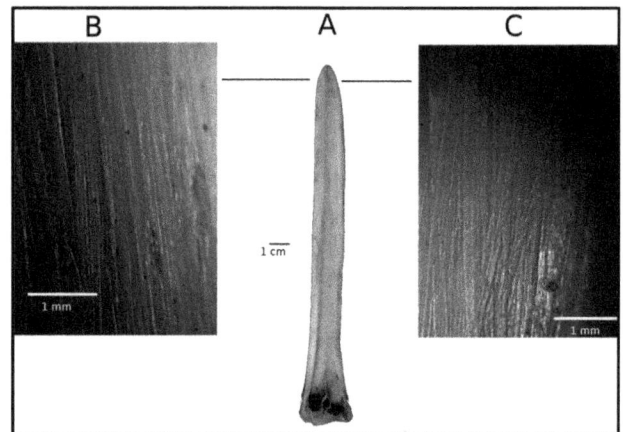

Figure 3. A) Experimental artifact N° 13, Used as Shuttle; B) surface before use, 110x; C) Surface After use (+1000 strokes), 110x. Note the intensive polish

ARCHAEOLOGICAL OBSERVATIONS

A total number of eight archaeological artifacts present micro-wear related with the results of the work on wool. Of these, five may be attributable to the technological category of "batten", known by the Andean region weavers as "Wichuña" (artifact used to tight the fibers in the loom to get a most resistant and compact woven); and other two as "shuttles", used to transport the warp in the loom.

Five archaeological artifacts (registered with codes H4-13-B, H2-40/50A, H4-13-C, E2-7 & W2-3), had very

similar use-wear patterns, with thin striations, transversely oriented to the axis of the workpiece, slightly invasive with polished cusps, cross-linked and ungrouped, covering portions of the distal and medial portions of the tool; without rounding and with scattered polishes (Figs 4, 5).

Artifacts D7-30/35 and E1-10, meanwhile, exhibit traces revealing fine and noninvasive use-wear, arranged longitudinally to the axis of the artifacts and parallel to each other, but not grouped into specific points on the bone micro-topography, but rather scattered in the distal portion. The same happens to the polished, without present rounding, similarly to the traces observed in the experimental artifact number 13, used as a shuttle for weaving in loom (Fig. 6).

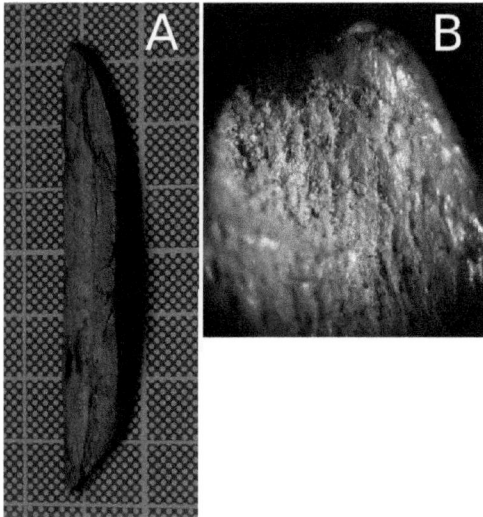

Figure 4. A) 2W-E3 archaeological tool.
B) 40x Metallographic image or distal portion

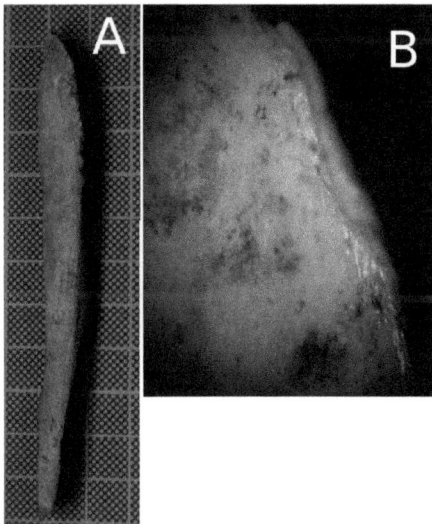

Figure 5 A) H2-40-50 archeological Tool.
B) 40x metallographic image at distal border

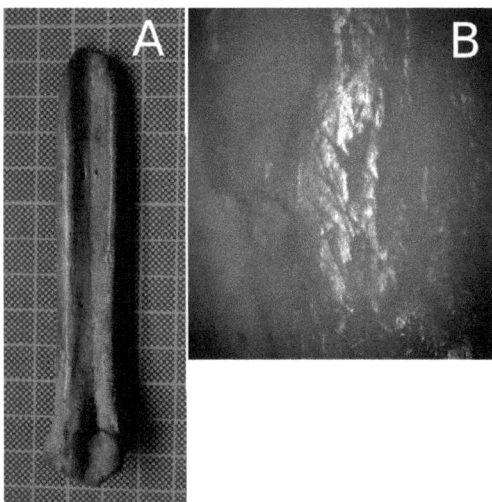

Figure 6. A) E1-N9 Archaeological Tool.
B) 40x Metallographic Image at Medial Portion

DISCUSSION

The work of weaving seems to have a discrete development in Tulan-54 site. Although evidence of working in wool are clear, the lowest number of this tools in relation to those artifacts oriented to the leather work, seem to correspond to a textile manufacturing strategy focused to the community, not to the exchange. Assuming textile work as a product for domestic consumption, fits well in a social system oriented to the maintenance of herds of *Lama glama* as draft animal, in conjunction with the hunting of wild camelids (*Lama guanicoe* and *Vicungna vicugna*) for meat (Cartajena, Núñez, & Grosjean, 2007; Núñez, Cartajena, Carrasco, De Souza, *et al.*, 2006), both animals form which the groups could obtain also raw materials like leather, fur and fibers.

Although loom textiles have almost not been recovered yet from Tulan-54, as stated by Dransart (1991); the presence of shuttles and pressers, is a clear sign of its production. At the same time, the abundance of wool and fleece, clearly suggests the interest of these communities in the camelid fibers. In relation to the previous point, the presence of artifacts with a very particular configuration, as D7-30/35, H4-14-B7, (and probably E17-D), which are interesting for their peculiarity, and had been described in a fairly lax terms as "loom battens" during the early stages of the bone tool analysis, after this study, could, with some certainty, be defined as shuttles.

CONCLUSIONS

As noted in this paper, the experimentation results of a model of thought linked to a modern conception of reality, in which the objective and subjective factors presents in all experiments, should be evaluated in the context of deductive methodological strategies. Although, the testing of hypotheses through experimentation allows assessment of empiric results in contrast to the expected results, the observation of unexpected phenomena may be relevant, allowing the reentry of new approaches. That is, even in the context of a deductive strategy, new elements, born of empirical observations are useful to enhance the interpretations. There are not an struggle between empiric and logic, on the contrary, the possibility of strengthening the deductive model, highlighting novel observations to be included within a new cycle of knowledge production. Although, the relationship between experience with archaeological materials and experimentation as formal process has tended to relegate the first to look as strictly didactic or exploratory, the fact is that in the same experimental process formal, there is always an experiential component which allows new insights to the problems addressed.

In the case of the presented paper, observation is particularly relevant the observations of some technological aspects, specifically in the degree of polish in the artifacts considered as "shuttles". At the beginning of the experimental process, the pieces used were not intensively polished, leaving small irregular portions on the tool, which made impossible to use them in the loom. Once regularized completely the entire surface through intense polishing, the effectiveness of the piece substantially improved, achieving optimal results.

Even when this statement might seem as secondary in the general framework of the evaluation process of the materials, the fact is that it changes radically previous interpretations about technological processes for the artifacts recovered within the ceremonial temple. As noted in a previous work (Santander, 2009), some tools recovered had an intense polish, and considered as an intensive preparation of the artifacts, with a view to his deposition within the Tulan-54 site as an elaborated offering. By developing an experimental strategy, and specifically the consideration of a subjective variable, as the relative usefulness of the tool, is possible to question the original interpretation offering a techno-functional explanation to the formatization process of the tools, independent, in any case of the particular characteristics of the remains covering the ceremonial temple Tulan-54.

Acknowledgments

I compromise my gratefulness to Lautaro Núñez, Isabel Cartajena, Carlos Carrasco and Patricio de Souza, Main Researchers of the 1020316 and 1070040 Fondecyt national projects in which were recovered the artifacts analyzed in this paper. Likewise, my gratitude to Stefano Grimaldi for his guide on the preparation of this research. The development of the present work was developed with the support of in the Quaternary and Lithic Industries of the Instituto Terra e Memoria de Mação, (Portugal), the Institut Català de Paleoecología Humana i Evolució Social (IPHES) from Catalunya, Spain and the Department of Geology of the Universidad de Chile.

References

BAENA, J. (1997) – Arqueología experimental: Algo más que un juego. *Boletín de Arqueología Experimental, 1*, 4-5.

BENAVENTE, A. (1981) – *Chiu-Chiu 200: Un Campamento de Pastores*. Universidad de Chile.

BUC, N. (2011) – Experimental Series and Use-Wear in Bone Tools. *Journal of Archaeological Science, 38*(3), 546-557. doi:10.1016/j.jas.2010.10.009.

BUC, N.; LOPONTE, D. (2007) – Bone Tool Types and Microwear Patterns: Some Examples from the Pampa Region, South America. In C. Gates St-Pierre & R. Beauchamp Walker (Eds.), *Bones as Tools: Current Methods and Interpretations in worked Bone Studies* (pp. 143-157). Oxford, UK: BAR Publishing.

BUC, N.; SILVESTRE, R. (2006) – Funcionalidad y complementariedad de los conjuntos líticos y óseos en el humedal del nordeste de la Provincia de Buenos Aires: Anah'\i, un caso de estudio. *Intersecciones antropología, 7*(1-2), 129-146.

CARTAJENA, I., NÚÑEZ, L.; GROSJEAN, M. (2007) – Camelid domestication on the western slope of the Puna de Atacama, northern Chile. *Anthropozoologica, 42*(2), 155-173.

DRANSART, P. (1991) – Llamas, herders and the exploitation of raw materials in the Atacama Desert. *World archaeology, 22*(3), 304-319. Retrieved from http://www.informaworld.com/index/924436687.pdf.

GONZÁLEZ URQUIJO, J.E.; IBÁÑEZ ESTÉVEZ, J.J. (1994) – *Metodología de Análisis funcional de instrumentos en sílex* (p. 301). Deusto: Universidad de Deusto.

GRIFFITTS, J.L. (1993) – *Experimental Replication and Analysis of Use Wear on Bone Tools*. University of Colorado.

GRIFFITTS, J.L. (2006) – *Bone tools and technological choice: Change and stability on the Northern Plains (North Dakota)*. The University of Arizona. Retrieved from http://gradworks.umi.com/32/37/3237584.html.

GRIMALDI, S. (2003) – Riflessioni personali sullo studio sperimentale di industrie litiche del Paleolitico medio-inferiore. In P. Bellintani & L. Moser (Eds.), *Archaeologie sperimentali: metodologie ed esperienze fra verifica, riproduzione, comunicazione e simulazione* (pp. 203-208). Trento.

KEELEY, L.H. (1980) – *Experimental Determination of Stone Tool Uses: A Microwear Analysis* (p. 266). University of Chicago Press.

NÚÑEZ, L. (1999) – Fase Tilocalar: Nuevas evidencias formativas en la Puna de Atacama (norte de Chile). En Formativo sudamericano. Una reevaluación. In P. Lederberger-Crespo (Ed.), *Formativo sudamericano. Una reevaluación.* (pp. 227-242). Cuenca: Abya-Yala.

NÚÑEZ, L.; CARTAJENA, I.; CARRASCO, C.; DE SOUZA, P. (2006) – Temprana arquitectura ceremonial en el área de Atacama (Norte de Chile). In A. Franco, M. Justin Jennings, & A. Drusini (Eds.), *Actas del simposio internacional sobre arqueología del area centro sur andina*. Lima, Perú: Instituto Francés de Estudios Andinos.

NÚÑEZ, L.; CARTAJENA, I.; CARRASCO, C.; DE SOUZA, P.; GROSJEAN, M. (2006) – Emergencia de comunidades pastoralistas formativas en el sureste de la Puna de Atacama. *Estudios atacameños, 32*, 93-117. doi:10.4067/S0718-10432006000200008.

NÚÑEZ, L., MCROSTIE, V.; CARTAJENA, I. (2009) – Consideraciones sobre la recolección vegetal y la horticultura durante el Formativo Temprano en el sureste de la cuenca de atacama. *Darwiniana, 47*(1), 56-75.

NÚÑEZ, L.; SANTORO, C.M. (2011) – El tránsito arcaico-formativo en la circumpuna y valles occidentales del centro sur andino: hacia los cambios "neolíticos". *Chungara, Revista De Antropología Chilena, 43* (Número Especial 1), 487-530.

OSBORNE, C. (1965) – The Preparation of Yucca Fibers: An Experimental Study. *Memoirs of the society for American Archaeology, 19* (contributions of the Waterhill Mesa Archaeological Project), 45-50.

SANTANDER, B. (2009) – Modelos Secuenciales para Tecnología Ósea durante la Transición Arcaico-Formativo en Atacama, El caso de la Quebrada Tulan. In P. López, I. Cartajena, C. García, & F. Mena (Eds.), *Zooarqueología y Tafonomía en el Confín del Mundo* (pp. 45-58). Santiago: Universidad Internacional Sek.

SANTANDER, B. (2010) – *La industria ósea y su uso en materiales animales blandos. Una aproximación traceológica a un conjunto arqueológico del norte de Chile.* Instituto Politécnico de Tomar, Universidade de Trás-os-Montes e Alto Douro, Museo Nacional de Historia Natural, Universidad de Ferrara, Universitat Rovira i Virgili.

SANTANDER, B. (2011) – Los huesos como herramientas para un mundo en cambio. El conjunto artefactual óseo del sitio TU-54, región de Antofagasta, Norte de Chile. In Organización de Jóvenes en Investigación Arqueológica (OrJIA) (Ed.), *Actas de las II Jornadas de Jóvenes en Investigación Arqueológica* (pp. 393-397). Madrid: Libros Portico.

SCHEINSOHN, V. (1997) – *Explotación de Materias Primas Óseas en la Isla Grande de Tierra del Fuego.* Universidad Nacional de Buenos Aires.

VERGÈS, J.M. (2002) – *Caracterització dels Models d'Instrumental Lític del Mode 1 a partir de les Dades de l'Anàlisi Funcional dels Conjunts Litotècnics d'Aïn Aanech i El-Kherba (Algèria), Monte Poggiolo i Isernia La Pineta (Itàlia).* Universitat Rovira i Virgili.

EARLY DIAGENESIS OF UNGULATE CRANIA IN TEMPERATE ENVIRONMENTS: AN EXPERIMENTAL APPROACH

Cláudia COSTA

UNIARQ; FCHS – Universidade do Algarve, Campus de Gambelas, 8005-139 Faro, Portugal
ccordeirocosta@gmail.com

Nelson ALMEIDA; Pedro CURA

Quaternary and Prehistory Group (Geosciences Centre, UC, uR&D 73, FCT – Portugal);
Archaeology and Integrated Territory Management Research Group (UNESC, CNPq, Brasil);
ITM, Earth and Memory Institute and Museum of Prehistoric Art of Mação, Portugal
nelsonjalmeida@gmail.com   0pedrocura@gmail.com

Hugo GOMES

Quaternary and Prehistory Group (Geosciences Centre, UC, uR&D 73, FCT – Portugal);
IPT, Polytechnic Institute of Tomar; ITM, Earth and Memory Institute, Portugal
hugo.hugomes@gmail.com

Sara CURA

Quaternary and Prehistory Group (Geosciences Centre, UC, uR&D 73, FCT – Portugal);
ITM, Earth and Memory Institute and Museum of Prehistoric Art of Mação, Portugal
0saracura0@gmail.com

Abstract: *The acquisition of a corpus of data related to taphonomy and early diagenesis is crucial for the understanding of archaeological records. For that it is necessary to reproduce experimentations in controlled environments that allow inter-studies comparison.*

With the aim of monitoring taphonomic and early diagenetic alterations, seven ungulate crania were buried in different depositional environments in the region of Alto Ribatejo (central Portugal). The exhumed specimen CrOvcp1, buried for a total of 319 days in a sandy environment, still presented larvae activity and some organic matter. In this paper we discuss the experimental protocol developed, its applicability and future perspectives.

Key words: *Early stages of diagenesis; taphonomy; temperate environment; experimental protocol*

Résumé: *L'acquisition d'un corpus de données se rapportant a la taphonomie et diagénèse initiale est cruciale pour la compréhension des registres archéologiques. Pour cela il est nécessaire de reproduire des expérimentations sous des environnements qui permettent des comparaisons inter-études.*

Avec pour but de faire le monitorage des alterations taphonomiques et diagénétiques initiales, sept crânes d'ongulés ont été enterrés sous des environnements dépositionels différents, dans la région du Alto Ribatejo (Portugal central). L'individu CrOvcp1 exhumé après être enterré pendant 319 jours dans des sables, présentait encore de l'activité des larves et de la matière organique. Dans cet article on discute le protocole experimental développé, son applicabilité et les perspectives pour l'avenir.

Mots-clés: *Stades initiaux de la diagénèse; taphonomie; environnement tempéré; protocole expérimental*

INTRODUCTION

Zooarchaeology uses experimental and naturalistic analyses in order to produce actualistic data. The obtained information allows the realization of inferential transpositions and comparisons with the archaeological record, the main objective being the acquisition of information related to taphonomy, i.e., alterations occurring during the transition of parts of an organism from the biosphere into the lithosphere (Efremov, 1940). It is a complex process that involves the interference of several agents and processes that cause biological and physico-chemical modifications in bones and teeth, during partial or total burial (Lyman, 1994). Several taphonomy experimental researches were developed in the last years in the Iberian Peninsula (Igreja *et al.*, 2007; Blasco *et al.*, 2008; Cáceres *et al.*, 2009; Lloveras *et al.*, 2012; Saladié *et al.*, 2013). However, to our present knowledge, the same is not happening with the study of animal carcasses from an early diagenetic point of view.

The participation of the Quaternary and Prehistory Group (Geosciences Centre, University of Coimbra, Portugal) in several interdisciplinary projects (Oosterbeek and

Bastos, 2007) allowed the development and implementation of an experimental protocol dedicated to the study of these problematic. The buried elements (ungulate crania and mandibles) result from interdisciplinary experimental research projects focused on lithic industry functional analysis, taphonomy and bone technology (Cristiani et al., 2009; Santander, 2010; Costa et al., in press). The main objectives are: (i) to contribute to the growing corpus of data related to the study of early diagenetic alterations in temperate climates, by monitoring general trends in different sedimentary environments of Alto Ribatejo (central Portugal), and (ii) acquire data for the development of a predictive model related to the programming of activities dependent on the degree of preservation of bones (e.g., DNA and isotopic analysis, Lee-Thorp and Sealy, 2008).

EARLY STAGES OF DIAGENESIS: A BRIEF SYNTHESIS

The study of the early stages of diagenesis comprises extremely diversified variables of which the soil characteristics where the elements are deposited are crucial. Several recent research projects are focused on the development of "diagenetic parameters", as for example histological integrity, protein content, crystallinity/porosity changes and chemical exchanges (Hedges and Millard, 1995; Hedges et al., 1995; Nielsen-Marsh and Hedges, 2000; Fernández-Jalvo et al., 2010). The impact of these parameters seems to increase proportionally with the time of burial. Although the details of that correlation are site dependent or site-specific, it is possible to see general patterns or inter-site correlations (Nicholson, 1996; Nielsen-Marsh and Hedges, 2000).

Besides burial duration, bone preservation also depends on burial environment (Hedges, 2002). During soil formation, occur several physico-chemical and biological alterations and processes (Azevêdo, 2008) that can influence early diagenesis. Rainfall, for example, influences the burial hydrological dynamics interfering with the mineral component (Hedges and Millard, 1995) and affecting the existence or absence of corrosion on bone and teeth surfaces (Fernández-Jalvo et al., 2010).

Soft tissues decomposition depends mainly on burial temperature (but also humidity) (Vass, 2010; cf. Carter et al., 2010) and soil temperature relates to air temperature and depth of burial (Child, 1995ab). Climatic conditions affect soil pH (Nicholson, 1996) and microbial or fungi action (Collins et al., 2002; Jans et al., 2004). Extreme temperatures (or temperature sudden changes) reduce microbial activity making that the only mechanism of collagen degradation is chemical hydrolysis (Collins et al., 2002; Fernández-Jalvo et al., 2010).

In terms of soil pH, the death of microorganisms may cause punctual increases in the surrounding environment pH due to the liberation of ammonia and other microbial metabolic (Child, 1995ab). Neutral environments or with a slightly alkaline pH tend to favour bone survival because bone minerals will not be as prone to dissolution (Andrews, 1995; Child, 1995b). In these environments microbial action is optimized in discrete areas of destruction – sub-micron spongiform porosity (Turner-Walker et al., 2002). In extremely alkaline soils a tendency towards the creation of exfoliations on bone surface and dentine exists; in acid soils a tendency towards a faster destruction of soft tissues (Fernández-Jalvo et al., 2002) and a catastrophic mineral dissolution (Nielsen-Marsh et al., 2007) is evident. The burial surrounding vegetation is also important due to possible taphonomic modifications (vermiculations) and to the presence of humus (Andrews, 1995; Nicholson, 1996).

THE REGION: ALTO RIBATEJO, CENTRAL PORTUGAL

The Alto Ribatejo (central Portugal, Western Iberia) corresponds to a ~2,500 km^2 area located in the central northern sector of the Lower Tagus Basin. The relief is generally bellow 600 meters of altitude above sea level and affected by deep fluvial incision. The regional geomorphological features are strongly related to the geology of the substrate (Martins et al., 2009).

This region comprises three main geomorphological units: the Hesperian Massif, the Estremenho limestone Massif and the Lower Tagus Cenozoic Basin (Fig. 1). The Pleistocene deposits consist of karstic cave fillings in the limestone areas, fluvial terraces, colluvium and aeolian sands. The Holocene is mainly represented in the valley floor infill (Rosina, 2004). Acid soils are predominant in the region and, as a consequence, few osteoarchaeological remains are found, some exceptions being cave contexts in the most northwest part of Alto Ribatejo (Davis, 2002), some rare megalithic monuments (Figueiredo, 2010) and fluvial terraces on the Tagus valley (Rosina, 2005).

Alto Ribatejo is characterized by a temperate Mediterranean climate divided between the thermomediterranean and supramediterranean steps (Blanco Castro et al., 1997). According to the Digital Environment Atlas ([Accessed 13 Dec. 2012] http://sniamb.apambiente.pt/webatlas) from the Portuguese Environment Institute (data from 1931 till 1960), the annual average temperature for this region is between 12.5°C and 17.5°C. The solar radiation is relatively homogeneous in the entire area (annual average between 145 Kcal/cm^2 and 150 Kcal/cm^2) with the lowest values in the most northeast and higher values in the most east areas. Rainfall maximum values are found on areas of higher altitude and minimum values (between 600 and 700 mm) on the Tagus valley.

The Alto Ribatejo important geomorphologic variability, regional relevant micro-variability and different ecological sub-regions were a key factor on human occupation over time (Oosterbeek et al., 2010). The diversity of this territory makes it a privileged region for

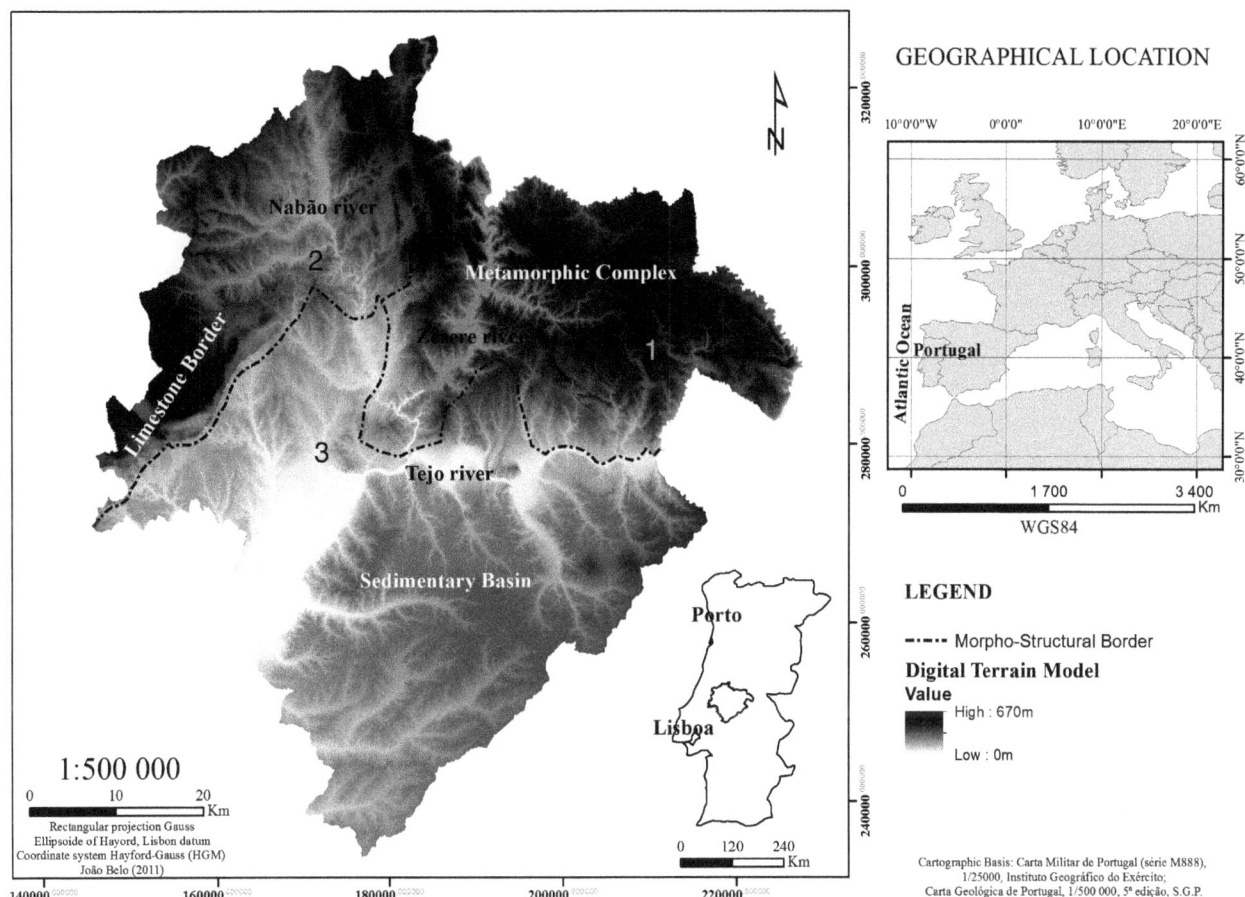

Figure 1. Digital Elevation Model (DEM) of the Alto Ribatejo region (central Portugal) and geographic location of selected burial sites: 1 – Museum backyard (Mação); 2 – Agricultural land (Tomar); 3 – Fluvial terrace (Barquinha)

the creation of an experimental taphonomic and early diagenetic corpus of data, allowing future correlations with other areas of western Iberia.

MATERIALS AND METHODS

Experimental protocol

So far, five ovicaprid (CrOvcp1-5) and two wild boar (CrSus1-2) crania plus mandibles were buried at 20/30 cm depth in several sedimentary environments (Tab. 1).

The selection of these elements allows the monitoring of alterations in both bone and teeth. The specimens CrOvcp1-3 and CrSus1-2 were buried on sandy soils located in the Museum of Prehistoric Art of Mação (Portugal), in its origin of anthropic character, in order to allow a more detailed monitoring. The remaining specimens, CrOvcp4-5, are located in different soils, comparable to deposits were archaeological and/or paleontological contexts were identified. The definition of the burial time (average of 4 years) is based on observations produced during the experimentation, this way allowing the acquisition of data at two levels: exhumation of several elements with a comparable time of burial (synchronic) and during an hypothetical chronological timeline (diachronic).

An experimental protocol comprising a mandatory filling working-form with the selected main relevant information was developed and implemented. Before the inhumation the elements were identified and observations related to *ante mortem* manipulations were registered (e.g., tongue extraction, area of segmentation, presence of soft tissues). The first specimen, CrOvcp1, was exhumed in order to evaluate the soft tissues decomposition and plan posterior actions. CrOvcp1 (crania and mandible) was previously disarticulated on the occipital area, the tongue was removed and the elements were buried without further modifications.

Burial location: vegetation and sedimentary deposits

The burial area of the specimen CrOvcp1 is located between a wall and a mulberry (*Morus nigra*), 50 cm away from the wall and 100 cm away from the mulberry. Depending on the size of the surrounding treetops this area is differentially sheltered during the day and year.

The sedimentary deposits characterization was made by grain size and pH analysis. Three soil samples were collected, the first sample before the burial and the remaining samples during the exhumation, one inside the pit were the element was buried and another on the internal space of the mandible. pH analysis followed Watson and Brown (2010), using a precision scale

Table 1. Specimens already included in the experimentation

ID	Species	Age	Element	Date of Burial	Exhumation	Soil description
CrOvcp1	*Ovis aries*	Adult	Cranium+Mandible	08/2008	05/2010	Sandy soil (Museum backyard)
CrOvcp2	*Capra hircus*	Adult	Cranium+Mandible	05/2008	2013 (scheduled)	Sandy soil (Museum backyard)
CrOvcp3	*Ovis aries*	Adult	Cranium+Mandible	08/2009	2015 (scheduled)	Sandy soil (Museum backyard)
CrSus1	*Sus scrofa*	Juvenile	Cranium+Mandible	03/2009	2013 (scheduled)	Sandy soil (Museum backyard)
CrSus2	*Sus scrofa*	Juvenile	Cranium+Mandible	04/2010	2014 (scheduled)	Sandy soil (Museum backyard)
CrOvcp4	*Ovis aries*	Adult	Cranium+Mandible	11/2010	2018 (scheduled)	Calcareous soil (agricultural land, Tomar)
CrOvcp5	*Ovis aries*	Juvenile	Cranium+Mandible	11/2010	2020 (scheduled)	Sandy soil (fluvial terrace, Barquinha)

Table 2. Results of the physico-chemical characterization of the CrOvcp1 burial. pH

ID	Provenance	Colour (Cailleux)	Description	pH (H_2O)
1	2 meters away from the burial	M70/71 (yellow)	Friable sediment with low organic content – coarse sand with silty matrix	6.34 Sub-acid
2	In the burial	N65/67 (orange)	Sediment with high clay and organic matter component – very coarse sand with silty-clayish matrix	6.56 Sub-acid
3	Sediment in the mandible	P67/69 (brown)	Silty-sandy sediment with high organic matter decomposition – coarse sand with silty-clayish matrix	7.56 Neutral

(Toledo AB_204) and a pH measurer (Clison Micrograph 2000) calibrated with buffer solutions (pH=4, pH=7) at 20°C. The sediments were dissolved in distilled water, homogenized and correlated with the Pratolongo scale (Costa, 2004). Soil samples were macroscopically analysed using a grading scale (Bllot and Pye, 2001).

Main climatic variables

Daily averages for air temperature, air humidity and rainfall during the time of burial were obtained. In the case presented, due to the costs involved with the *in situ* installation of an hygrometer, monitoring was made by using the data of the Water Resources National Information System meteorological station of Abrantes (model Davis Vantage Pro2 Plus), located around 13 km from Mação ([Accessed 10 Oct. 2010] http://meteoabrantes.no-ip.info/).

RESULTS

Specimen condition

The exhumation of the specimen CrOvcp1 was on May 2010. Some fur, skin and soft tissues remnants were visible on small areas of the bone surface at an initial state (primary or secondary) of arthropods larvae activity (*sensu* Gennard, 2007). No content was left in the interior of the crania and the mandible was fully disarticulated.

A macroscopic observation with a hand lens (4x) and a strong incident light was made after washing the

elements with water and no macroscopic alterations were registered. The elements were in a stage 0 of weathering (Behrensmeyer, 1978) and, although an almost direct contact occurred with roots from the surrounding vegetation, vermiculations were not perceptible in the bone and teeth surfaces. Darker coloration spots resulting from differential percentage of remaining fat in certain parts of the crania were evident.

Sediment pH

According to the Pratolongo Scale (Costa, 2004) the burial environment is considered sub-acid to neutral (Tab. 2). The comparison of the different samples pH values indicates that the pH of the sediment adjacent to the burial was 1.22 pH values higher than the surrounding areas. This occurrence is possibly a consequence of the soft tissues decomposition, however, the influence of other non-measurable external processes cannot be fully discarded.

Climatic conditions

Due to an external error only the data of 579 days (94% of the total time of burial) was made available, lacking alternated days from January, February and March of 2010. The air temperature data reveals a distribution near to normal (minimum of 0,7°C, maximum of 29,3°C) with a daily average temperature of 14,7°C during half of the burial time. The air relative humidity revealed an asymmetric data distribution with two extreme values: 19%, representing an extremely low air humidity, eventually related with reading errors, and maximum values of 100%. Humidity levels average was above 73% during half the time of burial. Concerning rainfall,

Table 3. Main climatic indicators distribution during the CrOvcp1 burial time

		Humidity (%)	Temperature (°C)	Precipitation (mm/h)
N	Valid	579	579	579
	Missing	0	0	0
Mean		72,45	15,1769	1,4549
Median		73,00	14,7000	,0000
Mode		72	9,40[a]	,00
Std. Deviation		15,243	5,64356	3,83452
Skewness		-,404	,164	5,521
Std. Error of Skewness		,102	,102	,102
Kurtosis		-,217	-,697	51,338
Std. Error of Kurtosis		,203	,203	,203
Minimum		19	,70	,00
Maximum		100	29,30	50,60
Percentiles	25	62,00	10,7000	,0000
	50	73,00	14,7000	,0000
	75	85,00	19,8000	,6000

a. Multiple modes exist. The smallest value is shown

although absent during 75% of the time of burial, the daily average revealed a highly asymmetric distribution reaching extremely high values (maximum 50,6 mm/h) (Tab. 3).

DISCUSSION

The first exhumation represents a very preliminary stage of the experimental protocol implementation but allows the elaboration of some considerations. After 619 days buried in a sub-acid coarse silty sand environment, with an average of 72% of air relative humidity and without precipitation registered in the major part of the burial, the specimen CrOvcp1 still had soft tissues with larvae activity in early stages of development.

Besides the experimentation produced in Wales, United Kingdom, that consisted on the monitoring of around 100 elements from animal carcasses deposited in different time periods reaching 20 or 30 years (Fernández-Jalvo *et al.*, 2010), other analogous experiments are being developed, for example, on the South of Sweden (Magnell, 2010). Several wild boar long and articular bones, without meat but with remaining soft tissues, were left on ground and buried in different environments. Focusing the sandy environment, the soft tissues decomposition occurred between 12 and 18 months of burial and, similarly to the CrOvcp1 specimen, no weathering was evidenced on those elements (Magnell, 2010).

In our case-study, the sediments pH had a slight increase of around 1.22 values (from sub-acid to neutral), possibly related to the soft tissues decomposition. The decomposition of organic matter is generally a

phenomenon caused by microbial action. During this phase some gases are released as a result of oxidation, mainly carbon dioxide, methane and other soluble molecules (Bolan *et al.*, 1991 *apud* Weiner, 2010, p. 57). If the decomposition occurs under an anaerobic environment, other microbes are active and the pH decreases. Nevertheless, in the initial phases of decomposition the pH may rise due in part to the formation of ammonium carbonates (Kirchmann and Witter, 1992 *apud* Weiner, 2010, p. 57). Organic content, high temperatures and humidity favour microbial activity. Focusing the CrOvcp1 specimen, the absence of rainfall during the major part of the time of burial might have detained that process, partially explaining the existence of larvae after 619 days of burial. Also, the sediment pH near to neutral possibly contributed to the preservation of organic matter.

FINAL REMARKS

Only the repetition of this experimentation will allow the acquisition of a pattern of organic matter preservation in these environmental conditions. For this to be possible it is extremely important to make a rigorous description of the sedimentary environment (grain size, pH) producing quantitative data that strengthens the interpretations, this way allowing comparisons between different burial sites and environments. The comparison of early diagenesis modifications would also be reinforced by a detailed description of the alteration stage by quantifying the organic matter present and also larvae activity.

The exhumation of the elements after a longer burial period will allow us to start working on bone and teeth mineral structure alteration rhythms. The inclusion of more and other type of elements (long and articular bones), in different states (fresh, dry, thermo-altered, fractured, without soft tissues), including new quantitative indexes (soil temperature and humidity) and deposits (lacustrine and karstic environments) is already being prepared.

Acknowledgements

Authors would like to thank Cristiana Ferreira, Luís Santos, Lídia Catarino, Teresa Ferreira and Leandro Infantini for valuable comments and help during the elaboration of the protocol and data interpretation. Palmira Saladié and Rebecca Dean commented on a previous draft and João Belo made the cartography. Hugo Gomes benefits from a FCT research scholarship (Portugal, Rupscience project, PTDC/HIS-ARQ/101299/2008). Nelson Almeida benefits from a FCT PhD individual scholarship under QREN – POPH – Typology 4.1. – Advanced Training, subsidized by the European Social Fund and by national MEC funds (SFRH/BD/78079/2011).

References

ANDREWS, P. (1995) – Experiments in taphonomy. Journal of Archaeological Science. 22, p. 147-153.

AZEVÊDO, M.T.M. (2008) – Solos: a pele da Terra. In Mateus, A. coord. – Solo: a pele da Terra [On-line]. Lisboa (Departamento de Geologia FCUL). [Accessed 15 Sep. 2011]. Available at http://geologia.fc.ul.pt/documents/163.pdf, pp. 6-11.

BEHRENSMEYER, A.K. (1978) – Taphonomic and ecologic Information from bone weathering. Paleobiology. 4: 2, p. 150-162.

BLANCO CASTRO, E.; CASADO GONZÁLEZ, M.A.; COSTA TENÓRIO, M.; ESCRIBANO BOMBÍN, R.; GARCIA ANTÓN, M.; GÉNOVA FUSTER, M.; GÓMEZ MANZANEQUE, Á.; MORENA SAIZ, J.C.; MORLA JUARISTI, C.; REGATO PAJARES, P.; SAINZ OLLERO, H. (1997) – Los Bosques Ibéricos: una interpretación Geobotánica. Barcelona: E. Planeta. 572 p.

BLLOT, S.J; PYE, K. (2001) – Gradistat: a grain size distribution and statistics package for the analysis of unconsolidated sediments. Earth Surface Processes and Landforms. 26, p. 1237-1248.

BLASCO, R.; ROSELL, J.; FERNÁNDEZ PERIS, J.; CÁCERES, I.; VERGÈS, J. (2008) – A new element of trampling: an experimental application on the Level XII faunal record of Bolomor Cave (Valencia, Spain). Journal of Archeological Science. 35: 6, p. 1605-1618.

CÁCERES, I.; ESTEBAN-NADAL, M.; LLUC BENNÀSAR, M. (2009) – Disarticulation and dispersal processes of cervid carcass at the Bosque de Riofrío (Segovia, Spain). Journal of Taphonomy. 7, p. 129-141.

CARTER, D.O.; YELLOWLEES, D.; TIBBETT, M. (2010) – Moisture can be the dominant environmental parameter governing cadaver decomposition in soil. Forensic Science International. 200, p. 60-66.

CHILD, A.M. (1995a) – Towards an understanding of the microbial decomposition of archaeological bone in the burial environment. Journal of Archaeological Science. 22, p. 165-174.

CHILD, A.M. (1995b) – Microbial taphonomy of archaeological bone. Studies in Conservation. 40, p. 19-30.

COLLINS, M.J.; NIELSEN-MARSH, C.M.; HILLER, J.; SMITH, C.I.; ROBERTS, J.P.; PRIGODICH, R.V.; WESS, T.J.; CSAPÒ, J.; MILLARD, A.R.; TURNER-WALKER, G. (2002) – The survival of organic matter in bone: a review. Archaeometry. 44: 3, p. 383-394.

COSTA, C.; ALMEIDA, N.; GOMES, H.; CURA, S.; CURA, P. (in press) – A monitorização das alterações diagenéticas em crânios de ungulados: um exemplo de experimentação em Zooarqueologia. Xelb. Silves. Actas do 8º Encontro de Arqueologia do Algarve "Arqueologia e as outras Ciências".

COSTA, J.B. (2004) – Caracterização e constituição do solo. Lisboa: Fundação Calouste Gulbenkian. 528 p.

CRISTIANI, E.; CURA, S.; GRIMALDI, S.; GOMES, J.; OOSTERBEEK, L.; ROSINA, P. (2009) – Functional analysis and experimental archaeology: the Middle Pleistocene site of Ribeira da Atalaia (Central Portugal). In Araújo, M.; Clemente-Conte, I., eds. – Proceedings of the workshop on "Recent Functional Studies on Non-Flint Stone Tools, Methodological Improvements and Archaeological Inferences" (Lisbon 2008), CD-ROM. ISBN 978-989-20-1803-4. Available at http://www.workshop-traceologia-lisboa2008.com.

DAVIS, S.J.M. (2002) – The mammals and birds from Gruta do Caldeirão, Portugal. Revista Portuguesa de Arqueologia. Lisboa, 5: 2, p. 29-98.

EFREMOV, J.A. (1940) – Taphonomy: a new branch of paleontology. Pan-American Geologist. 74, p. 81-93.

FERNÁNDEZ-JALVO, Y.; SÁNCHEZ-CHILLÓN, B.; ANDREWS, P.; FERNÁNDEZ-LÓPEZ, S.; ALCALÁ MARTÍNEZ, L. (2002) – Morphological taphonomic transformations of fossil bones in continental environments, and repercussion on their chemical composition. Archaeometry. 44, p. 353-362.

FERNÁNDEZ-JALVO, Y.; ANDREWS, P.; PESQUERO, D.; SMITH, C.; MARÍN-MONFORT, D.; SÁNCHEZ, B.; GEIGL, E.; ALONSO, A. (2010) – Early bone diagenesis in temperate environments. Part I: surface features and histology. Palaeogeography, Palaeoclimatology, Palaeoecology. 288, p. 62-81.

FIGUEIREDO, A. (2010) – Rituals and death cults in recente prehistory in Central Portugal (Alto Ribatejo), Documenta Praehistorica. 37, p. 85-94.

GENNARD, D.E. (2007) – Forensic entomology: an introduction. West Sussex: Willey-Blackwell. 244 p.

HEDGES, R.E.M.; MILLARD, A. R. (1995) – Bones and Groundwater: towards the modeling of diagenetic processes. Journal of Archaeological Science. 22, p. 155-164.

HEDGES, R.E.M.; MILLARD, A.R.; PIKE, A.W.G. (1995) – Measurements and Relationships of Diagenetic Alteration of Bone from Three Archaeological Sites. Journal of Archaeological Science. 22, p. 201-209.

HEDGES, R.E.M. (2002) – Bone diagenesis: an overview of processes. Archaeometry. 44: 3, p. 319-328.

IGREJA, M.A.; MORENO-GARCÍA, M.; PIMENTA, C.M. (2007) – Um exemplo de abordagem experimental da interface traceologia lítica/arqueozoologia: esquartejamento e tratamento da pele de um corço (*Capreolus capreolus)* com artefactos de pedra lascada. Revista Portuguesa de Arqueologia. Lisboa. 10: 2, p. 17-34.

JANS, M.M.E.; NIELSEN-MARSH, C.M.; SMITH, C.I.; COLLINS, M.J.; KARS, H. (2004) – Characterization of microbial attack on archaeological bone. Journal of Archaeological Science. 31, p. 87-95.

LEE-THORP, J.; SEALY, J.C. (2008) – Preface. Beyond documenting diagenesis: the fifth international bone diagenesis workshop. Palaeogeography, Palaeoclimatology, Palaeoecology. 266, p. 129-133.

LLOVERAS, L.; MORENO-GARCÍA, M.; NADAL, J. (2012) – Assessing the variability in taphonomic studies of modern leporid remains from Eagle Owl (*Bubo bubo*) nest assemblages: the importance of age of prey. Journal of Archaeological Science. 39, p. 3754-3764.

LYMAN, R.L. (1994) – Vertebrate Taphonomy. Cambridge: Cambridge University Press. 552 p.

MAGNELL, O. (2010) – Weathering and diagenetic changes of wild boar bones in five different environmental settings [On-line]. BoneCommons, Item #1344 [Accessed 28 Nov. 2012]. Available at http://alexandriaarchive.org/bonecommons/items/show/1344.

MARTINS, A.A.; CUNHA, P.P.; HUOT, S.; MURRAY, A.; BUYLAERT, J.P. (2009) – Geomorphological correlation of the tectonically displaced Tejo River terraces (Gavião-Chamusca are, Portugal) supported by luminescence dating. Quaternary International. 199, p. 75-91.

NICHOLSON, R.A. (1996) – Bone degradation, burial medium and species representation: debunking the myths, an experimental based approach. Journal of Archaeological Science. 23, p. 513-533.

NIELSEN-MARSH, C.M.; HEDGES, R.E.M. (2000) – Patterns of diagenesis in bone I: the effects of site environments. Journal of Archaeological Science. 27, p. 1139-1150.

NIELSEN-MARSH, C.M.; SMITH, C.I.; JANS, M.M.E.; NORD, A.; KARS, H.; COLLINS, M.J. (2007) – Bone diagenesis in the European Holocene II: taphonomic and environmental considerations. Journal of Archaeological Science. 34, p. 1523-1531.

OOSTERBEEK, L.; BASTOS, R.L. (2007) – Arqueologia Trans-Atlântica. Erechim: Habilis. 331 p.

OOSTERBEEK, L.; CURA, S.; CARRONDO, J.; GARCÊS, S.; GOMES, H.; TOMÉ, T. (2010) – Pré-História do Alto Ribatejo. Zahara. Abrantes. 15, p. 77-88.

ROSINA, P. (2004) – I depositi quaternario nella Media Valle del Tago (Alto Ribatejo, Portogallo centrale) e le industriche litiche associate. Unpublished PhD thesis. Università di Ferrara. 206 p.

ROSINA, P. (2005) – Os terraços fluviais e a fauna associada. In Marques, L., ed. – Paleontologia e Arqueologia do estuário do Tejo: actas do I seminário. Montijo/Lisboa: Ed. Colibri, p. 63-70.

SALADIÉ, P.; RODRÍGUEZ-HIDALGO, A.; DÍEZ, C.; MARTÍN-RODRÍGUEZ, P.; CARBONELL, E. (2013) – Range of bone modifications by human chewing. Journal of Archaeological Science. 40: 1, p. 380-397.

SANTANDER, B. (2010) – La industria ósea y su uso en materiales animales blandos: una aproximación traceológica a un conjunto arqueológico del norte de Chile. Unpublished Master thesis. Universidade de Trás-os-Montes e Alto Douro, Instituto Politécnico de Tomar. 180 p.

TURNER-WALKER, G.; NIELSEN-MARSH, C.M.; SYVERSEN, U.; KARS, H.; COLLINS, M.J. (2002) – Sub-micron spongiform porosity is the major ultra-structural alteration occurring in Archaeological bone. International Journal of Osteoarchaeology. 12, p. 407-414.

VASS, A.A. (2010) – Beyond the grave: understanding human decomposition. Microbiology Today. 28: 1, p. 190-193.

WATSON, M.E.; BROWN, J.R. (2010) – pH and lime requirement. Recommended soil test procedures for the North Central Region, North Central Regional Research Publication. 221, p. 13-16.

WEINER, S. (2010) – Microarchaeology: beyond the visible archaeological record. Cambridge: Cambridge University Press. 414 p.

BETWEEN TOOLS AND ENGRAVINGS: TECHNOLOGY AND EXPERIMENTAL ARCHEOLOGY TO THE STUDY OF CACHÃO DO ALGARVE ROCK ART

Neemias SANTOS DA ROSA
Quaternary and Prehistory group of GeoSciencesCenter Unit (uID73 – FCT), Brazil
neemias_of@hotmail.com

Sara CURA; Sara GARCÊS
Prehistoric Art Museum of Mação, Quaternary and Prehistory group of GeoSciencesCenter Unit (uID73 – FCT), Portugal
0saracura0@gmail.com   saragarces.rockart@gmail.com

Pedro CURA
Prehistoric Art Museum of Mação, Portugal
0pedrocura@gmail.com

Abstract: *This paper aims to present an experimental work developed under the studies about the Cachão do Algarve rock art (Central Portugal). In this context, we tested the feasibility of producing rock art engravings on greywacke supports through the use of lithic tools formatted according to characteristics of macrolithic industries found in the archaeological context of the Tagus Valley. The results of this work allowed us to create hypothetical operative chains through which could had been produced the rock art of the site, what is absolutely important for an attempt to understand the technological behavior of prehistoric populations that occupied the region during the Holocene.*

Keywords: *Rock Art, Technology, Experimental Archaeology, Tagus Valley*

Résumé: *Cet article vise à présenter un travail expérimental développé dans le cadre des études sur l'art rupestre du Cachão do Algarve (Portugal Centrale). Dans ce contexte, nous avons testé la faisabilité de la production de gravures rupestres dans grauwacke à travers l'utilisation d'outils lithiques formatées en fonction des caractéristiques des industries macrolithiques trouvés dans le contexte archéologique de la Vallée du Tage. Les résultats de ce travail nous a permis de créer hypothétiques chaînes opératoires par lesquelles pourrait avaient été produites l'art rupestre du site, ce qui est absolument important pour tenter de comprendre le comportement technologique des populations préhistoriques qui ont occupé la région pendant l'Holocène.*

Mots clés: *Art Rupestre, Technologie, Archéologie Expérimentale, Vallée du Tage*

INTRODUCTION

The experimental work which led to this paper was developed as part of a master's thesis entitled "Contribuição para o estudo do Complexo de Arte Rupestre do Vale do Tejo (Portugal): o sítio Cachão do Algarve". Its main goal was to test the feasibility of producing rock art engravings on greywacke supports, using to engrave, lithic tools of quartzite and quartz knapped according to the characteristics of the macrolithic industries found in Tagus Valley, flakes from the production of those tools and natural pebbles of the same raw materials.

The observation of the empirical data generated by such technical action allowed us to analyze important aspects of the technological process (behavior of raw materials during the procedure, percussion techniques more efficient, morphologies tools more appropriate for the work, etc.), enabling to propose hypothetical operative chains through which could have been produced much of the Cachão do Algarve rock art.

It is worth noting in this regard the importance of this approach, since the study of rock art technology through Experimental Archaeology provides a more accurate and concrete approximation of the artistic phenomenon in prehistory, minimizing the "subjectivism and free interpretations without empirical support" which, unfortunately, are so recurrent in this field of study (Sanchidrían, 2001:14).

THE CACHÃO DO ALGARVE SITE

Located in Vila Velha de Ródão, central Portugal, the Cachão do Algarve is one of the seventeen sites that are officially part of the known Tagus Valley Rock Art Complex (TVRAC), certainly one of the biggest and most important exponents of Post-Paleolithic rock art in Europe.

Identified on the greywacke from the right bank of the Tagus River during the first half of August 1972, since the beginning the Cachão do Algarve drew attention for

Figure 1. On the left, the rock 101 from Cachão do Algarve (Baptista, 1986:44)
and on the right, an example of latex molds produced over the engravings

its large platforms in position predominantly horizontal or gently sloping, red-brown staining and polished over millennia by the waters of the river, thus becoming excellent supports to production of a large amount of engravings by pecking (Fig. 1) (Baptista, 2011; Serrão, 1978).

But the construction of two dams (Fratel Dam and Cedilho Dam) in the stretch of river where were located the first sets of engravings would cause the Cachão the Algarve to be submerged by the waters of the Tagus in the end of the 1970s, together with the most other rock art sites of the complex.

However, before this event, members of the Group for the Study of the Portuguese Paleolithic were able to perform the rescue, with expressive urgency, of most engravings identified, something unprecedented in the country.

To accomplish this work, the methodology used was based on the record of that rock art by creating molds of liquid rubber (latex), a technique learned in France with Michel Brézillon, who had used that method for the study of prehistoric engravings in the Sahara desert (Fig. 1) (Baptista, 1974; Sande Lemos, 2011).

Thus, under the aforementioned thesis, the 301 molds from Cachão Algarve site were traced through direct tracing, according to a methodology developed by Abreu *et al.* (2010) and Abreu & Jaffe (1996). From this activity, we performed a typological classification of the rock art engravings and built the corpus formed by these. In total, we identified 18 anthropomorphic figures (1.10%), 21 zoomorphic figures (1.29%) and 1592 ideomorphic figures (97.61%).

But, as the main objective was the technological approach about the engravings, we also proceeded to the analysis of the technical aspects of each engraving and developed the experimental work presented here.

A HYPOTHESIS TO BE TESTED

Assuming that "an experiment is, by definition, a method to establish a reasoned conclusion, against an initial hypothesis, by trial or test," we focused our experimental procedure on the problem relating to the possible tools used as engraver elements in the production of Cachão do Algarve rock art (Reynolds, 1999:157).

This is, however, a matter markedly problematic because in any rock art engraving study the tools used to engrave are rarely found, either due to their absence in the archaeological context, for different reasons, or because the lack experience of researchers to identify them among other lithic artifacts recovered (Alvarez *et al.* 2001).

In the study of Cachão do Algarve, this is precisely the case. Having the engravings been produced on the greywacke banks of the Tagus River, it was not possible the formation of an archaeological context near the engraved supports, where could be found the tools used to produce that rock art.

Without any material evidence about the tools and the characteristics of the formative action of the engravings, we had only a few information from the literature produced about TVRAC, in which some authors eventually voiced their opinions on what kind of tools could have been used to perform the pecking on the rocky support close to the river. Serrão (1972), for example, believed that the engravings had been produced with any pointed tool, while Santos (1985) claimed be lithic or metal tools (without any opinion about the morphology) and Baptista (1986) advocated the use of quartz or quartzite pebbles (not defining if they would be knapped or used in its natural state).

Understanding the Cachão do Algarve engravings predominantly as Neolithic representations – according to the chronological framework proposed by Baptista (1981)

– we observe the characteristics of lithic industries of this period found in archaeological context of the region.

Immediately, we direct our attention to the so called macrolithic industry, strongly characterized by the exploration of quartzite and quartz (in a lower frequency) to produce knapped pebbles, mainly choppers.

This lithic industry, initially known as Languedocense, is very present in Neolithic contexts existent along the Tagus Valley, where is always found on the surface, either alone (in concentrations varying density) or in association with pottery elements, polished tools and other findings of Holocene chronology (Oosterbeek, 1994; Grimaldi, 1998; Cruz *et al.* 2000).

Such lithic artifacts were produced by direct percussion with a hard hammer, on pebbles usually of rounded morphology, abundant raw material in the area and whose origin is related to processes of formation and erosion on the conglomeratic levels of the fluvial terraces present in the region (Grimaldi, 1998).

Thus, emerged the following main question:

- It would be possible to produce rock art engravings on greywacke supports using lithic tools of quartz and quartzite knapped in accordance with the techno-morphological characteristics of the macrolithic industry found in the Tagus Valley?

Considering this possibility and finding on the macrolithic industry of Tagus Valley the techno-morphological features that, we believed, would be *a priori* fundamental to allow efficient use in the production of rock art engravings, we decided to set up the lithic tools necessary to carry out our experiment according to the characteristics evident in that industry.

Another issue that contributed to this choice, was the fact that in the course of a field work conducted in 2011 on the rock art site of Cachão de São Simão were identified macrolithic tools in the area close to where the engravings are, just 3 km from the Cachão do Algarve.

Appeared, then, some other questions:

- Regarding the raw materials, would be more efficient for the work the tools of quartzite or quartz?
- Based on your techno-morphological characteristics, what would be the tools more efficient for the work?
- Between the techniques of direct percussion and indirect percussion, which one would be the more efficient with respect to the results obtained in the pecking and investment of time and energy necessary to complete the action?
- The occurrence of impact points with distinct morphological characteristics in the same engraving would be more connected to wear the active zone of the same tool or the use of various tools to get the work done?
- The record of rock art engravings by molding latex is reliable?

Obviously, we were aware that, probably, the Cachão do Algarve rock art was not produced according only a single model of operative chain. However, for reasons of time, would not be feasible to test a large number of other operative possibilities to achieve the same goal. So, we focused our efforts on trying to prove, or disprove, the viability of some of the many possibilities.

Thus, the production of the Cachão do Algarve engravings through a technological process in which were used macrolithic tools would be the hypothesis experimentally tested by us.

THE EXPERIMENTAL WORK

Intending to rigorously test the hypothesis constructed and seeking to answer the questions that arose, we developed the experimental work.

We selected nine distinct morphologies of tools (Grimaldi, 1998), which had a good prehension to perform the technical gestures involved in pecking and morphology of the edge between pointed and convex.

Figure 2. Rock art motifs selected to be engraved during the experimental work. Respectively, from left to right: 16.4 cm x 7 cm (CAL63B M664), 60 cm x 50 cm (Gomes, 2007:93) and 8 cm x 7.5 cm (CAL103 M165)

The obtaining of the raw materials to produce the experimental lithic tools and the selection / procurement of the rocky supports to be engraved occurred in a location with the same geological characteristics of the area where is located the Cachão Algarve.[1]

In such a place were collected 28 pebbles (14 of quartz and 14 of quartzite) and selected nine supports of greywacke, fixed and with large dimension – that would be engraved there – and 2 platforms of the same raw material that would be transported to be engraved in the area of experimental activities of the Instituto Terra e Memória (ITM).

Then,were knapped 16 tools (8 in quartzite and 8 in quartz). The remaining 12 pebbles were kept in their natural forms. To complete the experimental collection, it

---

[1] The place selected was the Ocreza Valley, integrated in the CARVT and where is located an area for activities of Experimental Archeology, duly registered in the IGESPAR.

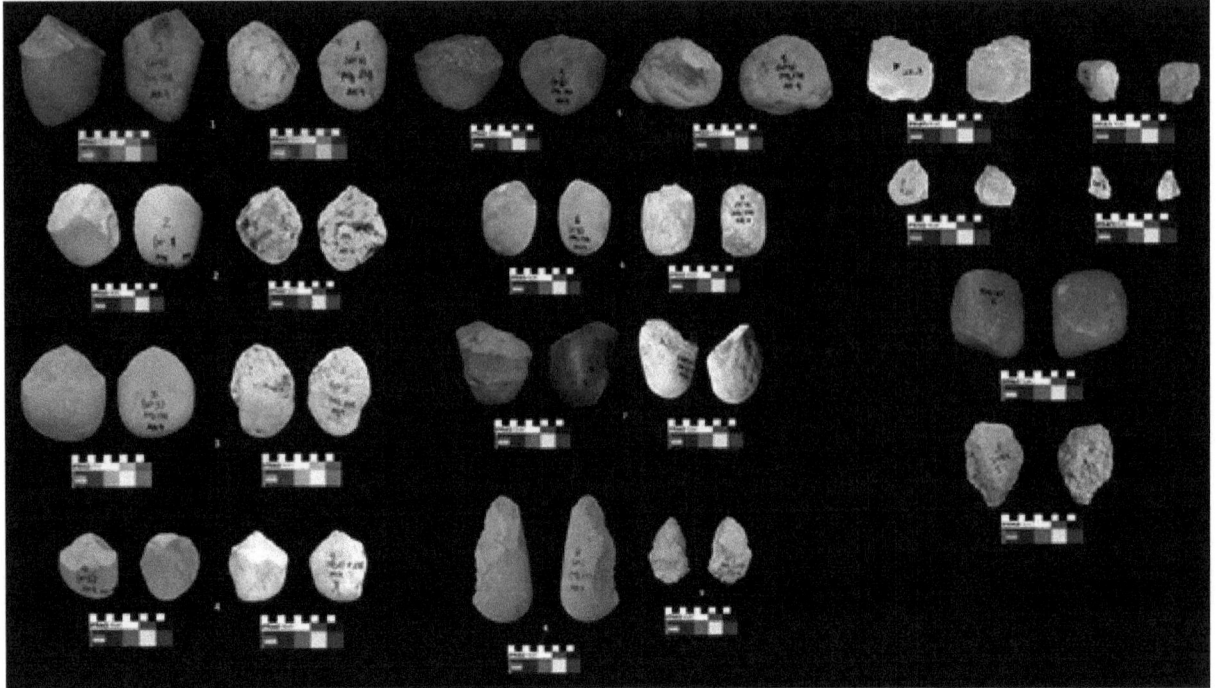

*Figure 3. Lithic material used in the experimental work. On the left and center,
choppers and knapped pebbles. On the right examples of flakes and natural pebbles*

was selected 15 quartzite flakes and 15 quartz flakes for use in indirect percussion. We prioritized the choice for cortical flakes, since such flakes are the most present on the macrolithic industries evidenced in the archaeological context of the region (Fig. 3).

All supports selected were further marked with a red ink with long durability, to avoid that the experimental engravings being confused with archaeological ones.

Thus, were produced 34 experimental engravings, in accordance with different combinations of tools and techniques, aiming to test the viability of the technical operation in question.

To perform this action, we used the following materials: 7 choppers in quartzite, 7 choppers in quartz, 1 knapped pebble in quartzite, 1 knapped pebble in quartz, 5 flakes in quartzite, 11 flakes in quartz, 6 natural pebbles in quartzite, 6 natural pebbles natural in quartz, 1 soft hammer (*Buxus simper virens*), 1 hard hammer (quartz).

With this tools were produced 10 experimental anthropomorphic figures, 10 zoomorphic ones and 10 ideomorphic ones, according to the following combinations of tools and techniques:

- quartzite chopper + direct percussion.
- quartzite chopper + indirect percussion.
- quartz chopper + direct percussion.
- quartz chopper + indirect percussion.
- quartzite flake + indirect percussion.
- quartz flake + indirect percussion.
- quartzite natural pebble + direct percussion.

- quartzite natural pebble + indirect percussion.
- quartz natural pebble + direct percussion.
- quartz natural pebble + indirect percussion.

Given the characteristics of the zoomorphic motif, with some traces thicker and other thinner, were also produced 4 further engravings by the following combination:

- quartzite chopper + direct percussion and quartzite flake + indirect percussion.
- quartzite chopper + indirect percussion quartzite flake + indirect percussion.
- quartz chopper + direct percussion and quartz flake + indirect percussion.
- quartz chopper + indirect percussion and quartz flake + indirect percussion.

Then, we reproduced the three rock art motifs selected with the same dimensions and traits of the archaeological ones (Fig. 4).

During the actions, the experimenter struck the rocky support in perpendicular and oblique directions, always in bidirectional movements. His gestures ranged between 70° and 90° in relation to support, having been the first angle to extracting a greater quantity of matter of the rocky surface and the second employee in order to give more depth to the pecking.

The whole process was recorded in detail before, during and after his execution by filling in forms created specifically for the experiment and making photographs and videos.

Figure 4. Productionof the experimentalrock art engravings

Besides the lithic tools have been properly measured and weighed before the experiment, their active zones were photographed, measured and had their angles information on their conservation status recorded after 1.200, 1.000 and 2.000 impacts. Any revivals that were able to eventually change their morphology has also been recorded.

After action is complete, these tools were photographed under the same perspective that were before and during the experiment, while the engravings were carefully recorded in the general scope and focuses more on the specific characteristics of pecking performed and traces of engraving.

In the list of materials used to record the experimental processes are: specific forms to the lithic tools and engravings, 2 photographic cameras Canon 600D, 1 photographic camera Nikon D80, 1 caliper, 1 scale, 1 meter angles and 1 stopwatch.

Then all experimental engravings were recorded by direct tracing, which, besides setting up a formal record, allow us to compare them with the tracings made later on the latex molds produced in the next stage.

Finally, in a last stage of the work, we did the production of latex molds of the experimental engravings (Fig. 5), and also their record by direct tracing, at the laboratory. We used this activity: 10 kg latex, 1 brush roll, 4 brushes 30 m gauze.

To produce the molds, we follow exactly the same methodology used by the researchers who have shaped the rock engravings of the Tagus Valley in the 1970s, which is described in detail in Baptista (1974) and Querol *et al.* (1975). Briefly, we can describe the procedure as follows: after the rock surface has been cleaned with water, was awaited and after drying it was applied a first layer of latex.

After approximately 30 minutes, when the first layer was dry, we proceeded to the application of a second one. This process being repeated until the fifth layer of latex, when was applied a layer of gauze over the entire surface.

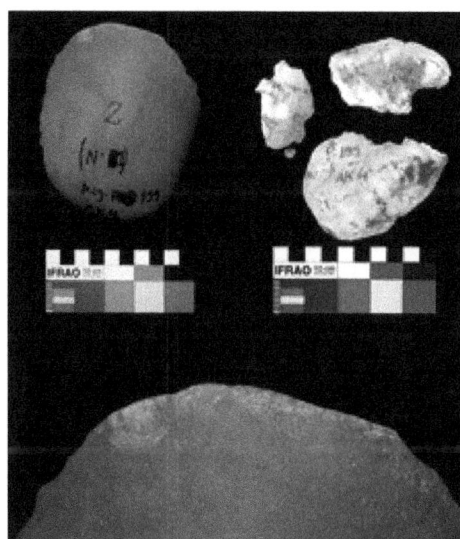

Figure 5. Mechanical damage suffered by the quartzite and quartz tools after their use in the engraving of the zoomorphic figures by direct percussion

After this last application, the process performed for the initial layers again be repeated until the tenth layers were completed. After complete drying, the mold was carefully removed from the rock surface, to thereby prevent occurrence of tearing.

RESULTS

Having successfully produced 34 experimental rock art engravings on greywacke supports, we consider absolutely feasible to produce that kind of representation through the use of lithic tools in quartz and quartzite knapped according to the characteristics of the macrolithic industries of the Tagus Valley, the flakes from the production of those tools and natural pebbles of the same raw materials.

However, it is worth noting that although has been possible to produce engravings with all tools tested under direct and indirect percussion, the level of efficiency shown by each of them was quite different, varying mainly according to the type of raw material that were composed and the morphology of its active zone.

Observing the behavior of quartzite and quartz, it was possible to identify a large difference between them, because the tools produced in quartzite responded much more satisfactory with regard to the occurrence of mechanical damages generated by the impacts resulting from the activity performed.

The quartzite choppers suffered little changes in their active zones, usually only a few small detachments (on average 0.5 cm x 0.5 cm) on the lower face of the edge, after 2000 impacts. In turn, the quartz choppers presented shredding, occurrence of large chipping (on average 2 cm x 1.5 cm) and fractures on the active zones already after suffering 10 impacts, until the completion of the engraving and making the edges constantly abrupt (80° / 90°), which reduced its efficiency and required frequent revivals. In some cases, there was even a complete fracturing of the tool (Fig. 5).

This fact was reflected in the characteristics of the pecking performed with quartz tools, which were less deep (0.1 cm or less) and more imprecise than those made by quartzite tools, because the steadily fragmentation of the artifact during the action hampered the realization of accurate technical gestures.

Such behavior was also evident on the flakes and natural pebbles. In the case of the flakes, the high level of fragmentation of the quartz made it necessary to use a larger amount of raw material. While to produce fully a zoomorphic figure only under indirect percussion using flakes, for example, was required 1 quartzite flake, to perform the same action it was necessary to use 4 quartz flakes.

Based on these data, although the use of quartz for the production of engravings is feasible, quartzite is much more able to perform that action.

Among the most effective tools stood out the quartzite choppers with active zone of pointed morphology and angle between 55° and 60°. Such tools were used by direct percussion and produced accurate and incisive pecking up to 0.2 cm deep.

Regarding the flakes, those in quartzite with semi-circular edge morphology and angle of the active zone between 35° and 45° were the ones with a better result. With an excellent performance when used under indirect percussion to perform finer traits as legs andantlers of zoomorphic figures, with these flakes could easily produce traces with an average thickness of 0.5 cm, depth 0.2 and U section.

But when used to engrave full zoomorphic figures the efficiency decreased, because its active zone rather narrow (0.2 cm) was not adequate to fill large areas by pecking. To fill the torso area of that kind of rock art motifs through their points of impact of linear

morphology and under indirect percussion, for example, it was necessary 100 minutes and around 15,000 impacts, namely, a high investment of time and energy.

To engrave the anthropomorphic and ideomorphic figures under the same technique that flakes showed once again large efficiency, producing precise and regular lines, being also efficient to eliminate the cortex layer of rock surface.

About the two pebbles knapped on both faces, used under indirect percussion, that one of quartzite (active zone whit convex morphology and angle of 60°) has been more effective in the action, producing a pecking depth (0.3 cm) and regular, although his great length (19.5 cm) has made it become difficult to control during the performance of the movements.

Finally, between natural pebbles, quartzite were also the most effective, although they produced a pecking shallow and too "rough" in achieving the zoomorphic, quite different from the original pecking. Its dominance was conditioned also by the aforementioned weakness of quartz to damage caused by the impacts.

Another interesting finding from the results of the experiment is that before to be a product of the use of different tools in a single engraving, or a large variation in the angles of gestures used by the engraver, the occurrence of pecking with different morphologies are much more connected to the wear process of the active zone of the engraver tool. That is valid for both quartzite and quartz.

For example, in the case of a tool with a pointed active zone morphology and angle of 50°, the occurrence of damage could remove its pointed shape and change the angle to 70°. This change will to modify the morphology of the pecking from a rounded morphology to a straight morphology, also presenting a lesser depth.

Regarding the techniques of direct and indirect percussion, we measure their effectiveness in comparing both the quality of pecking obtained on the support and investment of time and energy necessary to complete the intended action.

Thus, according to the parameters it was evident the higher efficiency of the pecking technique by direct percussion.

Using as an example the pecking through that technique and with the use of choppers of both raw materials, it is possible to realize that the result is more precise, smooth, controlled and also deeper (average 0.2 cm) (the dimensions of traces vary depending of the active zone dimensions). On the other hand, the pecking made by indirect percussion results more inaccurate, irregular, with large amount of cortex within the traces and with an average depth that tends not exceed 0.1 cm.

In our view, this is due to the fact that by direct percussion the engraver is able to control more

Table 1. Summary of average time and average of impacts necessary to perform each rock art engraving according different combinations of tools and techniques

Average time of production/ Average of impacts for production	Anthropomorphic figure	Zoomorphic figure	Ideomorphic figure
Chopper dir. perc.	11 min./1.840 impacts	31 min./6.150 impacts	8 min./1.590 impacts
Chopper ind. perc.	22 min./4.200 impacts	94 min./15.950 impacts	14 min./2.240 impacts
Chopper dir. perc. + flake ind. perc.	–	65 min./14.445 impacts	–
Chopper ind. perc. + lasca ind. perc.	–	116 min./16.975 impacts	–
Nat. pebble dir. perc.	5 min./1.220 impacts	27 min./5.250 impacts	3 min./580 impacts
Nat. pebble ind. perc.	23 min./3.855 impacts	89 min./13.800 impacts	7 min./1.155 impacts

adequately both made gestures as the intensity of the applied force, thus producing a pecking more controlled, precise and incisive.

Regarding the investment of time and power is glaring the difference seen between the two techniques, as can be seen in the Tab. 1.

Based on these data, it is clear that in addition to better results with regard to the quality of pecking, the direct percussion require a smaller investment of time and energy, as require the completion of a smaller number of impacts to achieve the same goal in a shorter space of time.

The last of the results presented here concerns the level of reliability of the record of engravings by molding latex, widely discussed topic in the studies about the molds of the Tagus Valley rock art.

With the production of the experimental molds, their record by direct tracing and the comparison of these tracings with those made directly on the experimental engravings, was possible attest to a considerable degree of reliability for this type of record. Elevenmolds were produced and nine of them recorded the engravings completely and with detail.

The other two remaining molds were not able to record the engravings completely. Some of their traits become invisible and, therefore, was not possible to carry out the direct tracing decal. We believe that such failure on the record can be related to the presence of a shallow pecking (less than 0.1 cm) forming the engravings on which the molding was unsuccessful.

However, it is very important to draw attention to the damage on the rock surface by the molding process in latex. Upon withdrawal of all experimental molds after they are dry, parts of the rocky surface, and of the engravings, were uprooted and remained glued on the latex. This fact demonstrates why this is a method already in disuse and which should be avoided to the maximum by researchers. From what we can see, their use on archaeological engravings can cause a great risk of destruction.

HYPOTHETICAL OPERATIVE CHAINS OF PRODUCTION FOR THE CACHÃO DO ALGARVE ROCK ART

First, in the words of Lévi-Strauss (1975), we must remember that it is always valid to form hypotheses, if they are coherently constructed and based on empirical data. In this context, we consider much more useful hypothesize about a problematic issue than simply not doing and to close the investigation when it is still far from its possible limits, blaming for this investigative lethargy the lack of an archaeological context in perfect condition to perform the work, a condition that in prehistoric archeology, and even more in rock art, we know, is pretty rare.

The Experimental Archaeology, more than a study procedure, is a method of contrasting hypotheses through experimentation, which when rigorously developed from a clear issue of work, permits to support (or to deny) the viability of interpretative hypotheses about prehistory, built with base on technical processes developed today (Baena, 1997; Coles, 1979; Reynolds, 1999).

Therefore, from the results obtained by the experimental work, which sustained the viability of the tested hypothesis, we now present, in a summary way, the proposal of three hypothetical operative chains by which could had been produced a large part of the Cachão do Algarve engravings. Before that, however, it's important to remember that we understand the term "operative chains" as the series of operations involved in any transformation of matter carried by humans (Lemonnier, 1992).

To build such proposal, we performed a comparison between the original molds and the experimental ones, with the intention of identifying which combinations of techniques and tools generated the experimental engravings most similar to the archaeological ones.

Analyzing first the anthropomorphic figures, the experimental engraving that result more similar to the archaeological one on technical aspects, was that produced by direct percussion with gestures variants between 70° and 90° and through the use of a quartzite

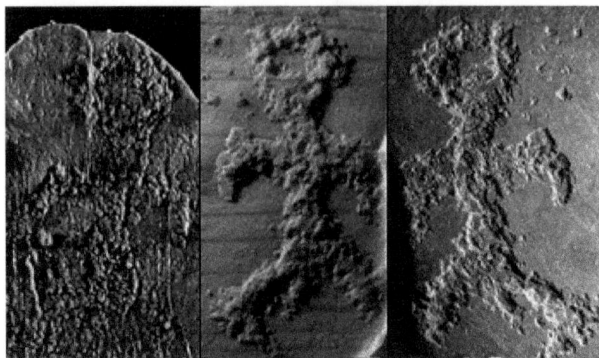

Figure 6. Comparison between the archaeological anthropomorphic figure present in the original mold CAL63B M664 (left) and the experimental one (center and right)

chopper with pointed edge morphology presenting angle of 60° (Fig. 6).

In this case the pecking that forms this experimental engraving, as that which forms the original anthropomorphic figure appeared prominently deep (0.25 cm), indicating the achievement of precise and incisive impacts on the rocky surface which promoted the complete removal of the cortex within the traits. Being that rock art motif representative of the typological category to which it belongs, both in figurative as regarding the technical characteristics of the pecking, we can extrapolate this comparison for at least 44% of anthropomorphic figures analyzed in the study of the site.

Regarding the zoomorphic figure, the experimental engraving most similar to the archaeological one was that produced by two different combinations of techniques and tools.

This engraving was made through the techniques of direct and indirect percussion, having been used for the direct a quartzite chopper with pointed edge morphology and angle of 55° and for the indirect a quartzite flake with semi-circular edge morphology and angle of 35°. In the first case, the gestures of the experimenter varied between 70° and 90°, while in the second were performed perpendicularly (90°) to the rocky support.

Through direct percussion were recorded the torso, neck and head of the animal, creating a pecking wider (about 1 cm), thick, with irregular section and impact points higher and deeper. By indirect were performed the legs and antlers of the zoomorphic figure, through a pecking that formed continuous lines with thickness of 0.5 cm, depth of 0.2 cm and U section.

Finally, the experimental engraving performed with a natural quartzite pebble (pointed active zone an angle of 90°), used under direct percussion using gestures between 70° and 90°, was the most similar to the archaeological ideomorphic figure. The pecking produced appeared markedly irregular, discontinuous and shallow, which can

be extrapolated to 65% of the circles identified in the Cachão do Algarve.

It can be seen, therefore, the occurrence of a different operative chain different for each type of rock art motif. But although they differ in the course of its stages, with regard to obtaining raw materials the process would be the same for all of them.

In the area close to the Cachão do Algarve can be seen a vast presence of pebbles of quartz and quartzite, being the first most abundant. Thus, there would be a selection of a specific raw material for the activity, namely the quartzite instead of quartz, probably because the latter present a low efficiency (what has been proven during the experimental work).

Therefore, the production of lithic tools could be performed locally, without needing to transport raw materials or pre-formatted tools from another areas.

Regarding the morphology of the tools, would be privileged the production of choppers with pointed edge morphology and angle of approximately 60°, creating active zones efficient to produce an accurate and incisive pecking, being simultaneously resistant to mechanical damage caused by the impacts. Such tools would be used by direct percussion to perform impacts in angles between 70° and 90° relative to the surface of the rocky support.

The flakes from their production would also be utilized, preferably the cortical flakes with dimensions suitable to the realization of a good prehension. These would be used under indirect percussion with wood hammer, through gestures predominantly perpendicular to the engraved surface, producing continuous and detailed lines such as antlers of deer.

To realize engravings structurally simpler which not require a high technical improvement, it would be possible to use natural quartzite pebbles with pointed active zones to strike directly on the rocky surface obliquely and perpendicularly.

After the action has been completed, the tools could be discarded or reused on site to produce more engravings, if they had even a satisfactory level of efficiency or were undergoing some revival.

Below is a summary of the three hypothetical operative possibilities related to use of macrolithic industries in the production of the three types of engravings typical of the Cachão do Algarve (Fig. 7):

FINAL CONSIDERATIONS

Given all that has been exposed so far, we can conclude that the results of our experimental work reinforce the possibility of a relationship between the Cachão do Algarve rock art and the macrolithic industries present in

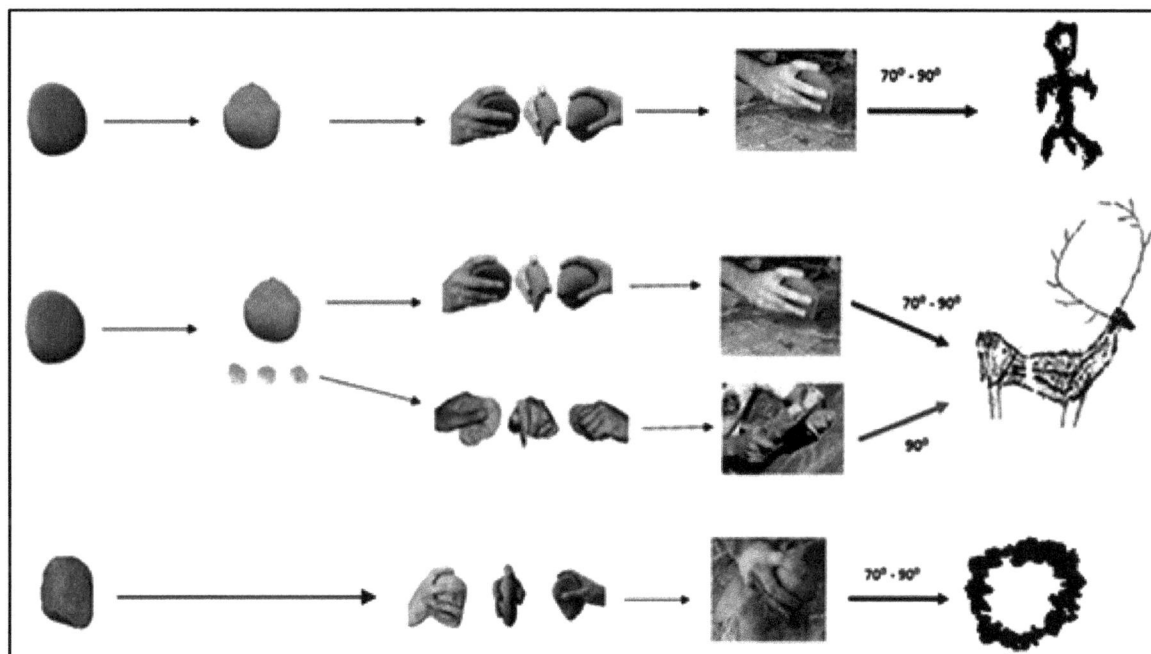

Figure 7. Operative possibilities for the production of the Cachão do Algarve rock art engravings in a hypothetical technological process in that would be used macrolithic tools to engrave

the archaeological context of the Tagus Valley, contributing to a better understanding of the possible technological behavior of prehistoric populations that occupied the region.

Obviously, the information generated by Experimental Archaeology, however useful they may be, absolutely not set a "bridge" to the minds of prehistoric men, since we belong to a culture very different from that in which were immersed the societies of the past (Sampaio & Aubry, 2008). However, it is once again important to emphasize the need to conduct experimental approaches in the context of technological studies, because like would say Leroi-Gourhan (1986:11), the technology must first be experienced, only after being conceived.

References

ALVAREZ, M. [*et al.*] (2001) – The use of lithic artefacts for making rock art engravings: observation and analysis of use-wear traces in experimental tools through optical microscopy and SEM. Journal of Archaeological Science 28. p. 457-464.

BAENA, J. (1997) – Arqueología Experimental algo más que un juego. Boletínde. Arqueología Experimental 1. Madrid. p. 3-5.

BAPTISTA, A.M. (1974) – O complexo de arte rupestre do Tejo: processos de levantamento. Congresso Nacional de Arqueologia. Porto. p. -. Atas.

BAPTISTA, A.M. (1981) – A Rocha F-155 e a Origem da Arte do Vale do Tejo. Monografias Arqueológicas. GEAP. Porto. 85 p.

BAPTISTA, A.M. (1986) – Arte rupestre pós- glaciária. Esquematismo e abstracção. História da Arte em Portugal. Do Paleolítico à Arte Visigótica. Lisboa. Publicações Alfa. p. 30-55.

BAPTISTA, A. (2011) – 40 anos depois – a arte do Tejo no seu labirinto. Açafa Online 4. p. 2-11. [Consult. 01 Dec. 2011] Available in WWW:_URL: http://www.altotejo.org/acafa/acafa_n4.html_.

CRUZ, A.; GRIMALDI, S.; OOSTERBEEK, L. (2000) – Indústrias macrolíticas do pós-glaciar no Alto Ribatejo. In Sanches, M.; Arias, P. (coord.) Neolitização e Megalitismo da Península Ibérica. Actas do 3º Congresso de Arqueologia Peninsular. Porto: ADECAP. vol. III, p. 47-61.

COLES, J. (1979) – Experimental archaeology. London. 234 p.

GOMES, M.V. (2007) – Os períodos iniciais da arte do Vale do Tejo (Paleolítico e Epipaleolítico). Cuadernos de Arte Rupestre. Lisboa. Nº 4. p. 81-116.

GRIMALDI, S.; ROSINA, P.; FERNANDEZ, I. (1998) – Interpretazione Geo-Archeologica Di Alcune Industrie Litiche "Languedocensi" del Medio Bacino del Tajo. In Cruz, A.; Oosterbeek, L.; Reis, R. (coord.) Quaternário e Pré-História do Alto Ribatejo (Portugal), Arkeos 4, Tomar. CEIPHAR. p. 145-226.

LEMONNIER, P. (1992) – Elements for an Anthropology of Technology. AnnArbor, Michigan. 176 p.

LEROI-GOURHAN. A. (1986) – Evolução e Técnica II. O Meio e as Técnicas. Edições 70. Lisboa. 357 p.

LÉVI-STRAUSS, C. (1975) – Antropologia Estrutural. Tempo Brasileiro. Rio de Janeiro. 445 p.

OOSTERBEEK, L. (1994) – Echoes from the East: the Western network. North Ribatejo (Portugal): an insight to unequal and combined development, 7.000-

2.000 B.C. Dissertaçao de doutoramento, London University.

QUEROL, M. [*et al.*] (1975) – El complejo de Arte rupestre del Tajo (Portugal). Crónica del XIII Congresso Arqueólogico Nacional (Hueva, 1973). Seminário de Arqueologia. Zaragoza. p. 237-244.

REYNOLDS, P. (1999) – The nature of experiment in archaeology. Experiment and Design in Archaeology. OxbowBooks. Oxford. p. 156-162.

SAMPAIO, J. & AUBRY, T. (2008) – Testar e recriar em arqueologia: balanços e perspectivas. Arqueologia Experimental. V. 4. p. 11-22.

SANCHIDRIÁN, J.L. (2001) – Manual de arte prehistórico. Ariel. Barcelona. 549 p.

SANDE LEMOS, F. (2011) – Vale do Tejo – A Ventura da Arte Rupestre. Açafa Online 4, p. 2-22 [Consult. 02 Dec. 2011] Available in WWW:_URL: http://www.altotejo.org/acafa/acafa_n4.html_.

SANTOS, M.F. (1985) – Pré-História de Portugal. Biblioteca das Civilizações Primitivas. 3a Ed. Editorial Verbo. Lisboa. 214 p.

SANTOS DA ROSA, N. (2012) – Contributo para o Estudo do Complexo de Arte Rupestre do Vale do Tejo: o Sítio Cachão do Algarve. Dissertação de mestrado. Universidade de Trás-os-Montes e Alto Douro / Instituto Politécnico de Tomar / Universitat Rovira i Virgili / Muséum National d'Histoire Naturelle / Universitade gli Studi di Ferrara.

SERRÃO, E.C. [*et al.*] (1972) – O Complexo de Arte Rupestre do Tejo (Vila Velha de Ródão-Nisa): Notícia Preliminar. Arqueologia e História IV. Lisboa. p. 9-38.

SERRÃO, E.C. (1978) – A Arte Rupestre do Vale do Tejo – Primeiras contribuições para uma periodização do Neolítico e do Calcolítico da Estremadura portuguesa. Porto. p. 5-14.